mexico unmanned

SUNY series in Latin American Cinema

Ignacio M. Sánchez Prado and Leslie L. Marsh, editors

mexico unmanned

The Cultural Politics of Masculinity
in Mexican Cinema

Samanta Ordóñez

Cover: Digitized frames from the film *Batalla en el cielo* directed by Carlos Reygadas, co-produced by Mantarraya producciones.

Published by State University of New York Press, Albany

© 2021 State University of New York

All rights reserved

Printed in the United States of America

No part of this book may be used or reproduced in any manner whatsoever without written permission. No part of this book may be stored in a retrieval system or transmitted in any form or by any means including electronic, electrostatic, magnetic tape, mechanical, photocopying, recording, or otherwise without the prior permission in writing of the publisher.

For information, contact State University of New York Press, Albany, NY
www.sunypress.edu

Library of Congress Cataloging-in-Publication Data

Name: Ordóñez, Samanta, author.
Title: Mexico unmanned : the cultural politics of masculinity in Mexican cinema / Samanta Ordóñez.
Description: Albany : State University of New York Press, [2021] | Series: SUNY series in Latin American cinema | Includes bibliographical references and index.
Identifiers: LCCN 2021030192 (print) | LCCN 2021030193 (ebook) | ISBN 9781438486291 (hardcover : alk. paper) | ISBN 9781438486284 (pbk. : alk. paper) | ISBN 9781438486307 (ebook)
Subjects: LCSH: Masculinity in motion pictures. | Motion pictures—Mexico—History. | Motion pictures—Social aspects—Mexico. | Motion pictures—Political aspects—Mexico.
Classification: LCC PN1995.9.M34 O84 2021 (print) | LCC PN1995.9.M34 (ebook) | DDC 791.43/652110972—dc23
LC record available at https://lccn.loc.gov/2021030192
LC ebook record available at https://lccn.loc.gov/2021030193

10 9 8 7 6 5 4 3 2 1

Contents

List of Illustrations   vii

Acknowledgments   xi

Preface   xiii

Introduction   1

Chapter One
Old Macho Mythologies in New Mexican Cinema—*Y tu mamá también* and *Rudo y Cursi*   37

Chapter Two
Demystifying Machismo in *Batalla en el cielo* and *Post tenebras lux*   73

Chapter Three
Manufacturing Malformed Masculinities in *Heli*   107

Chapter Four
Neoliberal Masculinities between Romance and Realism in *Te prometo anarquía*   145

Afterword   183

Notes   191

Works Cited   207

Index   215

Illustrations

Figure 1.1	Julio (Gael García Bernal) and Tenoch (Diego Luna) compete with one another in the swimming pool (*Y tu mamá también*).	53
Figure 1.2	Julio and Tenoch indulge in synchronous masturbation (*Y tu mamá también*).	54
Figure 1.3	The minor character Chuy (Silverio Palacios), a local fisherman soon to be expelled from his home along with his family, cheerfully plays soccer with the protagonists (*Y tu mamá también*).	62
Figure 1.4	Beto (Luna) and Tato (García) return home to their rural community much the worse for wear after their disastrous foray into the transnational world of professional soccer (*Rudo y Cursi*).	68
Figure 2.1	Ana (Ana Mushkadiz) gazes at her chauffer, Marcos (Marcos Hernández), from the rear seat of the stationary vehicle (*Batalla en el cielo*, 2005).	86
Figure 2.2	Close-up shot of Marcos's face in profile from a perspective implicitly aligned with Ana's gaze (*Batalla en el cielo*).	86
Figure 2.3	Another subjective shot from Ana's point-of-view emphasizes Marcos's corpulence and unkempt appearance with a close-up of his frayed, sweat-stained undershirt (*Batalla en el cielo*).	89

Figure 2.4	Marcos lies motionless in a cadaverous posture after his sexual encounter with Ana (*Batalla en el cielo*).	90
Figure 2.5	A print of Théodore Géricault's *A Horse Frightened by Lightning* from Marcos's perspective (*Batalla en el cielo*).	91
Figure 2.6	El Siete (Willebaldo Torres) speaks from the podium at an Alcoholics Anonymous meeting (*Post tenebras lux*).	98
Figure 2.7	Another AA group member, El Sapo, stands at the same podium (*Post tenebras lux*).	99
Figure 2.8	The explicit act of violence Juan commits against his dog remains mostly unseen from the audience's perspective throughout this static shot (*Post tenebras lux*).	101
Figure 3.1	The image of decapitated heads is included as a banalized visual element of generic television news coverage of drug violence (*Heli*).	125
Figure 3.2	The brutalized body of Beto (Juan Eduardo Palacios) hangs from a pedestrian bridge whose rectangular structure subtly mirrors the shape of a cinema screen (*Heli*).	126
Figure 3.3	The protagonist (Armando Espitia) appears bound and gagged, and with his captor's boot pressed on his head in the opening shot (*Heli*).	126
Figure 3.4	An inverted mirror image of the opening shot reappears approximately midway through the film (*Heli*).	127
Figure 3.5	One of the anonymous boys observing the torture records the scene on his cellphone camera with the intention of posting it online (*Heli*).	131
Figure 3.6	A high-angle shot minimizes the protagonist's stature from the implied perspective of members of the violent paramilitary police force (*Heli*).	140

Figure 3.7	A forced perspective technique similarly reduces the apparent size of the protagonist relative to the forces that threaten him (*Heli*).	141
Figure 4.1	Miguel (Diego Calva) gazes up longingly at his lover, Johnny (Eduardo Eliseo Martínez), in the opening sequence of *Te prometo anarquía*.	158
Figure 4.2	This shot of Miguel and Johnny having intercourse centers Miguel's expression of desire and pleasure, while Johnny faces away from the camera (*Te prometo anarquía*).	159
Figure 4.3	A long shot of Johnny contextualizes him in the urban environment, avoiding any suggestion of his emotional interiority (*Te prometo anarquía*).	161
Figure 4.4	An obscured shot of Techno (Diego Escamilla Corona) shows him collapsed on the floor of a subway train carriage while Miguel prepares to drag him onto the platform (*Te prometo anarquía*).	166
Figure 4.5	A long shot of the protagonists on a pedestrian overpass shows Miguel evidently undergoing a crisis while Johnny consoles him (*Te prometo anarquía*).	178

Acknowledgments

This book was written with significant institutional backing and with the intellectual and emotional support of many individuals. The initial seeds of my research on Mexican masculinities were planted in classes and conversations with Debra Castillo while I was a graduate student in Romance Studies at Cornell. Simply the best dissertation advisor and mentor anyone could hope for, Debra was unfailingly supportive and always generous with her excellent feedback and insightful suggestions. Over countless discarded drafts of dissertation chapters, she enabled me to define my intellectual path and gave me the confidence to find my own voice. I also benefited from the advice and encouragement of other members of my dissertation committee, Edmundo Paz Soldán, Gerard Aching, and Amy Villarejo. I must also thank Amy and Debra for opening the door for me to become a teaching assistant in the Performing and Media Arts Department. The experience of working with Sabine Haenni in her excellent global cinemas class was absolutely formative.

At Wake Forest University, I must appreciatively recognize Erica Still for organizing Faculty of Color initiatives and for creating a network of mutual support that helped me to feel at home as a new faculty member. José Villalba has been another steadfast supporter in the administration. In my own department, I have had the good fortune of being surrounded by amazing colleagues. Fellow cinema specialist Anne Hardcastle, who chaired Spanish and Italian throughout my first years at Wake, has been a reliable source of advice and camaraderie. I thank Irma Alarcón, Jane Albrecht, Diego Burgos, Andrea Echeverría, Margaret Ewalt, Jerid Francom, Mary Friedman, Olga Furmanek, Luis González, Linda Howe, Bruce Jackson, Tiffany Judy, Rémi Lanzoni, Kathryn Mayers, Sol Miguel-Prendes, Roberta Morosini, Carmen Perez-Muñoz, Teresa Sanhuenza, Jessica Shade Venegas,

Kendall Tarte, Silvia Tiboni-Craft, Claudia Valdez, José Luis Venegas, Nicholas Wolters, and Boston Woolfolk for their kindness and collegiality. Thanks also go to Dean Franco for his ongoing support of my projects, Wanda Balzano for showing interest in my work and inviting me to the Women's, Gender, & Sexuality Studies Colloquium, and Vinodh Venkatesh for engaging thoughtfully with me during his visit from Virginia Tech.

Much of the writing process of this book took place during a leave granted by the Wake Forest College of Arts and Science. Direct support also came from the WFU Humanities Institute, which awarded me a Summer Writing Grant in 2019. The Provost's Office provided additional backing in the form of funds for travel to conferences, giving me opportunities to share my ideas and engage in rich discussions with others in my field.

Thanks to Rebecca Colesworthy, James Peltz, and Ryan Morris at SUNY Press, and to the series editors, Ignacio M. Sánchez Prado and Leslie L. Marsh. Two anonymous readers provided thoughtful suggestions that were incorporated into the final text. Fragments of chapter 2 first appeared in "Carlos Reygadas's *Batalla en el Cielo* (*Battle in Heaven*) (2005): Disarticulating the Brown Male Body from Myths of Mexican Masculinity," *Studies in Spanish & Latin American Cinemas* 14, no. 1 (March 2017): 77–94.

Special thanks go to Carlos Reygadas and to David London at Splendor Omnia Studios for helping to secure the cover image from *Batalla en el cielo*.

From the very beginnings through to the completion of this work, no one has given me more support and love than my partner, Patrick Crowley.

This book is dedicated to the memory of my father, Pascual Ordóñez Cruz.

Preface

My earliest encounters with the mythical being known as the Mexican macho took place in the living room of my childhood home in an isolated Coahuila mining town named after another mythic model of manliness: Hercules. On one of the two television channels available in the late 1980s, I witnessed the Herculean trials and triumphs of Pepe el Toro, incarnated by Pedro Infante, in the classic trilogy of melodramas directed by Ismael Rodríguez, films that were by then almost four decades old. With the nearest cinema located several hours away by mostly unpaved roads, my introduction to Mexico's filmmaking tradition came from the relatively regular television broadcasts of landmark productions from the *cine de oro* archive. The first film of Rodríguez's three-part saga, *Nosotros los pobres* (We, the Poor) (1947), introduces the male protagonist, Pepe el Toro, as a humble carpenter who enjoys a relatively settled life in a close-knit urban community until it is abruptly overturned by a series of hardships and misfortunes. Despite having little money, Pepe goes happily and vigorously about his working day, spends quality time with his daughter, Chachita (Evita Muñoz), reveres his incapacitated mother (María Gentil Arcos), hangs out with his *cuates* (buddies), and woos his beloved Celia (Blanca Estela Pavón). Pepe has many personal flaws but these only serve to accentuate his virtues. He is ferociously stubborn but fundamentally kindhearted, quick-tempered but compassionate. Ultimately, his positive qualities far outweigh his defects. He is brave, handsome, physically strong, charming, playful, expressive, and always ready with a song. Replete with sudden tragic turns and forced resolutions, the trilogy's overarching narrative strains the suspension of disbelief even by the standards of Golden Age melodrama, hence much of the enduring appeal rests with Infante's iconic embodiment of Pepe el Toro. Enjoying these movies as a young girl in the 1980s necessarily implied overlooking many elements of the plot and dialogue that now stand out as abhorrent, including the naturalization of male privilege and outright misogyny. Although it was perhaps impossible not to perceive that the female characters occupied denigratingly subordinate positions relative to Pepe el Toro, some part of me was nonetheless captivated by the pathos of Infante's performance and blinded by the positive ideals he represented. Yet, even as I allowed myself to be partially entranced by his cinematic spectacle, I could not help but notice that neither my own father, who worked as an office-bound human resources manager, nor the fathers of any other children I knew came close to approximating any facet of Infante's quintessential Mexican manliness. The men of Hercules had about as much in common with national cinema's mythic macho as they did with the heroic son of Jove.

The discrepancies between the Mexican characters portrayed in classic films and my own contemporary social experiences were rather plain to see. In Hercules, as well as in other communities I had known, it was easy to observe that people's daily lives were not organized around strong communal bonds as they were onscreen. Public displays of emotion were very rare, and absolutely no one was predisposed to spontaneous neighborhood sing-alongs. In the demeanors of men at work and at home, I saw no resemblance whatsoever to Pedro Infante's defining qualities, such as his passionate intensity, charming optimism, and aggressive assertiveness. In my childish effort to make sense of the differences between the performances in classic cinema I was growing to adore and the everyday reality I inhabited, it occurred to me that the Mexican character must have changed dramatically along with society as a whole in the decades since my favorite films had been made. When I asked my mother if my grandparents' lives had been closer to those of the characters in the movies, she swiftly disillusioned me, explaining that nothing like cinema's version of Mexico's past had ever actually existed. Sparing me most of the detail about the adversities that marked our family's past—of which I learned more as an adult—she told me enough to curtail my nascent romanticism about the period of Mexican history that gave rise to the "Golden Age" of film. She showed me the few existing family photos taken in Chihuahua in the 1940s and '50s, giving me a glimpse into the past experiences I was curious about. Although relatively little could be gleaned from these images, I could see well enough that, even as a young man photographed in his newish mechanic's coveralls emblazoned with the Goodyear Tire logo, my maternal grandfather appeared nothing like a personification of classic cinema's cheerful and passionate working-class Mexican macho. To me, he looked somber and serious. My mother also spoke to me of my grandfather on my father's side, whom I would meet on only a few occasions while he was alive. As a Nahuatl-speaking campesino in rural Veracruz obliged to cultivate land he did not own, his lived experience could hardly have coincided with the model of Mexican manhood celebrated in Rodríguez's urban melodramas—not to mention the offensive stereotypes offered up by so many *indigenista* films of the same era. After these conversations with my mother, the appeal of spending part of a Saturday afternoon watching Pedro Infante suffer, sing, and swagger on television was never quite as strong.

Some memory of these early lessons in media criticism stayed with me as I began to study Mexican cinema and masculinity in graduate school. Engaging with scholarship that described and analyzed Mexican nationalist filmmaking as the definitive ideological instrument of the postrevolutionary era gave me an understanding of the vexed relationship between the "real" Mexico and the nation dreamed up in film studios financed by the state as part of a didactic cultural agenda. My readings disclosed the paternalism and patriarchal impetus behind the pedagogical construction of a national film culture that sought to "Mexicanize the Mexicans," in the words of famed director Emilio "el Indio" Fernández.[1] Yet, I was dissatisfied with certain recurring assumptions in accounts of how this strategy was supposedly realized. The explanations often amounted to iterations of the same basic argument positing homogenous popular identification with the fictional characters and narratives depicted onscreen. Of course, there had to be some consequences to a mass audience's temporary attachment to an ideologically driven cinematic point of view, but it seemed to me that what many chroniclers and critics were proposing presumed the public's passive and natural submission to an imposed set of cultural codes and parameters. From this perspective, Mexican audiences did not go to the cinema to have a responsive encounter with interesting stories set in a dreamlike, semimimetic world, presented in a novel medium, and spoken in a language that was, for some, their own. Rather, they went to receive lessons in national identity, which they readily accepted and internalized despite glaring contradictions between their own lives and the fabricated myths displayed on the movie screen. In this way, according to some prominent thinkers, ordinary men apparently learned that the value of being an Infante-style macho was equivalent to that of being a modern Mexican.[2]

To my mind, this account did not hold up against the fragments of family history my mother had gathered to lift the enchantment that *cine de oro* had briefly placed over me as a child. Did my maternal grandfather have the opportunity or inclination to watch films while working to support his eleven children? Did he recognize aspects of himself reflected in Infante's portrayal of a sentimental auto mechanic in *Necesito dinero* (I Need Money) (1952, dir. Miguel Zacarías)? Did he see this performance as an aspirational model of masculinity to emulate? And were national cinema's lessons at all relevant to my paternal grandfather? Did film have any significant cultural resonance in his church-oriented rural community? Would he have adopted a new understanding of his masculine indigeneity had he watched Infante perform in *Tizoc* (1956, dir. Ismael Rodríguez)? Although I never had the chance to ask my grandfathers these questions, reflecting on them oriented my investigations toward gaps and fissures in Mexican cinema's combined projects of mythmaking, nation-building, modernization, and machismo.

As I continued to research film's formative role in naturalizing the unity between Mexican men and the mythology of the macho, I was glad to discover the work of scholars who shared some of my doubts about the totalizing completeness of popular identification with *mexicanidad*. In Susan Dever's *Celluloid Nationalism and Other Melodramas* (2003), Andrea Noble's *Mexican National Cinema* (2005), and Dolores Tierney's *Emilio Fernández: Pictures in the Margins* (2007), I found complex critical reassessments of the national film archive that highlighted its unsettled meanings and problematized existing accounts of its role as an influential cultural mediator between the patriarchal state and the masses. I also relished Sergio de la Mora's *Cinemachismo* (2006), which brought to light the paradoxes of Infante's performances of iconic machismo in Golden Age cinema. His analysis of masculinity as a system of power in Mexico provided significant inspiration for the ideas in this book. The alternative textual interpretations of classic films offered by de la Mora show that normative, ideologically constructed categories of gender identity and sexuality articulated in Mexican cinema acquired significant cultural authority yet nevertheless remained in a constant state of flux, always shifting in tense relation with disavowed otherness. The very possibility of representing the virile heterosexual macho ideal embodied by Infante, argues de la Mora, depends on its coarticulation with homoeroticism and male effeminacy. Unveiling the queerness that both regulates and enables cinema's invention of machismo constitutes de la Mora's major critical intervention. His work reveals eclipsed dimensions of the gendered and sexualized logic of male identification, creating openings for complex encounters with nonnormative desires and subjectivities in national film.

Thinking relationally about masculinity at its intersections with categories of male sexual otherness fractures the monolithic façade of Mexican machismo. Cinema's invention of the iconic macho necessitated not only promulgation of the stereotyped figures of the submissive woman and her untamed counterpart but also of the unmanly male. De la Mora examined the overshadowed but nonetheless necessary presence of homosexuality in classic cinema's portrayals of dominant heterosexual masculinity, but there are many other cracks in the illusory monolith of Mexican machismo, and peering deeper into these fissures reveals still more hidden facets of its oppressive power. The cultural logic that organized the projection of idealized male identities onto the movie screens of the Golden Age was not only directed by homophobic and misogynist precepts but was also closely aligned with racial capitalism. The correlation of these dimensions of machismo has been obscured by the emphasis given to effusive, celebratory representations of protagonists coded as "mestizos" from lower-class origins. In addition to studying cinematic gender formation, scholars like de la Mora, Dever, Noble, and Tierney have provided insightful critiques of problematic codifications of class and race by identifying contradictions stemming from the romanticized view of poverty, the distorted meanings of *mestizaje*, the whiteness of the film stars, the denigrating aesthetics of *indigenismo*, and so forth, but there has yet to be a full study of how these and other related dilemmas impinge on the popular appeal of the symbolic supremacy accorded to the macho.[3] This book does not consist of such a study, but it does propose that critical dialogues with Golden Age cinema's originary configurations of machismo contribute to a genealogical mapping of the dominant representational matrix that continues to assign malformed gender identities to racialized, lower-class Mexican men.

As a starting point for such dialogues, I suggest that the positive myth of the proud, dominant, melodious, hot-blooded macho celebrated in so many Golden Age films was composed in contradistinction to an adjacent cultural construct with an opposing set of features: a defective perversion of a proper Mexican macho, one not successfully formed as a man, or, more precisely, permanently and intrinsically malformed. This figure has many correlates in Mexican cultural discourse, particularly in the social psychology of Samuel Ramos and Octavio Paz, intellectuals who sought to explain the perpetual deferral of Mexican national modernity by diagnosing essential pathological defects in the male psyche. The malformed macho overlaps with the invented categories of "el pelado" and "los hijos de la chingada" formulated by these writers but extends beyond them to encompass an array of despised gender characteristics marking the legitimate social coordinates of justifiable violence, containment, exclusion, regulation, and discipline.[4]

In the sphere of national cinema, malformed man manifests as a threatening criminal, a bandit, a gangster, a pimp, a usurer, a cheat, a rapist, a thief, an alcoholic, an absent or abusive husband/father, an incompetent worker, an idler, an excessive gambler, a wastrel, a buffoon, a primitive barbarian. Any social authority he appears to hold is illegitimate. He is almost invariably of the lower classes, since the bourgeoisie and elite tend to have individualizable moral flaws and are often redeemable, while the signs of masculine malformation ascribed to the commoner tend to denote an inherent deficiency. Malformed man is often located somewhere on the spectrum between "indio" and "mestizo," categories reflecting the racializing logic that inaugurated an ongoing project of coloniality disguised as a process of nation-building, integration, and modernization. His complexion typically appears dark, his physiognomy may be some version of cinema's familiar "native" type, but his racialized otherness may be encoded by other signifiers, such as clothing (or lack thereof), hairstyle, and manner of speaking.[5] Whatever shape it takes, his malformation metonymizes racial inferiority. He may partly coincide with stereotypes of the effeminate or the homosexual, especially when manifested as a weakling or a coward. He more often exhibits frustrated or overaggressive heterosexual virility, sometimes implicitly masking repressed homosexual desire. Any attentive viewing of most Golden Age films will yield multiple sightings of, or allusions to, malformed man, for without his presence the idealized macho could not exist. He does not necessarily occupy the role of the principal antagonist as he may not make a worthy adversary for an archetypal hero or heroine. Very often, malformed man is a secondary character, or even merely a part of the mise-en-scène. He may provide a moment of comic relief, an incremental rise in narrative tension, or a temporary obstacle on the road to triumph or tragedy.[6]

A key premise of this book's arguments is that the matrix of codified masculinities in Mexican cinema contain meanings much like those Roger Bartra attributes to the metadiscourses pervading intellectual projects that sought to define the national character in terms of a distorted ontology whose parameters would be aligned with an authoritarian agenda. What Ramos and Paz and other elite members of the state-sponsored intelligentsia presented as the "definition of 'the Mexican' is rather a description of how he or she is dominated and, above all, how exploitation is legitimated" (Bartra 6).[7] Far more than definitive models of national identity to be emulated by ordinary male subjects, the spectacles of machismo in national cinema served as mechanisms to symbolically delineate broad constituencies of men marked as perniciously defective, helping to secure the continuance of Mexico's hierarchal social order throughout the postrevolutionary period. The insidious mode of power discursively enacted through the wider articulation of this pattern of dominant cultural meanings of masculinity transformed signs of unwanted difference or opposition into confirmation of the malformity, thereby selectively justifying violent forms of control on land, resources, and especially laboring bodies.

This strategy has proved adaptable over the long run of Mexico's state-led transition to a neoliberal economic regime in which cultural production in general, and cinema in particular, increasingly belong to the domain of transnational capitalism. In the new state-corporate alliance, private and public investments in Mexican filmmaking respond primarily to the logic of a marketplace of aspirational identities supporting the structural expansion of the current phase of global capitalism. Hence, the most revered expressions of masculinity in recent cinema tend to be structured in the cosmopolitan values of Western modernity rather than any kind of recognizable Mexicanness. Yet present-day networks of power rely on architectures of oppression built in the past. Today, vast populations of mostly impoverished Mexicans are being made ever more vulnerable, disposable, disappearable, and killable for the sake of securing the stability of the neoliberal order. The cultural politics that naturalizes this expansive social scenario of economic precarity, territorial expulsion, labor exploitation, disappearance, and violent death derives at least part of its discursive authority from a rearticulated repertoire of mythic malformed masculinities that originated with national cinema. The cultural repository of mexicanidad continues to exist as a sinister legacy of images and discourses frequently redeployed by neoliberal projects to reinforce contemporary perceptions of defective and dangerous men. Current filmmakers ineluctably contend with this heritage. Wittingly or not, many draw upon its ready supply of threatening and contemptible signs of masculine malformation, reproducing the dominant representational logic that organized earlier regimes of cultural politics. Others interrogate the protean figure of malformed man and its enmeshment with structures of power in the neoliberal state. These distinct trajectories of contemporary Mexican cinema are the main topic of this book.

Introduction

I. Rethinking Mexican Cinema, the Crisis of Masculinity, and the Patriarchal Contract

From the formative period of postrevolutionary nationalism through to the present era of neoliberal cultural politics, Mexican cinema has retained a paradigmatic preoccupation with representing defective masculinities. The codified regularities and symbolic symmetries that have endured in filmic imagery of deficient male gender performance reflect the underlying stability of certain currents of cultural mythology sustained through more than a century of transitions between various permutations of the modern capitalist nation-state in Mexico. The transhistorical continuity of these connective threads has been secured via the consistent reproduction of an array of archetypal masculine personae integrated with intellectually and politically authoritative categories and metanarratives constitutive of national projects of modernization and westernization. The colonial rationale that subsists beneath the modern rhetoric of equal citizenship, state sovereignty, progressive development, and economic emancipation manifests itself in sociopolitical practices of domination structured in long-standing fictions of racialized gender difference. Beginning in the sixteenth century, modern/colonial discourse represented indigenous and African people in Mexico and elsewhere as genderless beings approximate to children or animals, externalizing them from the purview of rational intersubjectivity and legitimating brutal forms of imperial conquest, subjugation, enslavement, and territorial expulsion.[1] Throughout much of Mexico's postindependence history, the invented premise of racial inferiority served to justify oppressive impositions of hierarchical gendering arrangements in the illusory guise of assimilative integration and mestizaje. This historical process, often understood to have culminated in the establishment of the postrevolutionary nation-state's patriarchal social order with the Mexican mestizo as its presumptive protagonist, in fact preserved racialized distinctions within the hegemonic gender system that cannot be accounted for solely in terms of masculinism and heterosexualism. As philosopher María Lugones asserts, much current gender analysis centers "a binary, hierarchical, oppressive gender formation that rests on male supremacy without any clear understanding of the mechanisms by which heterosexuality, capitalism, and racial classification are impossible to understand apart from each other" ("Heterosexualism" 187). In the absence of intersectional and decolonial approaches to thinking about racialized gender categories and class relations produced by modern/colonial power, "heterosexualist patriarchy has been an ahistorical framework of analysis" ("Heterosexualism" 187). In the case of Mexico, I suggest that historicizing the patriarchal gender system entails analyzing culturally prevalent myths regarding the mestizo's flawed masculine development, which remain discursively embedded in the national imaginary as internal threats undermining Mexican modernity. Cinema has been among the most potent cultural mediums for articulating these mythologized metanarratives and disseminating them throughout significant parts of society, thereby reinscribing the violent, disciplinary logic that enforces a class-regimented, racially hierarchized, heteronormative order. At the same time, Mexican film has also been a site for contesting and disassembling pejorative constructions of racialized, lower-class, male gender identity. This book examines cinematic resignifications of malformed maleness in the context of Mexican neoliberalism, turning critical attention toward specific films that appear to offer meaningful challenges to the well-established paradigm of transposing the frustrated promises of the modern state onto stereotyped figures of masculine deficiency.

Cultural myths of dominant Mexican masculinity are generally understood to have shared a lengthy, intricate, downward trajectory with national cinema. Formerly venerated symbols of Mexican manhood— *charros*, charmers, champs, and chums—canonized in popular classic films are thought to have followed a descending pathway marked by inertia, recurring crises, and protracted decay, paralleling the torturous spiraling decline of cinema itself as a viable sphere of national culture during much of the latter half of the twentieth century. This history has been ably told by Charles Ramírez Berg in *Cinema of Solitude* (1992), a study of Mexican films produced between 1967 and 1983.[2] In addition to addressing a confluence of material and political factors that fueled the slow self-immolation of the state-sponsored national film industry, Ramírez Berg recounts dozens of examples of movies whose stagnant portrayals of men are marked by stubborn adherence to moribund cultural codes of Mexican masculinity. In his view, cinema's failure to imagine new cultural models of male identity capable of withstanding economic uncertainty and accommodating changes demanded by feminism foretold the inevitable collapse of patriarchal national ideology and the sense of social coherence it once offered. Apart from rare exceptions, including several works by auteur director Jaime Humberto Hermosillo, who often struggled to find a domestic audience, the predominant trends of filmmaking during these decades of decline "reveal the desperate state of patriarchy in crisis" (Ramírez Berg 125). A running theme throughout Ramírez Berg's book is that national cinema no longer provided the "myth-making machinery" to counteract social tendencies toward alienation and estrangement (213).

Picking up more or less where Ramírez Berg leaves off, Ignacio Sánchez Prado's *Screening Neoliberalism* (2014) traces Mexican filmmaking's complex route from decrepitude in the late 1980s toward transformative revival by the turn of the new millennium. Although he finds fault with the discursive reproduction of the nationalist framework of cultural identity in Ramírez Berg's analysis (10–11), Sánchez Prado's continuation of the narrative of national cinema's demise reiterates the same basic point, attributing its failures not merely to political interference and economic malfeasance in the state institutions supporting and regulating the industry but also to the irrelevance of the repository of cultural myths of nationhood that continued to organize filmmaking long after they had exhausted their social meanings (5). To reinvent itself, Mexican cinema had to begin by "freeing its production from the nationalist imperatives that had defined the industry since its inception in the post-revolutionary period, in order to reflect the experiences of new social groups that were emerging along with the process of cultural remodernization brought about by the neoliberal economic and political model" (5). In Sánchez Prado's approach to this emancipated market-driven cultural economy, articulations of specifically Mexican masculine identity retain little significance, as he adopts a perspective that "steps outside both cultural concepts of the Mexican self and, more crucially, the idea that film is a 'representation' of any kind of 'Mexican culture'" (11). This reading strategy reflects his overall argument that appealing to "new social groups" involved adopting transnational aesthetic languages, setting Mexican filmmakers on a course toward a "properly post-national cinema—one that, beyond the acknowledgment of the limits of the nation, fully deterritorializes and undermines the codes of the national" (195). This process, as described in great detail by Sánchez Prado throughout his comprehensive study, was not at all straightforward, as it introduced new contradictions without even pretending to resolve the old ones, but it eventually constituted what many recognize as the full-fledged rebirth of Mexican filmmaking in the 2000s and 2010s.

Mexico Unmanned reexamines this transition to a new paradigm of filmmaking linked to neoliberal cultural politics in Mexico, specifically by questioning whether ties to nationalism's outmoded representational regime have truly been cut, particularly those ties binding images of Mexican men to a fixed set of predefined meanings of masculinity. This involves rethinking some deeply ingrained assumptions about the social and political purpose of Mexico's prevailing cultural fictions of manhood. For example, it is easily taken for granted that national cinema's rigid attachment to normative models and codes of masculinity merely reflected the ideological entrenchment of old-fashioned Mexican patriarchy. Filmic portrayals of strong, proud, virile men are understood to have reinforced dominant social narratives about Mexico as a male-centered nation, entitling all men—or at least those deemed sufficiently manly—to enjoy unquestionable privilege, an arrangement that neither the Mexican state nor Mexican men were willing to abandon. This overdetermining presupposition obscures the racializing dimensions of heteropatriarchal state ideology in Mexico and fails to recognize how masculine symbols have been consistently wielded for authoritarian purposes to disempower the majority of ordinary Mexicans, men and women alike. Without denying the reality of racialized men's co-option into systemic practices of gendered violence, homophobia, and sexual oppression in Mexico, this book offers an analysis of prejudicial myths of masculinity circulated in cinema as a contribution to the critical understanding of unjust power relations reproduced at the level of cultural politics and representation.

This work seems especially relevant at a time when both the nation-state and its hegemonic fictions of national culture are often presumed to have already been displaced and superseded—or are well on their way to being so—by entirely new structures of authority and symbolic registers. Globalization is commonly understood to imply the dissolution of conventional gendered social paradigms and labor regimes formerly organized around patriarchal cultural values that grant undeniable privilege to the autonomous male family-provider. For this reason, one finds countless references to a so-called "crisis" of masculinity that accompanies the transition to the neoliberal phase of capitalism, especially in societies like Mexico where the masculine has been so closely identified with nationalist political ideology and where the rise of new decentralized economic structures has been especially rapid and acute. From this perspective, evidence of a weakening state, including the collapse of one-party rule, may be interpreted as signifying that the nation's traditional model of manhood is swiftly going (or has already gone) extinct. Corresponding images of Mexican men supposedly threatened by this change have become commonplace in cultural representations as well as critical theorizing about the rise of criminal violence, the drug trade, and the impunity surrounding the mass murders of women in Ciudad Juárez and other parts of the republic.[3] Foundering in the destabilized labor market and having lost their exalted cultural status, social prestige, and the shelter of the patriarchal state, ordinary Mexican men supposedly respond with frustration, lawlessness, and chaotic violence. At the same time, it is often presumed that the demise of national masculinity liberates cultural space for new cosmopolitan embodiments of maleness, feminist political expression, and greater challenges to heteronormative binary codes of gender and sexuality. In this view, the originary constructions of Mexican masculinity may persist in fragmented or residual form as obstacles to be overcome by emancipatory politics and progressive values, but they are generally absent from the prevailing frameworks of subject-formation reflected in and cultivated by spheres of cultural production such as cinema. *Mexico Unmanned* attempts to put some pressure on these claims, not because I think conventional Mexican masculinity is alive and well as a viable and desirable framework for identity, but because its relationship to power has been thoroughly occluded by pervasive cultural mythologies. One can only posit the obsolescence of Mexican masculinity by reducing it to a set of state-sanctioned practices that empowered ordinary machos to dominate women and effeminate men. Such a move not only reproduces the cultural myths generated by nationalism but also obscures how contemporary rearticulations of these myths continue to be invoked in discursive rationalizations of violence affecting lower-class racialized Mexicans across all sexes, genders, and sexual practices. Part of my purpose in situating this discussion in relation to the national filmmaking archive is to demystify the persistent association between machismo and a supposed patriarchal contract between the nation-state and ordinary men. My book uses masculinity in the sphere of cinema as a critical vantage point for exploring how the Mexican state's approaches to authorizing exploitative violence against its own population have been reconfigured amid the transition from national to postnational cultural politics and the installation of a neoliberal economic regime.

As a point of departure, I contend that, at its inception, the sociocultural gaze constructed around masculine imagery in Mexico's national filmmaking tradition was designed to legitimate the oppressive subordination not only of women and sexual minorities but also of presumptively heterosexual men regarded as brown mestizos. Far more than encouraging these men's straightforward identification with appealing models of Mexican maleness, national cinema's originary macho images concretized a representational logic intended to symbolically unman most of the male population of Mexico by ensuring that brown bodies were socially perceptible as dangerously deficient in relation to a whitened masculine gender norm. Mexican cinema's myths of national masculinity have always functioned to naturalize the submasculine, racially inferiorized category of the malformed male.[4] The questions I pose in my critical dialogues with contemporary Mexican films and film studies concern the aesthetic and discursive mechanisms that enable this category, originally formulated within the nationalist imaginary, to be inherited and rearticulated by neoliberal cultural politics and incorporated into current postnational cinematic signifying practices. By masculine malformations, I mean gendered signs of human deficiency, intersected with categorial constructions of racial difference and meaningful indicators of distinct geographic origins and socioeconomic disparities, forming representational assemblages affixed to certain bodies marked as biologically male in order to make them intelligible as being less than men. Because masculine subjectivity has been conceived as indispensable to Mexico's variously defined projects of modernization and westernization throughout every stage of its history as a nation, being classified as a malformed male directly impinges on one's relationship to modernity, predetermining whether one can properly embody modern values and Western ideals. Although this sociocultural designation implies perceptions of unmanliness, it does not necessarily call into question the presumed heterosexuality of the designee, as I explain later. The work of other scholars shows that there undoubtedly exist related categories of malformed femininity articulated in Mexican cinema and other spheres of cultural production and social practice.[5] My study aims to complement scholarship dealing critically with the logic of power that problematically situates racialized women within the modern/

colonial gender system.⁶ What I claim at the outset is that national cinema's paradigmatic codifications of Mexican masculinities have contributed to the naturalization of distorted ontological conceptions of Mexican men in ways that have only rarely been acknowledged. My readings of contemporary cinema show that if filmmakers, film critics, and cultural theorists do not critically confront the received meanings of Mexican masculinity, they risk reproducing these distortions.

The broader implications of this book's arguments extend across the history of filmmaking in Mexico, but by focusing my analysis on films produced during the past two decades, I show how the recodification of myths of masculinity within a neoliberal framework of cultural politics problematizes the narrative of cinema's definitive break with the national.⁷ To be sure, the reforms that began to dismantle the state-sponsored film industry in the 1980s clearly reshaped the existing systems of production, distribution, and exhibition, particularly by introducing the necessity for private investment at every point of the process. Institutional reorganization and privatization in combination with new media technologies, redesigned infrastructure, demographic displacement, strategic marketing, expanded festival circuits, complex funding mechanisms and tax schemes, endemic piracy, as well as other factors, have generated substantively different patterns of filmmaking and spectatorship in Mexico today as compared with the early 1990s. Simultaneously, major restructuring of Mexico's systemic links to globalized flows of capital has significantly altered material conditions throughout most of the country, especially since the implementation of the original North American Free Trade Agreement (NAFTA) in 1994. These economic changes have occurred without bringing about the promised prosperity for a majority of Mexicans and without meaningful dissent from any faction of Mexico's political leadership. They have, however, undoubtedly modified the terms in which unequal power relations and capitalist exploitation are legitimated. Understanding the ongoing cultural consequences of these interfacing processes of neoliberal transformation is one of the major challenges for Mexican film studies today. It is my contention that examining representations of masculinity in recent Mexican cinema can illuminate the cultural logic that reproduces codes and discourses authorizing violent practices of social control in the neoliberal state. While acknowledging the evident ruptures separating current postnational filmmaking practice from the expired paradigm of national cinema, I trace lines of continuity, showing the parallels between shifting contours of malformed masculinity and evolving networks of power in Mexico.

II. Neoliberal Cultural Politics

Critical discourses examining Mexico's changing patterns of cultural politics in relation to the development of the neoliberal order have established some parameters for mapping out new arrangements at the level of symbol and praxis. Thorough treatment of the range of analytic frameworks formulated in response to Mexico's neoliberal experience exceeds the scope of my purposes in this introduction, but engaging briefly with certain critical tendencies to show where they intersect with my thematization of masculinity in recent cinema will open the way for the discussions contained in my chapters.

Accounts of neoliberalism often begin from an understanding of the meanings it holds as a theoretical doctrine of political economy. In this context, as defined by geographer David Harvey, the term encompasses the ideological proposal that "human well-being can best be advanced by liberating individual entrepreneurial freedoms and skills within an institutional framework characterized by strong private property rights, free markets, and free trade" (2). In certain respects, these ideas do not necessarily represent a significant departure from orthodox conceptualizations of capitalism as the ideal economic model for modern liberal-democratic societies at whatever stage of development. However, during the past several decades, the distinctive impact of neoliberal theory has been borne out globally (albeit unevenly) in the practical application of state strategies that ostensibly seek to optimize human liberty by maximizing market-based freedoms. While there is no single paradigm that has been universally followed by national governments implementing neoliberal reforms, some particularly illustrative policies favored by these regimes include limiting state spending on social welfare programs; privatizing formerly public sectors of the economy (e.g., health and education); designating special economic zones exempt from wider regulatory frameworks; deregulating financial markets and lending institutions; limiting the power of labor unions; reducing or removing environmental protections and controls on natural resources; dismantling state-owned enterprises; shifting to export-based models of industrial and agricultural development; imposing regressive systems of taxation; and eliminating barriers to transnational commerce (Harvey 6–9). While such policies may be designed to prevent governments from actively intervening in their own national economies in ways advocated by Keynesian theory, or from enacting protectionist measures that could constrain the movement of capital and commodities in and out of the country, this does not mean that neoliberal restructuring results in an overall reduction of state power. Instead, what these changes amount to, according to Harvey, is the creation of a new kind of "state apparatus whose fundamental mission [is] to facilitate conditions for profitable capital accumulation on the part of both domestic and foreign capital. I call this kind of state apparatus a *neoliberal state* The freedoms it embodies reflect the interests of private property owners, businesses, multinational corporations, and financial capital" (7; original emphasis). Making a similar point from a Latin American perspective, Verónica Gago writes that "neoliberalism is not the reign of the economy subordinating the political, but the creation of a political world (the regime of *governmentality*) that arises as the projection of the rules and requirements of market competition" (153; original emphasis). As institutionalized state policy, neoliberalism came into practice in Mexico in the early 1980s when the bankrupt federal government under the presidential administration of Miguel de la Madrid (1982–88) enacted austerity measures and deregulatory reforms designed by the International Monetary Fund, Wall Street banks, and the U.S. Treasury in return for massive financial bailouts (Harvey 99–100). These changes, originally justified by an immediate debt crisis, laid the groundwork for the state's definitive embrace of neoliberalism during the presidency of Carlos Salinas de Gotari (1988–94), who oversaw the process of drafting, promoting, and signing the free trade accord between the United States, Mexico, and Canada (Harvey 101–104). As of 2019, despite newly elected president Andrés Manuel López Obrador's declaration that "ya se terminó con esa pesadilla que fue la política neoliberal" (the nightmare that was neoliberal politics is now over), Mexico continues along the same politico-economic trajectory that has defined the current stage of global capitalism.[8]

The cultural consequences of neoliberalism in Mexico have been profound and pervasive across the spectrum of creative activity, but transformations in the sphere of cinema are of particular interest here.[9] Scholars such as Sánchez Prado and Misha MacLaird have given detailed accounts of the complex restructuring of state cultural institutions involved in the film industry during the early phases of the neoliberal transition. In the mid-1980s, the state-organized systems of subsidizing, promoting, and regulating film production and exhibition that had been assembled over several decades were targeted for reform. While certain institutional structures remained formally in place, access to state funding was ever more limited and Mexican filmmaking's survival would increasingly be determined by its ability to compete on the open market. As a result, the aesthetic languages that national cinema had long relied upon to communicate with Mexican audiences entered a transformative phase. Both MacLaird and Sánchez Prado underscore how the new imperative to attract private investment by producing marketable content was often in tension with institutional policies supposedly intended to support and protect Mexican cinema's status as cultural patrimony. The work of both scholars demonstrates that after some initial ambivalence toward the displacement of the nationalist representational regime, audiences and filmmakers gradually coalesced around a new set of signifying practices closely aligned with neoliberal values, making cinema "a particularly apt genre for studying cultural transformation in Mexico precisely because it follows the transformation of hegemonic political and social ideologies in a very organic way" (Sánchez Prado *Screening* 12). As MacLaird puts it, "the films, filmmakers, stories, and production methods embody this ideological grey area [of the transitional period]; that is to say, they *are* the transition" (4; original emphasis).

More than simply a set of policies producing a material shift from state-sponsored to consumer-driven models of cultural production, neoliberalism has become an analytic category that opens critical perspectives on restructured formations of citizenship, collectivity, and subjecthood mediated by consumption practices in the transnational marketplace of culture. By the mid-1990s, cultural criticism in Mexico had already begun to consider the complex consequences of neoliberal processes using new theoretical tools and frameworks, such as Néstor García Canclini's notion of the "consumer-citizen"—a way of moving beyond national cultural imaginaries to rethink the exercise of citizenship "without dissociating it from those activities through which we establish our social belonging, our social networks, which in this globalized era are steeped in consumption" (*Consumers and Citizens* 20). Influencing both Sánchez Prado and MacLaird, this approach facilitates analysis of the correlation between the dissolution of concepts of collective national identity and the reconstitution of social ties within heterogeneous, transnational cultural formations organized by shared consumption habits and preferences. Globalized media industries offer cultural commodities that foster a sense of belonging to deterritorialized communities of consumers, transcending local, regional, and national modes of identification. García Canclini defines several corollary processes that contribute to configuring neoliberal consumer-citizenship, including "the reformulation of patterns of urban settlement and coexistence" in large cities and the "rearrangement of the institutions and circuits for the exercise of public life" (*Consumers and Citizens* 24).

Interrelated changes in the infrastructural circuitry of citizenship, cultural consumption habits, socio-spatial organization, and concepts of collective belonging converge closely in the analysis of Mexican cinema's neoliberal transformations. At the same time as the state was withdrawing institutionalized support for film production, ticket prices were being deregulated, screen quotas for Mexican films were being removed, and state-operated cinemas were being sold off and gradually replaced by corporate multiplexes often located in shopping malls outside of city centers (MacLaird 21–44; Sánchez Prado *Screening* 75–88). In other words, moviegoing was becoming an activity restricted to affluent urban consumers who were more likely to own cars, to live in certain neighborhoods, and to be accustomed to consuming non-Mexican media and other cultural goods. Mexican film producers participated in this "class displacement of audiences" by introducing formal strategies and aesthetic codes derived from Hollywood genres, U.S. independent cinema (e.g., Sundance festival films), and television sitcoms, tailoring the narratives, characters, and representational spaces to the tastes and aspirations of Mexico's privileged classes (Sánchez Prado *Screening* 6). In this way, cinema in the neoliberal era increasingly comes to reflect a "separation between the cultural languages of different social classes and social geographies" (Sánchez Prado *Screening* 63). An important consequence of these patterns of partition is the emergence of discrete spheres of affective identification, as cinema's dominant genres and idioms of romance and empathy become the exclusive province of privileged consumers. By identifying specific correspondences between the aesthetic and narrative choices of filmmakers and the social and affective sensibilities connecting film audiences to shared networks of belonging, it becomes possible to analyze cinema in terms of a distinct neoliberal "structure of feeling" (Sánchez Prado "Regimes of Affect" 4).[10]

While recent Mexican film scholarship has concentrated on the predominance of cultural sensibilities associated with a small affluent class of neoliberal consumers, another set of related critical theorizations of neoliberalism in Mexico lays emphasis on political and cultural responses to the structural transformations of authority, practices of violence, and control over land, labor, and resources.[11] The fact that the advent of neoliberalism in Mexico historically coincides with the last phase of the PRI (Partido Revolucionario Institucional) regime's seven consecutive decades in political control of the state can lend false credence to the ludicrous claim that economic liberalization was a precursor to democratization. This deceptive fantasy is dissolved by the oppositional thinking and praxis embodied by the EZLN's (Ejército Zapatista de Liberación Nacional) mobilization of an armed uprising among indigenous communities in the state of Chiapas on New Year's Day 1994, followed by its nationwide campaigns of nonviolent resistance articulating the struggle against the neoliberal state as a continuation of five centuries of indigenous defiance of colonialism, genocide, cultural destruction, and capitalist exploitation. The critical writings and communiqués issued by members of the EZLN's Revolutionary Indigenous Clandestine Committee thoroughly refuted the state-corporate media's propagandistic political and cultural discourses about the social benefits of opening the economy to transnational trade and investment, contending that subalternized indigenous people and their territories would be ever more violently pillaged to fuel the export market and tourism economy: "En pleno auge del neoliberalismo . . . el sureste sigue exportando materias primas y mano de obra y, como desde hace 500 años, sigue importando lo principal de la producción capitalista: muerte y miseria" (At the height of neoliberalism . . . the southeast [region of Mexico] continues exporting raw materials and labor power, and, just as for the past 500 years, continues importing capitalism's chief products: death and misery) (EZLN *Documentos* 54).[12] These texts provide richly theorized and prescient accounts of neoliberalism's ruinous effects on Mexico's most oppressed communities, but always with a view toward the transformative possibilities of countering capitalist modernity's epistemic monologue by invoking the radically pluriversal cosmovision of "a world where many worlds can fit" (EZLN "The People the Color of the Earth" 106).[13]

The activist spirit of *zapatismo* partly informs the more recent work of Mexican cultural theorists such as Sayak Valencia and Irmgard Emmelhainz who examine neoliberal transformations. While they tend to develop their insights in dialogue with mostly European interlocutors, both of these thinkers acknowledge continuities with the earlier efforts of the EZLN to disentangle the rhetoric of progress, democracy, and economic salvation articulated by neoliberal cultural politics from the systemic violence and exploitation it serves to legitimate. In *Gore Capitalism* (2010), Valencia begins her theorizing from the Tijuana border zone, a locus she describes in terms of extreme crosscurrents between hyperconsumption and commercialized violence, that is, organized crime, kidnappings, contract killings, and the privatization and outsourcing of public security. The increasingly evident coexistence of these phenomena across Mexico comprises what Valencia calls "gore capitalism . . . the undisguised and unjustified bloodshed that is the price the Third World pays for adhering to the increasingly demanding logic of capitalism" (19). Gore is what happens when the neoliberal rationale of unrestricted commerce and limitless pursuit of entrepreneurial opportunity is followed through to its ultimate conclusions. It occurs globally, but most intensively in geographic locales where the imbalance of economic power is greatest, hence Mexico's northern border with the U.S. provides particularly fertile ground for its proliferation. For Valencia, the dystopian neoliberal transformation of Mexico has constituted a "breakdown of the State," as the government gradually ceded its power to the globalized marketplace, the underside of which is gore capitalism (40). By contrast, Emmelhainz, in *La tiranía del sentido común* (2016), starts not from the premise of a failed state but rather the exercise of "calculated sovereignty,"[14] the Mexican government's flexible strategy of using controlled violence to regulate zones of legitimate investment and commerce while selectively allowing other territories to be ruled by the vicissitudes of corrupt local authorities and criminal organizations, no doubt in coordination with Mexican oligarchs and distant agents of global capital (62). The coalescence of state structures of authority, including the military and police, with transnational systems of profiteering embodies the fundamental logic of neoliberalism, complemented and reinforced by the mass media and major spheres of cultural production (Emmelhainz 15–16). Emmelhainz's primary critical concern lies with the insidious colonizing mechanisms by which this logic becomes normalized in discourses and symbols that disguise state-organized violence and corporate exploitation as development and economic growth (17). She argues that the pervasiveness of the neoliberal rationale in everyday life, language, culture, social practices, spatial inhabitations, aesthetic regimes, and so forth, may be understood as a tyrannous "sensibilidad y un sentido común" (sensibility and common sense) (19).

Critiques of neoliberalism's oppressive colonial dimensions have not figured prominently in Mexican film studies. *Mexico Unmanned* seeks to open a space for these conversations by showing how representations of defective Mexican men function as transhistorical symbolic mechanisms for justifying state practices of violence and exploitation. This also implies that film studies can make significant contributions to the critique of neoliberal structures of power and capital acquisition by introducing nuanced, politicized analyses of specific aesthetic strategies and larger systemic patterns of cultural representation. Knowledge of cinema's role in the construction and circulation of pernicious stereotypes of Mexican masculinity can unsettle certain "common sense" assumptions that sometimes infiltrate even the most sophisticated theoretical accounts of neoliberal transformations. For example, while Valencia's treatise has been widely praised for its cogent analysis of the political and economic processes reshaping Mexico's relationship to global capitalism, her work is in fact suffused with unthoughtful essentializations, particularly related to her descriptions of monstrous "endriago subjects," impoverished men whose frustrated, emasculated condition makes them predisposed to use violence and criminality as a means of pursuing perverse kinds of social mobility (26, 106, 118).[15] These figures are central to Valencia's effort to theorize the epidemic of brutal cruelty associated with the drug trade that overshadows Mexico's experience of neoliberalism, yet her account of these men's overdetermined tendencies to engage in gore practices dovetails closely with official discourses and prevailing cultural narratives of the drug war. As Dawn Paley writes in a review article, "[Valencia] reproduces many of the same myths about the violence that are propagated by Mexican state forces and the judiciary and repeated *ad nauseam* by mainstream media" ("Countering"). I would add that these present-day myths have clear genealogical links to the originary formulations of Mexican machismo in national cinema and the logically corresponding construction of malformed masculinities that I am tracing in this book.

The current predominance of mass media depictions of violent criminals who have supposedly transformed Mexico's rural regions and provincial cities into war zones merits special attention as it illustrates how neoliberalism activates preexisting cultural fictions to advance a new political and economic agenda. Paley's recent work (with Simon Granovsky-Larsen) attempts to reframe the dominant depoliticized narratives on the criminal drug trade in Mexico and other parts of Latin America by showing how the phenomenon of organized violence has "more to do with extraction, production, finance, or social control than it does with cocaine or gangs" (3). She elaborates on this thesis in her monograph book *Guerra Neoliberal* (Neoliberal War) (2019), where she directly challenges the ruling discourses that represent the ongoing situation of widespread violence in Mexico in terms of overlapping conflicts between the state and drug cartels, and between rival cartels competing for control over "plazas" in bloody regional wars whose victims are either themselves involved in narco activity or are simply caught in the crossfire of frequent gun battles occurring in public. According to Paley, these accounts, reiterated time and again in official documents, news reports, intellectual analyses, and cultural representations, serve to confuse and distort the reality of the systemic violence that has taken shape under the dominion of the neoliberal state in Mexico (*Guerra* 12). She puts forward the compelling argument that "la llamada guerra contra el narcotráfico en México representa un cambio en la forma de gobernar en paralelo con la profundización del proceso neoliberal, a través de la aplicación de tecnicas ampliadas de guerra contrainsurgente" (the so-called war against drug trafficking in Mexico represents a change to the form of governing in parallel with the deepening of the neoliberal process via the application of expanded counterinsurgency techniques) (*Guerra* 13). In a similar vein, Oswaldo Zavala makes the case for the seemingly provocative position expressed in the title of his book: *Los cárteles no existen* (Cartels Do Not Exist) (2018). To be clear, neither Paley nor Zavala suggests that illicit substances are not being clandestinely trafficked across Mexico's northern border to be sold in the U.S. and elsewhere, but rather they contend that the myths surrounding this lucrative trade provide convincing discursive cover for the brutal exercise of state power on people and territories unrelated to drugs and organized crime. As Zavala explains, "La violencia *atribuida* a los supuestos cárteles . . . obedece más a las estrategias disciplinarias de las propias estructuras del Estado que a la acción criminal de los supuestos 'narcos'" (the violence *attributed* to the supposed cartels . . . arises from the State's own disciplinary strategies more than from any criminal action of the supposed "narcos") (8; original emphasis). Zavala's work discusses how cultural representations, such as novels, television series, and films, contribute to reinforcing depoliticized distinctions between criminals and victims that cohere with government's official rationale for waging an ongoing war against the narcos (21).

These authors offer important interventions in the analysis of the undeniable bloodshed that has transformed Mexico over the past decade and half, revealing patterns of correspondence between the interests of transnational capitalism and the expansion of the Mexican state's security apparatus predicated on dubious accounts of large-scale criminal activity. They argue that Mexico's mounting toll of deaths and disappearances, mass graves, and public displays of mutilated bodies are not at all consistent with claims of a war being waged between the state and organized groups of combatants of considerable strength, but instead with a one-sided campaign of repression being carried out against ordinary Mexicans by the state itself or with its complicity. Paley and Zavala pay careful attention to the rhetorical strategies and discursive mechanisms that are employed to classify individuals and whole communities as criminals and narcos in order to legitimate their deaths or to deny them justice as victims, or both. More than mere bureaucratic doublespeak or linguistic chicanery, the specific cultural idiom that has arisen around narcotrafficking in Mexico comprises a highly compelling set of codes assembled into social fictions imbued with the persuasive force of official truth (Zavala 9; Paley *Guerra* 12). In my view, however, this phenomenon cannot be satisfactorily interrogated without a fuller critical understanding of how the invented image of the criminal drug trafficker embodies elements of racialized gender malformation, a mythology that has long been cultivated by Mexican cinema. When considering what makes the "reality" of the drug war so seemingly incontrovertible, one cannot ignore the way in which so many narco narratives rely on a naturalized dichotomy of positive and negative masculinities intertwined with categorical hierarchies of race.[16] *Mexico Unmanned* seeks to contribute to the critique of the neoliberal state's discursive justifications of violence by exploring how they follow patterns established by the representational language of cinema to situate subjects in a gender matrix that dehumanizes them in terms of malformed masculinity.

The chapters in this book traverse the field of cinema produced during the past two decades in order to illustrate and question the role of Mexican gender mythology in the reproduction of neoliberal arrangements of social exclusion/belonging, emotional connectivity, political violence, and economic reasoning. These arguments may be provisionally assembled under the overarching claim that representations of men in the films I study register how masculine gender codes are articulated in terms of Mexico's contemporary cultural politics—that is, how masculinity is structurally and symbolically integrated with the current neoliberal configuration of the dominant system of power. The codified matrix of masculinities represented in recent cinema expresses the logic that designates gendered criteria of inclusion and exclusion, desirable and undesirable embodiments of male subjectivity. Rather than merely building a typology of differentiated masculinities, my interpretative method aims to link specific symbolic codifications to corresponding neoliberal processes of segregation, affective realignment, state violence, and systemic enforcement of social, material, and political inequalities reflected in the films. In other words, it shows how cultural meanings of neoliberal masculinities are constituted in conjunction with the practices, discourses, and power relations that have given shape to Mexico's current hegemonic order. My specific interest lies with examining the ways in which the films construct and contest malformed masculinities within and against the dominant representational regime of neoliberal cinema. I consider how certain films naturalize inscriptions of male gender defects, treating them as though they were inherent properties attributable to differences of race, class, or regional geography. In other cases, I engage with filmmakers whose work discloses the representational logic that makes malformations perceptible and socially intelligible.

The selection of films to be analyzed concentrates on work by directors known in Mexico for their independent/auteurist practice: Alfonso Cuarón, Carlos Cuarón, Carlos Reygadas, Amat Escalante, and Julio Hernández Cordón. I acknowledge the ambivalence inherent in the term "independent" filmmaking and its applicability to the directors in my corpus of study, especially considering that chapter 1 examines two of Mexican cinema's biggest box office successes of all time. I am also aware that this label itself has likely contributed to the commercial marketability of the films and the heightened transnational and domestic visibility of certain of these directors. Furthermore, I recognize that their achievements as independent filmmakers are both cause and consequence of the neoliberal restructuring in the film industry.[17] Taking into consideration the complex factors that have brought these individuals to relative prominence within their creative field, my goal is to use their films to engage an array of masculinity-related shifts in Mexican cultural politics rather than to assess their particular achievements as artists. Invoking auteurism often connotes a certain kind of critical practice that attempts to encompass the authorial vision of the individual director by privileging his or her stated or implied aesthetic intentions over the dialogic possibilities opened via critical engagement with the work, undermining supposed textual autonomy. The challenge, as I comprehend it, is to maintain a productive equilibrium between respect for the artist's distinctive purposes and the resultant multiplicity of meanings that emerge in the exercise of critical dialogue. My approach incorporates certain director-centric material gathered from interviews and commentaries, but without giving it undue weight in the balance of other input from scholars and critics as well as my own interpretative analysis. Each of the directors whose work I have selected make a unique contribution to cinema as a global art form and to filmmaking traditions located in Mexico, but by no means do I consider them to represent the strongest talent or most interesting projects of the past two decades. Nonetheless, the individuality of their creative practice is a consideration I take seriously, which is why I elect to organize my chapters around specific directors and films, or, in some cases, around particular pairings. I am conscious that my selection of primary research materials encompasses the work of a relatively homogenous cast of male filmmakers who share common sociocultural backgrounds and aesthetic-cognitive orientations, which makes evident persistent patterns of exclusion in the Mexican film industry that are replicated at least to some extent by criticism and scholarship.[18] My main objective in assembling the corpus for this book was to select representative work foregrounding questions of masculinity in the context of neoliberal cultural politics and changes in filmmaking practice. More specifically, my purpose involves addressing the historicity of the logic of power transmitted in the reproduction of cultural myths generative of malformed masculinities in the dominant representational regime of cinema. To elucidate this dimension of my argument more fully, I trace the lineage of this mechanism of control to its originary formulations in postrevolutionary nationalism.

III. Formations of Machismo

Much of the predominant mythology of modern Mexican masculinity is condensed by the ambiguous concept of "machismo." Idiomatic usage of macho-related vocabulary in ordinary speech must be interpreted relative to the variable self-perceptions and communicative intentions of speakers located in complex sociohistorical, cultural, and rhetorical situations. However, as a term for discursive analysis, machismo retains special currency in reference to an idealized model of virility and male solidarity considered integral to the project of mexicanidad, a concerted effort by nationalist intellectuals, artists, and state institutions to redefine the spirit of Mexicanness following the political chaos of 1910–20 (commonly referred to as a revolution). Of particular concern in this discussion are the macho characteristics affixed to archetypes of manliness portrayed in popular cinema. In his landmark study *Cinemachismo*, Sergio de la Mora writes that reinventing Mexico as a "macho nation" involved the creation of the "cult of a particular form of masculinity—and therefore also femininity and womanliness—that was aggressively promoted by the cultural nationalist post-revolutionary establishment" (2). In hundreds of films produced during what is known as the Golden Age of Mexican cinema—roughly the mid-1930s to the mid-1950s—filmmakers repeatedly returned to a shared set of visual, aural, and narrative strategies to naturalize the correlation between machismo and Mexicanness. Yet even in this context of vehement nationalism, the meanings of *lo macho* are not as straightforward or homogenous as they might initially appear. The fact that machismo needed to be "aggressively promoted" and "officially decreed" as the sine qua non of Mexican national identity already indicates not only its dubious status as a shared cultural value but also its contested significance as a categorial concept (de la Mora 2). Indeed, as de la Mora's work illustrates, national cinema's celebrations of an ostensibly settled definition of Mexican machismo consistently reflected "social anxieties and tensions over changing representations of masculinity and manhood as well as femininity and womanhood" (3). The dissonance surrounding gender and nationhood was not limited to postrevolutionary cinema, but pervaded literature, the arts, and intellectual discourse throughout other periods of Mexico's cultural history, as has been shown by scholars such as Robert McKee Irwin and Héctor Domínguez-Ruvalcaba.[19] In the decades following the revolution, however, the reconstituted state's emphasis on machismo as the cornerstone of national unity gradually transformed the male body into an overburdened locus for the exercise of patriarchal power.

Differing accounts of the ideological construct of Mexican machismo that emerge as the contingent and contested norm in cinema and other spheres of postrevolutionary cultural production have been given by the scholars mentioned above, but general agreement exists on two main constituent elements: phallic virility and strong homosocial affinity. These form a mutually reinforcing arrangement of codified male conduct while simultaneously generating a plethora of contradictions with potentially destabilizing effects that must be controlled and mitigated by compulsory misogyny and homophobia. The most obvious ideological appeal of correlating masculinity to the solidity of men's homosocial bonds lies with the allegorical correspondence between *compadrismo* and patriarchal nationhood. Heterosexual romance narratives continued to carry symbolic weight as metaphors for national unity,[20] but Mexican filmmakers, artists, and intellectuals placed extraordinary value on male-to-male intimacy as both a sign of patriotic camaraderie and "a structure of masculine formation" (Domínguez-Ruvalcaba 75). It is only in relationships between men that virile masculinity acquires its truest and fullest expression, thus "virility is grounded in homosociety" (Domínguez-Ruvalcaba 77). This potentially poses a paradox since, in theory, all men are already naturally endowed with virility, but because it is configured as relative rather than absolute, individuals are compelled to constantly compare themselves and compete with one another to establish and confirm their masculine prowess in public and private settings (Irwin xviii–xx; Domínguez-Ruvalcaba 83). These relational comparisons and rivalries among men most often play out within the heterosexual economy, entailing "traffic in women."[21] In the typical triangular erotic scenario, women are reduced to objects of possession and exchange that "both facilitate and block the physical and affective ties between men" (de la Mora 70). Homosocial behaviors inherently introduce the possibility of transgressing into homoerotics, hence prescribed contests based on heterosexual conquest serve as an ideological constraint on male-male desire. But since relations between men hold primary importance, substantial romantic ties to women may be misogynistically represented as "threatening and disruptive to the male bond" (de la Mora 88).

Homophobia imposes a regulatory limit on masculine intimacies, but also has a curiously ambivalent role in constituting virile machismo. Homosexuality in Mexico, like elsewhere, had been mostly unnamed and unrecognized throughout the nineteenth century, but it entered into the public consciousness in a profound way after the notorious scandal of the "famous 41," when Mexico City police arrested a group of presumed homosexual men attending a transvestite ball in 1901 (Irwin xi–xii, xxii). With this highly publicized incident, fear mongering about savage criminal sodomites and urbane pederasts became pervasive in the press, and male sexuality was increasingly a question for debate in many spheres of intellectual and creative activity (Irwin 115). In the postrevolutionary period, "effeminate" writers were condemned for the perceived lack of virility in their aesthetic practice, and some were personally denounced and attacked as homosexuals (Irwin 152; de la Mora 2). Yet the ideological framework of masculinity in postrevolutionary Mexico does not flatly disallow homoeroticism and male effeminacy, but rather accommodates them in conflictive ways, and even depends on them to establish and enforce normative heterosexual virility. The Mexican macho's obligatory revulsion toward the homosexual corresponds conversely to his homosocial affection toward his male companions/competitors, reflecting two sides of the same compulsion to establish virile supremacy. As Domínguez-Ruvalcaba writes, "The relationship between desire and hate is dialectic, never a definite opposition. Homophobia and male-to-male attraction appear interrelated in narratives of homosociety" (5). In national cinema, as de la Mora shows, this contradiction gets expressed in scenarios where "bonds between *cuates* deliberately criss-cross the boundaries between homosociality and homosexuality" (71). The stereotyped figure of the effeminate *joto* often serves to "define and affirm" machismo, especially in diegetic spaces where male sexuality comes under explicit scrutiny, such as brothels and cabarets (de la Mora 5).

The co-constitutive relationship between virility and homosociality also inscribes an ambiguous dimension of sensuality and sentimentality into postrevolutionary Mexican machismo. In the immediate aftermath of the revolution's violence, nationalist intellectuals often emphasized aggressive physicality and martial valor in their celebrations of the masculinity embodied by the heroic men who fought side-by-side to emancipate the nation from the dictatorship of Porfirio Díaz and his ill-fated successors (Irwin xxxii; Domínguez-Ruvalcaba 77). But the collective attribution of visceral strength and fierce bravery to Mexican men retained class and racial connotations entangled with the binary of civilization and barbarism, as these virile characteristics were intended to distinguish autochthonous masculinity from the un-Mexican effeteness associated with the Europhile *criollo* elite of the Porfiriato and the bourgeois intellectuals of the 1920s and '30s (Irwin xxix, xxxii). Savage masculinity, an asset during wartime, would be a liability to the progressive evolutionary process of mestizaje envisioned by the architects of postrevolutionary nationalism. The imperative to modernize the nation meant that a revised consensus on masculinity had to be negotiated, especially given that the capitalist trajectory of economic transformation was introducing more Mexicans into urban-industrial labor arrangements and social relations with altered gender requirements that had to be accommodated within mexicanidad. Film was to play an important role in this process of reconfiguring the dominant image of the Mexican macho, making it more amenable to modern sensibilities through sentimentalism, song, melodrama, and pathos.

In contrast to the inexpressive masculine stoicism that pervades Hollywood movies and some other Western film traditions, Mexican men are most often represented in Golden Age cinema as sensitive, passionate, temperamental subjects vulnerable to intense bouts of suffering and given to animated outbursts of emotion, traits that paradoxically affirm their manhood. Domínguez-Ruvalcaba observes that the melodramatic representation of masculinity in cinema "contradicts machista principles, deviating the ostentatious use of force toward the softness of sentiment"

(86). De la Mora argues that the codification of sentimental behaviors as legitimate modes of performing machismo in Golden Age film reflects an ideological strategy for coping with social anxieties surrounding modernization, including the transformation of gender roles through women's participation in politics and the labor force, along with rapid urbanization, advanced forms of industrial capitalism, and economic instability (70). In other words, the maintenance of the state's patriarchal order depended on the production of appealing models of masculinity that would show men how to respond to their apparent loss of prestige without feeling overly threatened. According to this view, cinema was to provide Mexican men with a necessary sentimental education that would allow them to continue to form strong homosocial ties and maintain their virility in a modernized society, increasingly distinct from the one their fathers and grandfathers had known.

Irwin, Domínguez-Ruvalcaba, and de la Mora, like most contemporary scholars researching Mexican gender identities, share a critical understanding of machismo as an ideological construction—an authoritative fiction adapted to the historically specific needs of an evolving national power structure—as opposed to an authentic expression of Mexico's masculine essence. They approach Mexican masculinity not as a singular unchanging entity, but rather in the pluralistic terms of its shifting "genealogy" (Irwin xxxvi); as a category that is "culturally produced not only as a perceived entity but also as a device for perception" (Domínguez-Ruvalcaba 1); or as a "a visible and highly contested system of power" (de la Mora 7). They are informed by theoretical frameworks such as Pierre Bourdieu's notion of *habitus*, which allows them to describe gender as a system of rules operating below the level of consciousness, invisibly reinforced through learned behaviors and subtly coercive social practices (Irwin xix; Domínguez-Ruvalcaba 165n2). They draw upon ethnographic and sociological studies of Mexican and transnational masculinities offered by scholars such as Matthew Gutmann and R. W. Connell to show how male gender takes multiple and diverse forms within and between distinct sociohistorical settings, variable economic conditions, and differently institutionalized systems of authority.[22] They take for granted that biological sex is not determinative of gender, and that the sexual binary itself is, as Judith Butler calls it, a "regulatory ideal whose materialization is compelled" (1). From this perspective, gender takes shape as a reiterative set of performances whose corporeal naturalization is sustained in sociopolitical relationships of power (Butler 7).[23] All of this amounts to saying that they take a view of the phenomenon of Mexican machismo that is significantly at odds with an earlier intellectual tradition that attempted to decipher Mexican man via the discursive objectification of his essential nature. That is, they stand at a critical distance from figures such as Samuel Ramos and Octavio Paz, whose studies of the national character represented Mexican masculinity as a problem with its genesis in the ontology of Mexican men themselves.

The ideas articulated by these highly influential writers, who formed part of Mexico's intellectual elite of the mid-twentieth century, are symptomatic of what Roger Bartra has described as a "vicious circle" in which "postrevolutionary Mexican society produces the *subjects* of its own national culture" (1–2; original emphasis). In other words, by describing aspects of mexicanidad as though they actually originated in the attitudes and personality traits of real Mexicans, Ramos and Paz perpetuated enduring stereotypes that acquired a life of their own, a life that sustains and is sustained by "imaginary power-networks" structuring the authoritarian nation-state (Bartra 2). Ramos's *El perfil del hombre y la cultura en México* (Profile of Man and Culture in Mexico) (1934) and Paz's *El laberinto de la soledad* (The Labyrinth of Solitude) (1950) helped to establish cultural concepts and definitions that became so well known among Mexicanists that they were, and still are often referred to in discussions independently of the canonical authors who invented them, partly confirming Bartra's point. Briefly, the work of both Ramos and Paz offered speculative philosophical and psychoanalytic assessments of pathologized features of the national ethos as embodied by its most emblematic subjects, that is, Mexican machos. Ramos draws upon Adlerian notions of inferiority and masculine protest to explain Mexican man's proclivity toward confrontational sexualized aggression as a means of masking his internalized sense of constitutional fragility (51). He invokes the archetypal semiprimitive, urban (sub)proletarian mestizo figure, *el pelado* (the flayed one), to characterize the conjunction of hypersensitivity and overdetermined self-assurance that exemplifies Mexico's conflict-ridden national identity, especially when positioned in comparison with the scientific and cultural achievements of European nations (52–57). Paz, for his part, builds upon Ramos's discussion of the *pelado* when formulating his definition of the *pachuco*, a stereotypical lower-class Mexican hoodlum who similarly engages in obsessive phallic posturing in order to experience a hollow sense of superiority (33–35). He famously appeals to a specialized idiom centered on the verbs *rajarse* (to crack) and *chingar* (to fuck) in order to emphasize even more explicitly the dimensions of erotic violence symbolically—or physically—enacted by Mexican machos who compulsively assert their virile dominance over women and other men (51, 99–100). Perhaps the most well-known piece of Paz's treatise is his account of how the allegorical recapitulation of the colonial conquest scenario in the national psyche causes Mexican men to view themselves as bastard sons of a traitorous mother, "hijos de la Malinche," condemned to live out their destiny in a frustrated condition of solitude (110–113).[24]

For contemporary scholars of Mexican masculinity, the writings of Ramos and Paz provide instructive illustrations of the assumptions that informed gendered discourses of nationhood during the formative period of postrevolutionary nation-building. The Mexican state had legitimated its rule by enlisting cultural institutions to invent a macho nation held together by cohesive bonds between men whose preferred form of government would naturally be patriarchal and paternalist, and while members of the intellectual establishment such as Ramos and Paz offered criticisms of this utopian vision, they did not contradict its underlying premises. In fact, by articulating the primitive and pathological perversions intrinsic to Mexican machismo, they not only affirm the desirability of authentic and properly socialized forms of virile masculinity, but also give clear expression to the rationale for authoritarian governance. As Pedro Ángel Palou explains, the defects embodied by Paz's Mexican types "son fundamentals para el control de los cuerpos individuales y de los grupos sociales que el Estado necesita para perpetuarse" (are fundamental for the control of individual bodies and social groups that the State needs in order to perpetuate itself) (27). If Mexican men are inherently predisposed to unruly masculine behaviors, the state's regulatory impositions are all the more necessary and justifiable. As Domínguez-Ruvalcaba writes, the image of Mexican masculinity that comes to the fore in the work of Ramos and Paz is that of "an obstacle to modernization" (98). In the context of the institutional reformation of Mexico's ruling party and the acceleration of capitalist development in which Ramos and Paz were writing, "to critique machismo is an expression of modernizing the nation" (Domínguez-Ruvalcaba 98). In this sense, as Bartra explains, critical intellectual discourses on the Mexican character, even when they run counter to the ideals of nationalism as expressed in murals, revolutionary literature, popular music, and cinema, "equally form part of the cultural process of the modern state's political legitimation" (6).

The myth of Mexican man's inadequacy to modern civilization coexists with the myth of his singular form of sentimental virility so frequently celebrated in Golden Age cinema, and their enmeshment is a key to the state's authoritarian strategies of control. For Domínguez-Ruvalcaba, males represented as 'subjects who cannot control their own impulses" are symbolically disempowered, for their inclusion within the legitimate boundaries of modern masculinity entails constant regulation under a "paternalist conception of government" (3). The sentimentalism of Golden Age cinema "configures a melodramatic exaltation of national masculinity" designed to keep hypersensual men feeling empowered but under the control of the state's "modern paternalism" (3). The archetypal male protagonist of Mexican melodrama "expresses his feelings through diatribes, screams, and tears. With those manifestations he establishes his power" (82), yet this dominance remains contingent upon his compliance with the hegemonic order. The excessive sensual nature of the Mexican man renders him always potentially unmanly, always approaching the dangerous liminal degree of machismo, and as the borders come into view, they must be policed by patriarchal law. Regulation of male gender performance, as outlined above, occurs within a field of homosociety, the outer edges of which are delimited by homophobia and misogyny (4). From this perspective, Mexican masculinity defines itself negatively by what it excludes, or, more precisely, by "a compulsive oscillation between desire and expulsion, acceptance and rejection" (5).

In their discussions of classic film, both Domínguez-Ruvalcaba and de la Mora, like Irwin in the field of literature, foreground this interplay of masculine desire and fear in order to dismantle the monolithic ideological structure of Mexican machismo. Cinema's consistent coarticulations of desirable masculine virility with undesirable male effeminacy and homosexuality along with misogynistic portrayals of women provide ample material for deconstructive cultural analysis that not only exposes the representational mechanisms sustaining patriarchal hegemony but also opens up the Golden Age archive to new readings, validating alternative modalities of historical and contemporary spectatorship and subject-formation. This is best exemplified by de la Mora's queer appropriation of Pedro Infante (73). While remaining in agreement with these authors, I argue that masculinity as a system of power in Mexico also encompasses forms of control and exclusion that exceed the enforcement of misogyny and homophobia. The invention of the macho as an assemblage of cultural myths brought to life on Mexican movie screens can be partially decoded by examining the dialectic of desire and rejection that emerges in his constitutional ambivalence toward gendered and sexualized otherness. Yet additional fissures and contradictions pervade the relationship between representations of the fully integrated and compliant modern macho and his male counterpart positioned as submasculine on the basis of an array of perceived gender deficiencies entangled with categories of racialized class difference.

IV. From Mestizaje to Malformation

Mexico's well-known nationalist myths of mestizaje as racial synthesis, along with corresponding currents of indigenismo, have been critically historicized more thoroughly and consistently than those of machismo.[25] This constitutes a paradox since the all-encompassing mestizo identity ascribed to the imagined universal subject of the patriarchal nation-state is always implicitly gendered male and therefore contingent on codifications of masculinity.[26] To be properly mestizo, one must be a macho, and vice versa. Disaggregating these categories, overlooking their historical interdependency, potentially leaves significant dimensions of mestizaje-based narratives of racial democracy, cultural homogenization, and male solidarity unchallenged. My analysis shows that examining the coarticulation of race and gender in the national imaginary is the only way to understand contemporary myths of malformed masculinity as products of history. Relatedly, representations of class difference in postrevolutionary popular films can appear somewhat inchoate when analyzed only in the conventional terms of modern capitalist social relations. Conceptualizing class as structurally enmeshed with race and gender enables me to consider how national cinema's constructions of Mexican subjecthood served to legitimate unequal distributions of wages and wealth. Most contemporary studies of Mexican masculinity, including those by Irwin, de la Mora, and Domínguez-Ruvalcaba, take at least some steps toward addressing how the normative boundaries of gender and sexuality have been established and enforced codependently with race- and class-based social categorizations. This kind of analytic move informs Irwin's insights on Ramos's recuperation of turn-of-the-century positivist discourses in criminology that had "dichotomized Mexican masculinity along class lines" (189), as well as de la Mora's critical opening toward the codified meanings of Infante's whiteness (86). Without taking anything away from these valuable contributions, I suggest that cracks in the veneer of modern Mexican masculinity reveal a category thoroughly interwoven with racializing arrangements of social, material, and political inequality. My position entails thinking of gender and sexuality as integral to, and inseparable from, the same classificatory logic that constructs hierarchies based on invented fictions of race in order to exercise control over laboring bodies, land, and resources.

The most prominent nationalist intellectual and institutional agendas on race in the postrevolutionary period were set forward as aesthetic, cultural, and educational programs rhetorically oriented around the social goals of progress, sovereignty, cohesion, development, and modernization.[27] The discursive and ideological parameters of these projects were largely inherited from earlier debates on *el problema del indio*, which had preoccupied and divided liberal thinkers throughout the Porfiriato (Lund 4). In brief, these discussions among scholars, statesmen, editorialists, anthropologists, and other *letrados* revolved around various theoretical strategies targeting Mexico's vast and diverse indigenous population for improvement and integration. From the late nineteenth century well into the twentieth, a relatively stable consensus held that "the Indian might exhibit a civilizational deficit, but this is merely the function of historical and environmental accidents; modernization will transform the Indian into a productive citizen; and good state planning can help achieve this goal" (Lund 13). The idealized outcome of this well-managed process would be the downtrodden native's assimilative and redemptive evolution into the mestizo, an imaginary figure based on the colonial concept of the half-caste but now reconceptualized as the racial expression of modern Mexican citizenship, statehood, and cultural identity. The mestizo became the emblematic representative of the national collective and its future trajectory, while the romanticized cultural image of the Indian served as an iconic symbol of Mexico's glorious past and primordial virtues. Initially formulated and concretized in philosophical, scientific, and political treatises as well as in spheres of fine art and literature, these two basic representational components of mexicanidad were swiftly incorporated into popular cultural forms, especially cinema, where they underwent further elaboration and modification as mechanisms for reproducing the national racial mythology.

This is not the place for an extended revisitation of the plurality of erasures and contradictions permeating nationalism's archetypal mestizo and indio personae, the artificial boundaries between them, and the codified roles they play in hegemonic social narratives. As I already mentioned, the parallel conceptualizations of mestizaje and indigenismo supporting postrevolutionary nation-building projects have been subjected to thorough critique in recent scholarship. What concerns me is how the specific cultural logic organizing these racial identity paradigms produces the masculine malformations represented in national cinema. This overarching question informs my discussion throughout the book as I consider how contemporary filmmakers contend with the embedded sociocultural meanings of masculinity historically linked to the representational regime of mexicanidad. I address some specific examples from the Golden Age archive in the first and second chapters, but here I limit myself to outlining three interrelated patterns of representational demarcation that illustrate the constitutive role of race in establishing categories of defective men. First, although indigenous and mestizo categories are conceptually discrete, they are also structurally linked in an ambiguous evolutionary relationship that is not strictly unidirectional. Characters in films may occupy a range of different positions *between* the two poles, where they are neither fully formed as mestizos nor identifiable as indios, at least not in the idealized terms typical of *indigenista* aesthetics. These intermediate figures may signify an ongoing progressive process of socialization and integration, or, by contrast, stagnation and potential regression to a prior stage of development. As Palou puts it, "El mestizo, de hecho nunca *es*, siempre *está siendo*, es un proyecto" (In fact, the mestizo never simply *is*, but is always *in the process of being*, he's a project) (101). Second, while there are many possible ways in which films may indicate a character's full realization of modern mestizo subjecthood, personifying machismo is perhaps the most definitive. By the same token, aberrant gender performance is often—though not always—suggestive of racial deficiency. The internal ambivalence and potential excess of machismo in combination with the variability of "race" in Mexico makes mestizo masculinity a highly unstable identity, requiring constant regulation. Third, physical features are, in theory, the least relevant dimension of the mestizo, since the category is intended to establish identification with a national cultural community more than a phenotype or biological essence. In the signifying practices of national cinema, however, the fullest expressions of mestizaje are almost exclusively represented by white bodies. A logical effect of this uniform corporeal imagery is to make brownness—and, to an even greater though perhaps less obvious extent, blackness—culturally synonymous with incomplete assimilation, premodern subjectivity, and defective masculinity.

The particularities exhibited by Mexican nationalism's invented parameters of racial classification corresponding to the salvational mythology of mestizaje facilitate critical decodings of cinema's constructions of the mestizo. Similarly, the idiosyncrasies of Mexican machismo call attention to themselves quite deliberately in film imagery and narrative, which makes the underlying contradictions more readily discernible. Representations of class difference in Golden Age films are less easily pinned down. One can venture to say that nationalist cultural productions were more interested in obscuring material disparities and clouding the economic relations constitutive of Mexican capitalism than they were in promoting any specific agenda of class-based affinities or antagonisms. This is not to suggest that Golden Age cinema ever came close to producing authentic or credible reflections of any aspect of Mexican social reality. Everything about these films is fundamentally distortive, but the patterns of distortion related to gender and race are more programmatically aligned with statist initiatives. Access to land, work, commerce, wealth, and social mobility is always contextually meaningful in specific films, yet it is challenging to identify any underlying ideological coherence in how these issues are thematized across the field of national cinema during the period in question. I propose that representations of capitalism's disproportional social outcomes in Mexican film are rationally connected to the goals of the patriarchal nation-state through the same logic that produces racialized categories of gender.

This perspective enables me to argue that the culturally codified myth of malformed masculinity functions as a colonial mechanism of control over capitalist production and its resources in postrevolutionary Mexico. The instrumentalization of invented racial identities to establish and naturalize unequal distributions of labor is the characteristic feature of what Aníbal Quijano calls the "coloniality of power," a particular form of domination that originated with the imperial conquest of América and extended globally over the course of centuries (536). Quijano's expansive theoretical account of the development of world capitalism as a process determined by a colonial model of power relations contributes to my understanding of the operative logic of racial classification in the modern Mexican nation-state.[28] Historically, the European rulers of colonial territories such as Mexico "associated nonpaid or nonwaged labor with the dominated races because they were 'inferior,'" while at the same time, "wage labor was concentrated almost exclusively among whites" (538). Variations of this dualist economic arrangement lasted well into the period of national independence and, in certain ways, continue to this day. Part of what enables the coloniality of racialized labor to remain hegemonic in the absence of formal colonialism is the Eurocentric cognitive perspective retained by the nationalist elite. Even as they professed to offer a new identity and a form of citizenship that would unite the national collective, the white *criollo* minority in control of the state and the larger social and economic power structures granted themselves sole rational authority to determine the meanings of Mexican modernity in relation to the global trajectory of human civilization. In doing so, they preserved a fictive view of "the differences between Europe and non-Europe as natural (racial) differences and not consequences of a history of power" (542). Certainly, some nonwhite Mexicans gained limited access to predominantly white social, economic, and political spheres via the route of assimilation, in exceptional cases rising to the very pinnacles of authority in the national order, bolstering the official narrative of mestizaje as a process of overcoming a civilizational deficit. However, beneath the liberal and postrevolutionary rhetoric of integration and development, the naturalized racial inferiority of the native remained the constitutive myth of modern Mexico, as evident in the violent colonial methods used to assert state/capitalist control over indigenous land and labor during the Porfiriato and into the postrevolutionary period (Lund 76). As capitalism demanded new resources to exploit beyond the rural land base, Mexico experienced rapid industrialization and mass urbanization in the decades after the revolution, transforming national socioeconomic structures and situating more nonwhite workers in waged labor arrangements, but without displacing the racial logic of coloniality.

From the beginning of the industrial expansion in the 1940s through the economic contractions of the '70s and into the cyclical crises of the '80s and '90s, right up to the present era of neoliberalism, race has continued to be a powerful instrument for dominating, regulating, and disciplining Mexico's workforce (in urban as well as agrarian contexts), but I argue that its role in shaping the trajectory of capitalism in Mexico is inseparable from predominant cultural myths of masculinity. My position on Golden Age cinema's function in reproducing these myths diverges from many standard accounts in the sense that I do not regard portrayals of working men in these films principally as pedagogical appeals to a plausible, attractive, imitable model of modern, masculine, lower-class, mestizo subjectivity. Without engaging in too much speculation about the unrecorded responses of ordinary urban workers and campesinos who may have been included in the original audiences for these films, I find it doubtful that many of them saw aspects of their potential selves reflected in these idealized images of the Mexican macho.[29] This is not to deny national cinema's capacity to generate cultural fictions with popular appeal across a broad spectrum of society, but only to suggest that the social meanings of masculinity they encode can be better assessed when the logic of coloniality is understood to be operative in the ideological processes of subject-formation. Quijano's insights make clear that the coloniality of power does not seek to transform the colonized into a modern citizen-subject but rather into an object of domination and exploitation. The colonial civilizing mission, and its prolongation under the guise of nationalist integration, offered a salvation narrative with a false promise at its core: no racialized group or individual could ever truly overcome the civilizational deficit of being nonwhite and non-Western since this difference was defined as a natural, essential inferiority. Identifying a significant gap in Quijano's theorizing, Lugones illuminates how gender is implicated in the logic of coloniality. She argues that, under conditions of colonial oppression, gendered identity is a distinction reserved for Western subjects: "Only the civilized are men or women. Indigenous peoples of the Americas and enslaved Africans were classified as not human in species—as animals, uncontrollably sexual and wild" ("Toward" 743). The civilizing mission gradually imposed a gender framework on colonized subjects, but not with the goal of establishing their full human equivalence to white, European, Christian men and women, but rather with the purpose of masking violence and preserving the racial hierarchy. Accordingly, the transformation from bestial beings to gendered human subjects was always perceived as partial, imperfect, and morally suspect, such that "males became not-human-as-not-men, and colonized females became not-human-as-not-women" (Lugones "Toward" 744). The perceptual judgments of colonized subjects' gender deficits from the standpoint of power justified the exercise of all manner of cruelty and violence on racialized bodies. I propose that national cinema's gendered images of working-class mestizos constitute a transhistorical reproduction of this classificatory rationale that authorizes practices of domination and exploitation in contemporary Mexico.

The aggregate effect of distortive and ambivalent fictions of Mexican masculinity comes into focus at the nexus of state-organized practices of violence and the cultural politics authorizing them. The symbolic archetypes, visual templates, and narrative patterns amassed for the distillation of masculine malformities in national cinema comprise a connective interface linking the modern state's racialized arrangements of exploitation, expulsion, dispossession, and detention to the logic of coloniality. Domínguez-Ruvalcaba suggests the need to map this network with his assertion that "Mexican masculinity is an invention of modern colonialism" (3), but his work does not fully take up the task. Further enhancements to this perspective can do more to overcome the distortion generated by the macho myths accrued to the Mexican man. Existing accounts of the social violence attributable to archetypal machismo tend to follow the vectors of misogyny and homophobia. Women, effeminate men, and homosexuals constitute masculinity's others, sources of fear whose violent subordination secures and is secured by heterosexual men's enactments of desirable homosocial virility. Cultural representations of normative macho identities are presumed to interpellate men as subjects of patriarchal law, which "authorizes the community to exclude, condemn, discriminate against, and coerce those whom the patriarchy defines as its others" (Domínguez-Ruvalcaba 6). This conceptualization is altered by the acknowledgment of the fuller historical array of categories of otherness signified by male archetypes who model racially defined gender defects, rendering them ineligible for full subjectivity within modern patriarchy.

Rethinking cinema's articulations of patriarchal law in this way necessarily modifies the terms of the supposed social contract between the state and individual machos. Rather than enabling positive self-recognition as citizen-subjects based on compliance with regulatory meanings and uses of the body, I suggest that cinema's myths of masculinity are designed to facilitate and legitimate the state's domination of men by making them perceptible as defective beings not quite up to the standards of modern manhood. Representational codes articulated by repeated images of socially dysfunctional, unintegrated, primitive, criminal, immoral, or rationally deficient Mexican men are correlatable to sociopolitical practices of exclusion, condemnation, discrimination, and coercion. Mexican national cinema constitutes an archive of codified masculine imagery that can be meaningfully interpreted at the differential between the idealized macho and his submasculine others, figures who are sexually marked as male but whose gender identity is malformed and misaligned with the norm.

Mexico Unmanned proposes that the myths stored in this cultural repository continue to have social consequences within neoliberal arrangements of power. The new representational regime has not simply discarded these mythologies, but rather transfigured them so that they continue to exert their authoritative effects. Codified gender malformities are as much an instrument of domination today as they were throughout the postrevolutionary period, though the precise mechanisms have undergone significant transformations. To map the shifting contours of masculine malformation is to locate nodes on the "imaginary networks of political power" where cultural myth interfaces with the exercise of state violence (Bartra 163). I suggest that contemporary film, when read in conjunction with this understanding of the cultural repository of masculinities in Mexican national cinema, facilitates such a mapping. To avoid confusing the map with the territory, criticism must historicize and denaturalize the embodied performances of maleness in film by treating them as symbolic markings referencing the accumulation of myths as opposed to the ontology of the Mexican. Unmanning Mexico, in this sense, also means interpreting these references as demarcations of domination writ large on the bodies of men.

V. Overview

Chapter by chapter, this book examines cinema that reflects—sometimes critically—the prevailing cultural politics of masculinity in contemporary Mexico. The intention is to show how the selected filmmakers either reflectively confront or uncritically reproduce a particular representational logic of gender malformation, which I argue exhibits structural continuities with a paradigm that achieved its most enduring expression in Golden Age cinema. Chapter 1 examines how *Y tu mamá también* (2001, dir. Alfonso Cuarón) and *Rudo y Cursi* (2008, dir. Carlos Cuarón) represent the consistent realignment between defective masculinities and racialized class hierarchies in neoliberal Mexico. Both films articulate recognizable codes of Mexican masculinity in the context of political and economic transformations associated with globalization and consequent social demands for reordered gender identities compatible with transnational capitalism. However, the narrative of the metropolitan middle-class and elite male characters in *Y tu mamá también* is organized by tropes of education and self-reformation, while the provincial rustics comically portrayed in *Rudo y Cursi* reiterate previously established discourses of failed masculinity, justifying exploitation and segregation. Reading these films together enables new perspectives on how the culturally progressive urban middle and upper classes retain a naturalized symbolic association with modern masculine subjecthood, while gender defects continue to be attached much more readily to portrayals of the rural poor in current Mexican cinema.

In chapter 2, I discuss a pair of films directed by Carlos Reygadas, *Batalla en el cielo* (Battle in Heaven) (2005) and *Post tenebras lux* (Light after Darkness) (2012), to illustrate how the filmmaker critically engages the signifying practices that sustain systems of social oppression in present-day Mexico. The director's self-reflexive aesthetic holds up a mirror to the contemporary politics of representation in postnational Mexican cinema in order to expose certain retentions from earlier portrayals of the nation's transition to modernity, particularly concerning the mythic conceptions of social power supposedly embodied by the urban, working-class mestizo male. The image of the *Batalla en el cielo*'s subjugated, enfeebled male protagonist marks deep discrepancies with the idealized male leads of classical Mexican cinema, but also reveals the logical necessity of denigrating the brown male body in order for machismo to be effective as myth. In *Post tenebras lux*, the film's upper-class protagonist embodies a colonizing gaze that observes and reifies the apparent deficiencies of subordinate men as a means of constituting and legitimating his own patriarchal masculine identity. Reygadas reveals the persistent contradictions of Mexican masculinity inscribed onto bodies whose racialized and classed gender performance is condemned as defective, providing rationalization for their ongoing exploitation in the neoliberal order.

Chapter 3 comprises an analysis of *Heli* (2013, dir. Amat Escalante), a film that calls attention to persistent symbolic imperatives configuring rural communities in economically marginalized areas of Mexico as nests of unruly, barbaric, malformed men engaged in drug trafficking and other criminal activities. I address the director's strategic mode of exposing the representational processes by which such fictive narratives of narco violence circulate in various forms of mass media, acquiring unquestionable status as "reality," only to be indexically redeployed in current cinema. By making these mechanisms visible, *Heli* suggests how contemporary definitions of normative masculinity distort social perceptions of male identities formed under conditions of extreme precarity. In my reading, Escalante's film shows that an ideological counterpart to the natural threat of barbaric masculine violence can be found in the tempering images of malformed rural men's peripheral integration into exploitative transnational labor markets.

My discussion of *Te prometo anarquía* (I Promise You Anarchy) (2015, dir. Julio Hernández Cordón) in chapter 4 considers processes of affective realignment in contemporary cinema that have created space for new masculinities while at the same time reproducing familiar patterns of exclusion. I read the film as a critical hybridization of romance and realism that attempts to redefine masculinity beyond the national heteropatriarchal framework of power without falsely ascribing a sexually emancipatory trajectory to neoliberalism. It offers a standpoint for considering the erasures produced by codes of empathy that seek to normalize homosexual desire in contemporary cinema. However, in the film's articulation of the dystopian dimensions of contemporary Mexico as a marketplace of gore, malformed masculinities reappear as naturalized phenomena.

Chapter One

Old Macho Mythologies in New Mexican Cinema—
Y tu mamá también and *Rudo y Cursi*

I. Bridging National and Neoliberal Masculinities

In the substantial critical bibliography on Alfonso Cuarón's *Y tu mamá también* (And Your Mother Too), diverging from predominant lines of interpretation that emphasize the film's deployment of transnational cinematic genre templates, formal strategies, and frames of reference, one finds many readings that offer suggestive links to the national tradition of filmmaking.[1] However, in my view, the meanings generated by Cuarón's allusions to the Golden Age archive have yet to be fully explored. The analytic framework I propose, which treats national cinema's models of masculinity as instruments for delineating categories of defective men, reveals transhistorical continuities in the cultural logic informing Cuarón's cinematic approach to gender politics in neoliberal Mexico. These arguments will be complemented by my reading of Carlos Cuarón's *Rudo y Cursi*, a comedy film that may be considered a companion piece to *Y tu mamá también* in several respects, including the return of the two principal male performers. In this somewhat dark parody of the sports genre, Gael García Bernal and Diego Luna play an impoverished pair of half brothers, respectively, Tato "el Cursi" ("the flashy one") and Beto "el Rudo" ("the rough one") Verdusco, whose unexpected rise to fame in the national soccer league is followed by a precipitous fall back into obscurity. The reappearance of the two leading men in roles representing a socioeconomic stratum far removed from the urban middle- and upper-class adolescents they played seven years earlier, Julio Zapata (García Bernal) and Tenoch Iturbide (Luna), elicits comparisons that, according to my perspective, disclose how masculinities in neoliberal Mexico continue to be defined in terms of detrimental mythologies and essentialisms entangled with the cultural politics of nationalism.

Y tu mamá también's symbolic invocations of mexicanidad, along with its oblique references to shared historical memory, have frequently been taken as invitations to engage in allegorical readings, many of which coincide in describing the film's challenges to traditional Mexican gender roles. According to Ernesto Acevedo-Muñoz, the film critically confronts the legacy of national cinema's "*machista* imaginary" by revising foundational myths of the treacherous figure of Malinche that perpetuate misogyny and sexist violence as intrinsic components of Mexican identity that underpin the patriarchal postrevolutionary social contract (40). Due to the narrative agency exercised by the main female character, Luisa Cortés (Maribel Verdú), Acevedo-Muñoz contends that the film constitutes a "counterepic" in which "the nation is rediscovered as a place of contradictions, where machismo is unveiled as a façade hiding homoerotic desires, where divisions of class are revealed as latent and leading to violent confrontation, and where instead of 'treachery' (like Malinche) the woman mediates all meaning" (47). While this approach suggests that Cuarón intends his film to replace traditional masculinist cultural ideology with a feminist agenda in order to inscribe a "new type of Mexican foundational fiction" (Acevedo-Muñoz 47), Elena Lahr-Vivaz comes to a different conclusion regarding the filmmaker's treatment of national collective identity. Making contrapuntal comparisons with classic formulas of Mexican melodrama, she shows how Cuarón revisits national cinema's conventions and archetypes "to challenge rather than to shore up the imagined, imaginary community of *nosotros*" (138). Borrowing a term from Roberto González Echevarría, Lahr-Vivaz understands recent Mexican films such as *Y tu mamá también* as "archival texts" that function as a "compilation and display of past myths of identity," but without seeking to establish or promote new mythologies (28). For her, the film assembles fragmented vestiges of Mexico's foundational fictions in order to signify the "ultimate failure of allegories of national identity in the decentered, globalized world of the twenty-first century" (161).

This attitude of exhausted resignation toward the collapse of nationalism is also highlighted by Sánchez Prado in his reading of the film as a response to the challenges posed by neoliberal transformations in

Mexican film culture. For him, *Y tu mamá también* marks the culmination of post-1988 Mexican cinema's gradual abandonment of all interest in collective cultural identity and sociopolitical discourse. In *Screening Neoliberalism*, Sánchez Prado analyzes the formation of a new paradigm of filmmaking that profoundly altered the aesthetics and ideologies that had been integral to national cinema for decades. These shifts, he argues, "are the consequences of deep transformations in the material practices of producing and consuming cinema, triggered by changes in the very idea of the role of culture in society developed under neoliberalism" (6). Sánchez Prado identifies Alfonso and Carlos Cuarón as key contributors to the earliest phase of this process with their first major collaborative film project, *Sólo con tu pareja* (1991), which assembled an innovative set of class-specific frames of reference, cultural codes, and formal strategies that, although largely unnoticed at the time of release, several years later would prove to be definitive ingredients in the development of Mexican romantic comedy, the most successful genre within the neoliberal paradigm. The flourishing of commercial cinema based on a "detached, depoliticized, and self-referential" film language pioneered by the Cuaróns in *Sólo con tu pareja* accelerated the demise of nostalgic "neo-Mexicanist" cinema preoccupied with surveying—and sometimes attempting to salvage—the wreckage of a shared national tradition (186). By the time of their second Mexican project, *Y tu mamá también*, the filmmakers were faced with an utterly transformed landscape of cinema and the problem of "how to reengage both the national and the political at a juncture where . . . the very possibility of doing so seemed preempted by the nonexistence of current and viable languages for such an enterprise" (185). According to Sánchez Prado, the film overcomes the dilemma "by using this impossibility as a central formal conceit, through its unique use of the voice-over" (185). Employing this device calls attention to the characters' own self-referential perspectives and "allows the social contradictions of Mexico to coexist in the space of commercial cinema" (188). This somewhat paradoxical strategy enables the film to offer a critical view of the fractured reality of Mexico's present without assuming any shared remembrance of a fictive past defined by homogenous wholeness.

While I find compelling the position Sánchez Prado takes regarding *Y tu mamá también*'s complete disengagement from national identity narratives, I also believe that he overstates his case by arguing that mexicanidad has no bearing whatsoever on the construction of the characters' social identities. Against the broader critical consensus, he claims that the film contains "no unequivocal Mexicanness, not even a problematic one" (193). Yet the formal presentation of the "impossibility" of Julio and Tenoch's engagement with complexly fractured Mexican realities outside their shared sphere of relative privilege would seem to depend on the provisional narrative coherence of their masculine bond configured by homogenizing cultural codes of machismo. Sánchez Prado consciously cordons off the gender dimensions of the film (184), so it is no surprise that his discussion largely bypasses the signs of Mexican masculinity suffusing the male protagonists' relationship. Without fully disputing the idea that *Y tu mamá también* is "uninterested in engaging with the nation as such" (192), my discussion seeks to account for the deployment of these recognizably idiosyncratic male gender performances. This involves rethinking the meanings generated by the film's narrative trajectory leading to the point when the protagonists catch up with what the implied audience already knows, that is, that the common ground established via their masculine homosocial bond is unsustainably replete with contradictions. I suggest that Cuarón attempts to dramatize the separation of individual subjectivity from specious nationalist fictions of collectivity by focusing on the gradual breakdown of the friendship between Julio and Tenoch, whose affective attachments are represented in terms of retrograde/immature Mexican masculinity. In order to set the stage for this drama of maturation and estrangement, the film turns to the foundational repository of mythic narratives of nationhood, especially those dealing with the establishment of a gendered social contract as articulated in Golden Age buddy films. In examining this dimension of *Y tu mamá también*, my approach partly coincides with that of Lahr-Vivaz, who suggests that Cuarón's main motive for referencing the archive of national cinema is to "refute . . . a static, allegorical rendering of the nation and its (idealized) subject" (13). However, I am more doubtful about the overall success of Cuarón's effort to articulate a decisive break with nationalism's myths of maleness. Despite his intent to offer a critique of the limiting structure of gender identities formulated by the politics of nationalism, Cuarón's work ends up reproducing and naturalizing elements of the same cultural logic that structures the ideals of Mexican masculinity in relation to malformed otherness in Golden Age cinema.

Throughout the film, Julio and Tenoch remain oblivious to the complex social realities surrounding them, but they gradually become more clearsighted regarding the falseness of the "Charolastra" pact that codifies their friendship in terms of fealty to a shared set of archaic masculinist-misogynist values. The apex of their illumination occurs when they realize that their individual desires and distinct class positions provide a more coherent basis for their identities than the traditional masculine essentialisms that previously united them. Their social privileges preclude any understanding of, or identification with, aspects of the "real" Mexico located beyond the horizon of their "detached, depoliticized, and self-referential" perspectives, but they ultimately attain a clearer comprehension of their own personal realities and identities as middle- and upper-class men. I argue that this transition serves to illustrate the cultural logic at work in neoliberal Mexican cinema's rearticulation of masculine signifiers recognizably derived from those invented by the films of the Golden Age. While expressions of traditional machismo in recent cinema no longer lay any legitimate claim to represent a national collective identity, they still deliver a potent symbolic charge by marking a clearly perceptible difference from the normative masculine subjectivities associated with globalization in Mexico. In the case of *Y tu mamá también,* the characters initially appear to be cultivating an illusory set of ideals that are predestined to collapse not only due to internal contradictions but also because they are thoroughly out of step with the prevailing neoliberal cultural politics of masculinity. Much like Tomás Tomás, the shameless womanizer in *Sólo con tu pareja,* who finally accepts the appeal of stable romantic monogamy—or, at least, learns to be more discrete about his sexual promiscuity—the protagonists of *Y tu mamá también* undergo individual transformations bringing them into closer alignment with the norms of global masculinity, suggesting that their apparent gender defects are merely the superficial products of a vestigial cultural matrix. They possess the bodies of men but must acquire gendered conduct appropriate to their social condition by way of a harsh education culminating in a disavowal of the defective codes of mexicanidad that facilitated their boyish friendship. This change cannot provide a conventional happy ending like that implied in *Sólo con tu pareja,* as it necessitates Julio's and Tenoch's close conformity to the class-specific demands of late capitalism. Yet, from the audience's perspective, it still represents a credible outcome because the renunciation of retrograde models of male subjectivity associated with the national is correlated to clear-sighted perception of the adjustments needed to assure their own positioning within Mexican neoliberalism.

Whereas in *Y tu mamá también* and *Sólo con tu pareja,* the urban middle- and upper-class characters are inherently capable of self-knowledge and self-regulation, making their identities separable from degenerate expressions of Mexican masculinity, Beto and Tato, the rural lower-class protagonists of *Rudo y Cursi*, embody an essentialized gender malformation that marks them as irredeemable machos. This difference, beyond illustrating contemporary commercial cinema's perpetuation of a representational framework predominantly aligned with Mexico's racialized class structure, supports my position that masculine signifiers derived from the originary film culture of nationalism continue to be meaningfully rearticulated in ways that affirm the ideology of the neoliberal state. Impoverished rural men, defined by a familiar array of unalterable gender defects, are legitimately excludible from the social order, and can even constitute a threat that warrants active measures to suppress and expel. By examining how Carlos Cuarón's follow-up to *Y tu mamá también* reproduces the same cultural reasoning that organized the earlier film yet generates a distinct set of narrative consequences for the protagonists, this chapter aims to draw some general conclusions regarding the determinative function of assemblages of class, race, and socio-spatial difference in neoliberal Mexico's prevailing cinematic discourses of masculinity.

Despite its wide distribution and significant commercial success, *Rudo y Cursi* has received far less response from critics and scholars than its predecessor. However, several of the existing commentaries recognize meaningful continuities pertaining to the treatment of traditional gender identities in both films. For example, according to Claudia Schaefer, the earlier production deploys established genre conventions of the road movie and "buddy" film to reinforce "strong male-to-male bonds that pose no threat to family structure or values," while *Rudo y Cursi* satirizes these formulas in order to "rupture . . . the myth of the bonds that held men and their families together" (50). But in spite of this parodic intention, the fraternal ties evinced in the more recent film's reprised pairing of the two leading male actors still "casts a vote of confidence for the continued support of men by men as the nation struggles down a road (movie) of its own" (52). Taking a somewhat distinct position, David Wood argues that *Rudo y Cursi* recuperates the exploration of "masculinity in crisis" from *Y tu mamá también* and uses the framework of the sports film to contribute to a "generalized questioning of gender roles and machismo that opens out well beyond football" (1370). Like Schaefer, however, Wood finds that the critique of patriarchal narratives in *Rudo y Cursi* does not fully decenter the familial foundations of nationhood as a unifying cultural construct: "The film is an affirmation of Mexico as a place of origin and a community, even if the bases upon which that community is constructed are undergoing profound change as a result of the erosion of hegemonic discourses, the crisis of masculinity and the drugs trade" (1372). In addition to foregrounding the two films' shared concern with gender and nation, both scholars also identify allusions to Golden Age Mexican cinema in the Cuarón brothers' work (Schaefer 55; Wood 1371).

While these critical approaches to *Rudo y Cursi* are not fully consistent with one another, together they do form a contrast with Sánchez Prado's explanation for why the film "belongs to the same paradigm as *Y tu mamá también*" (*Screening* 193). By making a farce of the "mythology of soccer as a structure of social ascendance," he explains, the film not only rejects outright the associated nationalist discourses of cultural unity often tied to triumphalist sports narratives but also ridicules neoliberal fantasies of individual self-realization, which appear especially absurd when extended to Mexico's rural poor (193). In other words, what Carlos Cuarón's film shares with its predecessor is not a desire to revisit questions of Mexican identity inscribed by the hegemonic discourses of the past, but the intention to do precisely the opposite by implicitly declaring such discourses to be dead and showing the available alternatives to be laughably irrelevant to most Mexicans. Both films express the "exhaustion of Mexican culture and the absurdity of its ideals amid the disappointment with and failure of the neoliberal model" (194). Once again, although partly in agreement with Sánchez Prado's position, I suggest that attending to *Rudo y Cursi*'s rearticulations of specific masculine codes from the tradition of national cinema leads to a revised understanding of the paradigm of neoliberal filmmaking in Mexico. For example, Sánchez Prado's preemptive response to criticisms of the film's "classist" depiction of impoverished rural characters as clowns is based on the claim that the humor arises from the privileged-class audience's shared recognition of the irrelevance of conventional narratives of sports heroism to those at the bottom of Mexico's socioeconomic hierarchy (193). My reading counters that, even if the film mocks the standard neoliberal success story, it is the derisory emphasis on the protagonists' naturalized gender defects rooted in cultural myths of mexicanidad that provides the primary narrative justification for their expulsion from the transnational world of professional soccer. The audience's dissociative laughter is therefore significantly authorized by the outmoded masculinity the main characters are unable to transcend for reasons that, according to the prevailing cultural logic of neoliberalism, are indeed related to naturalized conceptions of class difference and the racialized division of labor. The satire's appeal depends on its alignment with, and reproduction of, dominant assumptions regarding the essential incompatibility between neoliberal citizenship and lower-class masculinities. Taken together, my discussions of both of these films by the Cuarón brothers show that cinematic rearticulations of national identity paradigms in the political and cultural context of neoliberalism continue to function as representational mechanisms to legitimate and disguise ongoing processes of othering vast constituencies of Mexican men as malformed subjects.

II. The Meanings of Malformed Machismo

In order to disentangle the ostensibly critical/satirical perspectives offered by the Cuaróns' films from the rearticulated myths of Mexican masculinity instrumentalized by the dominant cultural politics of the neoliberal order, I must first briefly review some of the originary cinematic formulas that inaugurated the enduring legacy of machismo as a synonym of mexicanidad. The discussion will address how the nationalist codes of masculinity enunciated in popular Golden Age film genres, such as *comedias rancheras* and buddy films, not only affirmed positive ideals of manhood but also marked its outer limits. The tensions and conflicts at the liminal, regulatory boundaries of Mexican machismo unveil the inner structure of a hegemonic gender system organized by fictive essentialisms. This provides the analytic basis for examining how aspects of these myths have been reincorporated into gender-based strategies of legitimation/exclusion constituted within the dominant cultural politics of neoliberalism as reflected in both *Y tu mamá también* and *Rudo y Cursi*. Just as in postrevolutionary cinema, contemporary representations of masculinity can function to naturalize and dehistoricize categories of difference, symbolically reproducing unequal distributions of social power in Mexico.

As indicated in several of the critical responses to both films, allusions to traditional Mexican gender codes are apparent in the homosocial configurations of male-to-male bonds of friendship and fraternity enacted in the narratives. Critics draw parallels between the central pairing of male protagonists (and actors) in *Y tu mamá también* and *Rudo y Cursi* and the close relationships between men in Golden Age films in order to support claims concerning the Cuaróns' interest in reexamining gender-related contradictions of Mexican nationalism. While the masculine homosocial buddy dynamic undoubtedly exists in other major film traditions, including Hollywood, particularly Mexican variants were successfully introduced as narrative templates in the early phases of postrevolutionary national cinema and became integral to the hegemonic definition of machismo. Films comprising the nascent *comedia ranchera* genre were frequently organized around patterns of male companionship among gallant *charros* (cowboys/ranchers) whose romantic conquests and contests of physical bravery unfolded in nostalgic rural settings. Filmmakers quickly adapted and expanded these formulas into urban musical comedies, often focusing on camaraderie between working-class men in contemporary occupations. Studies of the postrevolutionary cultural politics of masculinity by scholars such as Héctor Domínguez-Ruvalcaba and Sergio de la Mora identify distinctive dimensions of male intimacy and solidarity represented in popular cinema of the 1930s, '40s, and '50s, illustrating how the relational parameters that define and legitimate macho identities onscreen reflect the historical scope and development of the patriarchal ideology instituted by the state. As de la Mora writes, the meanings of machismo constructed in cinema are "intimately linked to State power and to the highly contested gendered social contract extended to Mexican citizens in the post-revolutionary period" (6).

A prevalent trope in Golden Age cinema with particular relevance to my discussion of *Y tu mamá también* is the articulation of friendship pacts between men. In many films incorporating formulaic buddy elements, the male protagonists share tacit understandings of the codes organizing their relationships, but with surprising frequency, male-male agreements are spelled out in explicit terms, often with specific promises thematized in the narratives. These pledges of mutual fidelity, akin to marriage vows, grant priority to the masculine bond above any other commitment, especially above relationships to female lovers. This kind of accord organizes the two urban comedies, *A toda máquina* (Full Speed Ahead) (1951), and its sequel, *¿Qué te ha dado esa mujer?* (What Has That Woman Given You?) (1951), both directed by Ismael Rodríguez and both starring Pedro Infante and Luis Aguilar as a pair of motorcycling traffic patrol officers, Pedro and Luis, whose intimate friendship is continually tested by their competitive and jealous responses to one another's relations with women. Following many trials and tribulations, their masculine bond is finally confirmed along with their conjoint perpetual bachelorhood. De la Mora describes how these films activate a misogynist logic to represent women as a potential disruption of the homosocial contract enabling virile masculinity, but he also illustrates how the narrative interplay between homoeroticism and homophobia regulates the cultural meanings of machismo. Erotic triangles with a homosexual subtext are a common formula in many transnational variants of the male-oriented buddy film, but according to de la Mora, Mexican cinema of this period often placed a distinctive emphasis on sustaining affection between male companions, as opposed to Hollywood's tendency to separate male partners to enable their symbolic reintegration with the heteronormative order (88). This is best exemplified in ¿*Qué te ha dado esa mujer?* when the protagonists make—and ultimately honor—a "mutual verbal agreement on the primacy of their relationship predicated on the decision that women occupy a secondary role in their lives" (de la Mora 88). Another buddy comedy, *El gavilán pollero* (The Chicken Hawk) (1950, dir. Rogelio A. González), contains a very similar scenario in which two friends, José (Infante) and Luis (Antonio Badú), having symbolically sealed their oath of solidarity by mingling their blood, finally decide to rid themselves of Antonia (Lilia Prado), a vengeful lover who repeatedly attempts to turn them against one another. By expressing their mutual commitment in terms of an overt pact that involves swearing off women in order to protect homosocial hedonism, the male characters in these films "actively court homoeroticism only to barely repress and contain it through compulsory heterosexual opposite-sex couplings" (de la Mora 70). The resulting paradox is that the heteronormative codes of virility are reinforced by homoerotic suggestion precisely because the performance of Mexican machismo simultaneously raises and dispels doubts regarding sexual preference.

The contractual structure of male-male relationships as represented in Golden Age buddy films symbolically institutes a basic condition of masculine parity and affiliation, establishing a common ground where men compete on ostensibly equal terms and cultivate affection without directly transgressing homoerotic boundaries. Within this imaginary playing field, women are often reduced to exchangeable objects that facilitate the formation of homosocial bonds. This pattern may approach the hedonistic rejection of heterosexual monogamy, especially in urban comedy, but there are often additional regulatory parameters encoded into the portrayal of proper male conduct, which nonetheless underscore the underlying potential for immoderation. In the *comedia ranchera*, the norms of virile machismo frequently coalesce with the conservative rule of traditional family values, patriarchal codes of honor, and deference to maternal authority. For instance, in *Los tres García* (The Three Garcías) (1946, dir. Ismael Rodríguez) three male cousins (Pedro Infante, Abel Salazar, Víctor Manuel Mendoza) fiercely contend with one another to win the affections of their attractive female cousin (Marga López), who is visiting from the U.S. where she was raised by her American father (Clifford Carr). The men attempt to outdo each other with feats of bravery and dramatic declarations of sentiment, but they are all predisposed to certain excessive tendencies (e.g., pride, greed, vanity), so their grandmother (Sara García), whom they respect and fear, plays the role of disciplinarian, batting them with her cane as punishment for their overindulgences, but also as encouragement toward proper manly conduct. The gender-defining homosocial performance of heterosexual rivalry takes shape not only in the men's competitive relations but also in response to the reproachful matriarch's imposed "moral contention" (Domínguez-Ruvalcaba 83). The trope of motherly women censuring wayward men is often complemented by elements of narrative logic that represent female sexual autonomy as an affront to male honor and a justification for violence, creating an ethical structure that Domínguez-Ruvalcaba describes as a "misogynist fence" that constrains the "hedonist sovereignty of the macho" (83). As de la Mora reminds us, the reverence shown to maternal figures in these films also reflects the religious tradition of "*marianismo*, the institutionalized cult to Nuestra Señora de Guadalupe" (82). The patriarchal imperative to conserve the dichotomy of Guadalupe-Malinche, which configures women in binary terms as either virginal/motherly or whorish/treacherous, generates significant consequences for national cinema's approach to encoding virility in representations of homosocial relations between men. The moral restriction of powerful maternal bonds and the moral threat posed by unruly women form constitutive borders of the social space where men prove their legitimacy in competitive relations with other men.

In their research on male gender constructions in classic cinema, both de la Mora and Domínguez-Ruvalcaba underscore that, despite its outward appearance as an ahistorical monolith, Mexican masculinity remained in constant flux, its boundaries shifting in response to unsettled political, economic, and social conditions. Filmic narratives organized around the establishment of homosocial bonds between men via heterosexual rivalries and competitions over women constitute both a mainstay of Golden Age cinema and a site of a suggestive tension, contradiction, and paradox—that is, a structure of differences where masculinity comes more clearly into view as a system of power. Both scholars explore articulations of misogyny and homophobia in Golden Age films as reflections of the nation-state's historical efforts to impose a hegemonic gender system consistent with the overlapping projects of mexicanidad, modernization, and industrial capitalism. In agreement with their premise regarding masculinity's unstable enmeshment with the state's process of consolidating power and legitimating its own authority, I suggest that representations of homosocial bonding in national cinema also manifest signs of racialization and class segregation that were equally and inseparably consequential as regulatory mechanisms in the hegemonic codification of Mexican machismo. In addition to homophobic and misogynist boundaries, the legitimate terms of masculinity are also expressed in contradistinction to portrayals of primitive, dangerous, unintegrated men who threaten to subvert the patriarchal contract, thereby justifying the measures employed by the state to reinforce it.

These figures, whom I refer to as malformed males, represent the underside of Mexican machismo. They often convey a perverse resemblance to fully socialized machos but with discernible differences that mark them as improperly developed or insufficiently regulated. As discussed in the introduction, the term "malformation" attempts to capture how, during the postrevolutionary period, Mexican masculinity became internally dichotomized in alignment with the racializing project of mestizaje, which posited a false narrative of salvational transformation for the nation's nonwhite population. Mestizo identity ostensibly comprised a unifying cultural category of citizenship that transcended racial difference, but it contained within it the colonial imperative to embody a whitened form of modern subjectivity whose defining criteria inevitably excluded most inhabitants of Mexico. The possibility of achieving full mestizo subjecthood was governed by an invented hierarchy of distinctions between brownness and whiteness that encompassed not only ancestry and physical appearance but also language, aesthetic sensibilities, religious/spiritual practices, diet, dress, education, health and hygiene, labor, social habits, living spaces, family structures, domestic arrangements, and many other overlapping factors. In practice, mestizaje as a nationalist project involved a rearticulation of colonial logic equating whiteness with humanness. Perhaps above all else, being a Mexican mestizo depended on conforming with codified norms of masculinity and femininity that were almost always at odds with the historical conditions in which ordinary people lived. To be positioned outside of the preferred normative arrangements of gender identities and relations was to fall short of whiteness, and consequently to be considered less than human in the eyes of the mestizo state. The cultural parameters of gendered subjectivity have undergone significant shifts in recent decades with the transformations of global capitalism, the Mexican state, and their shared networks of power, but my discussions of current cinema in this book show that the hegemonic codes of masculinity in the neoliberal era continue to be co-aligned with racializing dichotomies. As I use the term, masculine malformation registers the transhistorical practice of classifying certain embodiments of maleness as essentially inferior in ways that intersect with dominant social hierarchies and patterns of racialization.

In the next chapter, I explain more about how this category functions in Golden Age film, but it is worth noting here that several of the buddy films and *comedias rancheras* mentioned above depict malformed men as submasculine counterparts to the main protagonists. This is perhaps most demonstrably apparent in *Los tres García*, as the three García cousins are paralleled by a trio of men from the rival López family (Luis Enrique Cubillan, José Muñoz, Manuel Roche). Although these two families have supposedly been involved in a transgenerational blood feud that caused the deaths of the protagonists' fathers, the film clearly emphasizes the inferior masculinity embodied by the López men. The differences are significantly coded in terms of whiteness, as the García family are upstanding town dwellers and landholders, while the López brothers apparently exist on the margins as rural bandits This makes them poor adversaries, and they are eventually caught and killed not by the García cousins themselves but by their grandmother's brown, bumbling, childlike manservant, Tranquilino (Fernando Soto), whose brother had also been murdered by the López family. Indeed, the García cousins' only substantial rivalry is with one another, and their practice of contending among themselves for superiority within the established norms of homosociality stands as the most important male gender distinction in the film. Socially unintegrated, racialized men appear unfit to participate as equals in the sphere of masculine competition governed by the paternalist state—or, in this case, maternal morality. It is beyond the scope of this chapter to discuss examples of malformation in each film analyzed by de la Mora and Domínguez-Ruvalcaba, but it should be added that in some buddy narratives, protagonists start out on the socioeconomic margins and gradually become integrated via the formation of homosocial bonds. This pattern is repeated in both *El gavilán pollero* and *A toda máquina*, though it is perhaps more obvious in the latter, where Pedro first appears as a lonely drifter with an uncertain past and ends up as a full member of the Mexico City Police Department's elite acrobatic motorcycle corps, where he further strengthens his ties to Luis in manly competitions overseen by the state. The myth of peripheral male mestizo subjects becoming integrated via masculine affiliations is essential to the ideological construction of Mexico's patriarchal social contract, but the implications of the racializing expression of this myth in cinema cannot be overlooked.

The cultural logic at work in these films reinscribes essentialized categories of social difference that subsist beneath the redemptive, integrative narratives. National cinema's male protagonists may have provided idealized cultural models of masculine prestige, fraternity, and constrained hedonism, but they also illustrated how these ideals were constructed as homologous with whiteness. Even when these characters professed to represent lower-class mestizo subjects, their corporeal images and performative attributes remained unmistakably identifiable as white, not only in terms of complexion or physiognomy but also in terms of speech, costume, posture, hairstyle, accoutrements, spatial location, and so forth. Because the racializing logic was sublimated into a wide array of codified imagery, it was not always necessary for malformed males to be played by actors with darker pigmentation, though this was a common pattern. The portrayal of these figures is related to, but should not be confused with, equally denigrating indigenista-style representations, which employed white actors and an aesthetics of exoticism to depict "indios" as childlike innocents who often come into involuntary conflict with modernity. The strategies for signifying normative Mexican machismo in Golden Age cinema systemically reproduced categorial distinctions between whiter and browner masculinities, aligning with the state's official agenda of mestizaje as a homogenizing framework for a national identity that privileged whiteness and Western modernity.

When discussing Mexican cinema's role in promoting and normalizing a certain set of codified ideals as the basis for a gendered social contract, it is crucial not to assume generalized indifference to race and class as barriers to national belonging. Cinema's invention of the macho as the paradigmatic image of the nation is often treated by critics and chroniclers as though it reflected at least a provisional popular consensus on how ordinary men wished to see themselves represented.[2] But for much of Mexico's population, consenting to recognize oneself in the iconic protagonists of the Golden Age films, even when they registered as lower-class mestizos, would mean buying into the same cultural politics and logic that had generated all manner of injustices, exclusions, expulsions, and impositions experienced throughout the violent colonizing process of postrevolutionary nation-building. According to Bartra, ordinary people would tend to see national culture "not as a reflection, but as a strange prolongation (or transposition) of their own daily reality" (173). He explains that prevailing images of "Mexicanness" invented by nationalist cultural institutions "are not fundamentally equivalent to social consciousness or ideology; as part of the Mexican culture they are, let us say, the prolongation of social conflicts by other media. In this transposition brews the myth of the Mexican, subject of national history and object of a peculiar form of domination" (173). This does not mean that no one other than fully integrated, passively conformist spectators could enjoy Golden Age films as entertainment. It does, however, suggest that significant segments of Mexican society would not readily identify with patriarchal myths that sought to erase or naturalize the violent domination through which the racialized and class-regimented postrevolutionary social order had been constituted. To properly historicize the mythic masculinities and malformations invented by these films, they must be read in conjunction with the coarticulated fictions of essentialized hierarchical race and class difference. My approach to the Cuaróns' films shows that they take for granted the universal internalization of the gendered social contract and omit any historicizing treatment of nationalist culture as a framework of domination. Of course, they are far from being alone, as these assumptions are widely shared, but the failure to see past them has consequences for their films' attempts to critique models of maleness associated with mexicanidad in the context of neoliberal cultural politics and reorganized structures of social control.

III. The Postnational Evolutionary Narrative of *Y tu mamá también*

Y tu mamá también presents Julio's and Tenoch's characteristic mode of masculine homosocial conduct as a symptom of self-delusion stubbornly rooted in archaic remnants of national culture. The narrative structure reflects a process of disillusion and detachment, in which the protagonists separate from one another and withdraw from their comfortable inhabitation of juvenile macho fantasia. Indeed, the road movie genre, relatively uncommon in Mexican cinema, is predicated on such a transformative uprooting, but if the pace of the journey in Cuarón's film is rather fitful and slow to start, this reflects his interest in illustrating the stagnant narrative dynamics of the buddy comedy and the corresponding models of male gender identity inherited from the past. The first thirty minutes of the film focus mainly on the boys' languid summertime routine in Mexico City before they actually get on the road to the Oaxacan coast with Luisa, and the trip itself is continually interrupted and delayed, not least by the boys' competitive antics. More than a hybridization of the Mexican buddy film with the transnational road movie genre, *Y tu mamá también* rather reflects the irreconcilability of a transformational travel narrative with outmoded formulas of representing male companionship derived from classics such as *A toda máquina* and *El gavilán pollero*.[4] Eventually, it is the road movie structure that prevails as the film sets the protagonists on a necessarily painful path of self-discovery. This does not mean that they experience a totalizing conversion or that their altered trajectory leads to an inherently desirable destination. At the end of the film, they find themselves in the same neoliberal Mexico with all its social conflicts and injustices, unlikely to be resolved despite the election of a new political party, but the mutual betrayals and harsh truths unveiled in the course of the journey appear to orient them in different directions, turning them away from the mirages in the desert of Mexican machismo where they both began.

Focusing on the narrative framing and performative enactment of this course adjustment in the film, I pose questions about its meanings and motives. What makes this change necessary to begin with? What presuppositions contribute to its credibility as cultural discourse in contemporary Mexico? My answers show how the film naturalizes and dehistoricizes the very same nationalist construction of male gender identity it proposes to critique. To support these claims, I begin with a discussion of the film's initial portrayal of the protagonists as throwbacks to an outmoded set of male gender codes reminiscent of Golden Age cinema. The clearest signs linking the main characters' starting point with traditional models of Mexican masculinity are to be found in the homosocial patterns that define their friendship and their relationships with women. The film's opening dialogue, between Tenoch and his girlfriend, Ana (Ana López Mercado), underscores his conventional attitude of male possessiveness and underlying insecurity, as he insists on a pledge of sexual fidelity, anticipating that she will be tempted to betray him during her summer holidays in Europe. His hypocrisy becomes self-evident soon afterward as he engages in misogynist boasting with Julio and another male friend, Saba (Andrés Almeida), while they prepare for a night of teenage hedonism, openly expressing hopes of hooking up with other young women in their circle of friends and classmates. This pattern is partially repeated in Julio's parallel dialogue with his partner, Cecilia (María Aura), during their brief sexual farewell. When Cecilia asks Julio, midcoitus, if he plans to go out partying that night following her departure to Italy, he assures her that he will be too despondent to enjoy himself during her summerlong absence. While double standards and hollow commitments in adolescent dating are hardly remarkable on their own, the film situates them within a larger symbolic assemblage enabling these behaviors to signify a pattern of correspondence with recognizable elements of paradigmatic Mexican machismo. The promises the boys make to their girlfriends are fundamentally empty, but the commitment they express to the male bond of friendship is taken as sacred. The contradictions are initially played for laughs, but the fact that they are eventually forced to recognize their oaths of fraternal loyalty to be as worthless as the pledges they made to their girlfriends in the opening sequences marks the major point of divergence from Golden Age buddy formulas. There is an implicit reference to, and contrast with, gendered patterns of trust and betrayal in films such as *El gavilán pollero* and *¿Qué te ha dado esa mujer?* where men's amorous attachments to women are dismissed in order to protect and prioritize masculine allegiances. The thematization of the sexual contract in the opening sequences foregrounds the significance of these issues throughout the rest of the film.

Other elements contributing to the initial framing of the boys' friendship in terms of the homosocial codes of mexicanidad include their competitiveness in physical activities and their ambivalence toward homoeroticism, as illustrated in sequences taking place at an exclusive country club, where they race against one another in the swimming pool and later masturbate in unison on the diving boards (figs. 1.1 and 1.2)

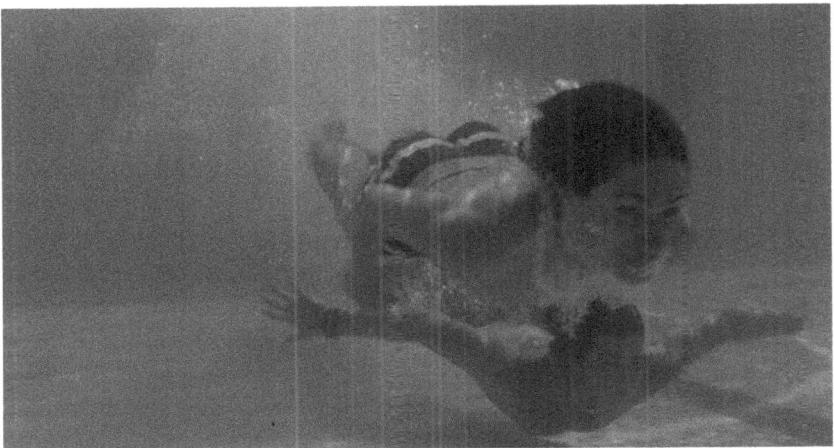

Figure 1.1. Julio (top; Gael García Bernal) and Tenoch (bottom; Diego Luna) compete with one another in the swimming pool (*Y tu mamá también*, 2001, dir. Alfonso Cuarón).

Figure 1.2. Julio and Tenoch indulge in synchronous masturbation (*Y tu mamá también*).

Their dialogue reflects the sexual tenor of their interpersonal rivalry as they make incessant comparative commentary on one another's genitalia. Of course, Golden Age cinema could not include such explicit homoerotic references in characters' speech, let alone anything comparable to *Y tu mamá también*'s shots of men masturbating, showering together, and engaging in nude horseplay, but the classic films often invented playful alternative ways to suggest male intimacy, such as when Pedro and Luis share a single set of pajamas in *¿Qué te ha dado esa mujer?* or when José and Luis exchange bodily fluids via a blood transfusion in *El gavilán pollero*. Another significant set of references to the canon of national film culture in *Y tu mamá también* are the *charrería* events and mariachi music during the wedding sequence. It is significant that these provide the backdrop to the boys' drunken tag-team exploits that include deflating the oversized ego of Tenoch's cousin Jano (Juan Carlos Remolina) and attempting to seduce his wife, Luisa, with a fictive description of a paradisiac beach called Boca del Cielo (Heaven's Mouth). The nostalgic framing evokes reminiscent links to the loquacious male characters in *comedias rancheras* such as *Los tres García*, who engaged in exaggerated seduction strategies and elaborate verbal jousting, often with subtle sexual inuendo, to establish their masculine prestige. Here, it should be added that the wandering camera's inclusion of aspects of the wedding that go unseen from the perspective of the protagonists, such as the meals being served to dozens of chauffeurs in the parking lot, creates critical distance from the self-enclosed sphere of nostalgia in order to place it under scrutiny.

One of *Y tu mamá también*'s most meaningful references to the codes of masculinity elaborated in the nationalist tradition of filmmaking is the "Charolastra" manifesto, which articulates the terms of the friendship between Julio and Tenoch, as well as two other friends, Saba and Daniel (who never appears onscreen), as a set of rights, commitments, or rules for life they each abide by in order to maintain their bond. Just as buddy movies of the Golden Age frequently incorporated pacts overtly affirming the primacy of male-male relations, Cuarón likewise activates this trope in his film, though obviously with the intention of highlighting the internal contradictions of the codified expression of masculinity. A point-by-point analysis of the puerile content of the charter would be somewhat superfluous, but a few remarks will suffice to illustrate the connections I find most significant. The inclusion of several clauses in the contract protecting each Charolastra's entitlement to indulge his own desires and impulses is perhaps unsurprising, given the behaviors represented throughout the first part of the film, but it resonates closely with the exercise of the exclusively masculine privilege of hedonism represented in Golden Age cinema. This emphasis on self-indulgence draws greater attention to the parts of the manifesto placing restrictions on male behaviors, particularly the prohibition against sexual relations with another Charolastra's girlfriend. This misogynist limit on masculine sexual freedom somewhat predictably proves to be the most consequential fracture in the homosocial system, for reasons I address below. The disparagement of Club América soccer fans as "putos" (fags) is not to be taken literally as an indication of underlying homophobic hatred or bigotry. Precisely because the film makes a point of representing the protagonists as being comfortable with homoeroticism, the deployment of this pejorative antigay language in their foundational text stands out as a discursive incongruity they are not yet prepared to confront. Their general blindness toward the heteronormative assumptions built into their contract leaves them unable to give a coherent explanation for their homosexual friend Daniel's withdrawal from the Charolastra collective. When they eventually transgress the tacit boundary of compulsory heterosexuality near the end of the film, it seems intended to illustrate their complete divergence from the hegemonic nationalist model of machismo, but without implying that they are both necessarily repressed homosexuals.[5]

The invented word "Charolastra" contains some ambiguous cultural resonances, as the characters explain that it derives from some misunderstood English song lyrics, adding that it conjures up the image of being a *charro* on the astral plain of consciousness, artificially expanded by drug use. The moniker also contains a faint echo of José Vasconcelos's *La raza cósmica* (1925), linking the transcendental utopianism of the nationalist intellectual's treatise on racial amalgamation to the boys' catalogue of shared ideals. One can detect at least a trace of antipositivist philosophy in the tenth clause, "La neta es chida pero inalcanzable" (The truth is cool but unattainable).[6] More than any one of its itemized tenets, however, it is the overall spirit of the Charolastra manifesto that strikes a chord with the metaphysical conception of mestizaje put forward by Vasconcelos. The boys' sublime confidence in the strength of their affective attachment mirrors Vasconcelos's optimistic faith that the evolutionary fusion of the world's dispersed peoples would bring about the "triumph of fecund love and the improvement of all the human races" (Vasconcelos 18). De-emphasizing the bio-racial premises of the theory, as well as its other logical inconsistencies, Leopoldo Zea argues that the aim of Vasconcelos's project was to cultivate an aesthetic attitude capable of envisioning the cultural and political integration of distinct social groups in "una relación horizontal de solidaridad" (a horizontal relationship of solidarity) (36). Similarly, being a Charolastra entails nurturing a shared set of sensibilities to support the fraternal feeling that unites individuals from different social backgrounds. The imperative to disavow or suppress consciousness of difference is an intrinsic source of tension and internal conflict, as illustrated by the omniscient narrator's description of the boys' mutual discomfort using the lavatories in one another's homes. The film represents Julio and Tenoch's obstinate adherence to this imperative, and their corresponding reproduction of the codes of patriarchal masculinity, as impediments to their personal growth. As long as they continue to delude themselves with vestigial myths derived from nationalist utopianism, they will remain suspended at an immature stage of development.

Cuarón's formal strategies, such as the offscreen narrator (voiced by Daniel Giménez Cacho) and independent camera, establish certain parallels between the contradictions suffusing the boys' illusory sense of shared identity and those pervading the dominant social narratives of contemporary Mexico. But there is a significant distinction apparent in the possibilities envisioned by the film for responding critically to these related phenomena. Even as the film acknowledges the unjust realities that exist beyond the main characters' field of perception, it does not provide a narrative standpoint to facilitate a sustained, coherent critique. Inequality and injustice appear endemic to the system, manifesting in ways that are seemingly disconnected from any identifiable cause or underlying motive. The historical agency behind the social deterioration is described in generic and abstract terms, apart from brief mentions of corrupt politicians like Tenoch's father (Emilio Echevarría), who was implicated in a contaminated corn scandal and had to flee to Canada with his family for eight months, or the president, who duplicitously denies state involvement in a recent massacre just before jetting off to attend a World Trade Organization meeting in Seattle. The narrator relates these details about the perfidious conduct of the ruling elite in the same observational tone used to describe a random traffic accident or an outbreak of foodborne illness, which contributes to the film's avoidance of direct ideological denunciation. Similarly, the camera's repeated pattern of lingering on scenes of repressive and violent policing in rural regions of the country as the main characters pass by unaffected registers the existence of these practices without subjecting them to critical questioning.

By contrast, the contradictory structure of the protagonists' masculine bond comes under persistent scrutiny, not only implicitly by the narrator's comments but also directly by Luisa, and ultimately by the boys themselves. Luisa sarcastically suggests that the Charolastra manifesto should be handed over to the government, drawing a correlation between patriarchal nationalism and the model of male gender identity the boys are perpetuating. She needles their narcissistic insecurities when she remarks that their girlfriends likely went to Italy in order to enjoy their own sexual autonomy. She plays an inadvertent role in exposing the rift between them when she has impromptu sex with Tenoch, and her decision to repeat the act with Julio the following day is motivated mainly by pity, as she assumes—quite correctly—that their fragile masculine egos may collapse entirely without the reinforcement they receive from one another. However, once the fissures are exposed, it becomes impossible to conceal them again. The betrayals the boys each reveal in their angry exchanges have been foreshadowed by the terms of the Charolastra pact itself. Indeed, that there was a need to make a specific rule against having sex with one another's partners suggests they anticipated its inevitable violation. The only way they could overlook the logical inconsistency between unfettered masculine privilege and mutual self-limitation to protect friendship and equality was by deluding themselves with myths about the transcendent sanctity of their bond. Despite each of them knowing that the contract had been broken already, neither Julio nor Tenoch was prepared to live without the mythology they had created to sustain their masculine identities.

The rupture of the protagonists' friendship during the road trip constitutes the film's critical narrative turning point, as they are forced to see their performance of masculinity in a different frame of reference, altering the standpoint they had been occupying together throughout much of their adolescence. The narrator's commentary affirms that the feeling of disillusionment deeply affects them both in ways analogous to the loss of innocence they experienced as children discovering their parents to be imperfect individuals with selfish desires. Even though they almost appear to make amends during the few idyllic days they spend together on the seashore, a significant change becomes evident during the sequence set in the cantina where they end up on the final night of the trip. Here, with help from copious amounts of alcohol, they begin to acknowledge truths that had not previously dared to approach, starting with earnest recognition of the class divide that separates them and the underlying resentments and prejudices it produces. Perhaps more importantly, they are finally able to unburden themselves of the lies that have covered up the true depth of their mutual betrayals. Liberating themselves from the fictive webs that had bound them to an illusory framework of masculinity brings on a sense of cathartic exultation, which, to me, is the best explanation for their indulgence of homoerotic desire. By transgressing the unspoken rule that is tacitly inscribed into the Charolastra code, the characters finally purge themselves of its distortive influence.

The movement toward disillusionment and demystification brings them finally to the point of accepting their separate identities as middle- and upper-class men in neoliberal Mexico. This is not presented as a straightforward, redemptive transformation, as the brief coda showing their final conversation does not provide much detail pertaining to their moral conduct. What it does suggest, in broad strokes, is that they have set themselves on different paths toward self-realization that conform to contemporary social expectations. The fact that they have opted for relatively conventional routes of professionalization (biology and economics) is less significant than the renunciation of their false sense of solidarity based on an imaginary set of ideals and commitments to a fictive identity. Tenoch's loss of appetite for writing seems intended to reflect his turn away from the broken myths of Mexican manhood that, if followed through to their ultimate conclusions, lead to outcomes akin to those embodied by his cousin Jano, an unacclaimed novelist and intellectual, whose constant infidelities resulted in the catastrophic failure of his marriage to Luisa. Of course, following in his father's footsteps to pursue a career in the upper echelons of the Mexican state's economic and political institutions will likely require Tenoch to weave a different kind of fiction. In accordance with the film's overall tendency to keep ideology in the background, the issue of whether the main characters might acquire a critical social consciousness is sidestepped in order to examine a particular stage in their personal development as young men.

Cuarón's effort to create a depoliticized and demythologized portrait of the protagonists' transformation against the historical backdrop of neoliberal restructuring and the end of single-party rule articulates an ambivalent critique of Mexican masculinity that, in my view, fails to break with the cultural logic inscribed in the nationalist cinema of the Golden Age. The film implicitly acknowledges the ideological origins of the specific codes of male conduct that comprise the gendered social contract modeled by the Charolastra manifesto, but in order to avoid engaging in an overtly political mode of questioning, Cuarón represents the antiquated macho behaviors of the main characters as naturalized and internalized. In other words, the premise of the film takes the originary cultural constructions of machismo and homosociality at face value, as though they were valid and credible representations of Mexican men, albeit now out of sync with a changing society. To motivate the film's narrative of transformation, Cuarón reproduces nationalism's myths of masculinity not simply as ideological signifiers to be voided and refuted, but as organic expressions of shared identity and affinity that are now obsolete and must be overcome at the personal level. In this way, the film obscures the historical gendering of Mexican national subjectivity even while attempting to dramatize the process of bringing masculinity up to date with present-day reality.

Examining the specific structure of Mexican masculinity reproduced in the protagonists' performances, along with the internal contradictions causing it to collapse and be transformed in the context of neoliberalism, reveals that Cuarón's critique does not actually seek to fully denaturalize the gender paradigm invented by postrevolutionary nationalism. The cultural reasoning expressed in the film reessentializes significant structural components of the invented male gender identity originated in national cinema. The codes that organize the bond between Julio and Tenoch are designed, above all else, to safeguard the exercise of masculine virility, hedonism, and self-indulgence, echoing the classic Mexican buddy films.

The utopian idea of transcendent fraternalism ostensibly provides the regulatory framework, placing certain limits and constraints on male conduct by prescribing homosocial rivalry, misogyny, and heteronormativity. But according to the logic of the film, the gender codes of the past, assembled in conjunction with fictive narratives of national cohesion, no longer effectively regulate male desires in the context of Mexican neoliberalism. Cuarón's film strongly suggests that the problem lies with the overarching myths of unity that attempt to erase class divisions and other categories of social difference and individuality. To embody a coherent expression of masculinity, individuals must reform and normalize their own conduct in alignment with their particularized social position, but the underlying self-indulgent impulses remain unquestioned. Julio and Tenoch attempt to justify their male egotism and self-interest within the terms of the Charolastra manifesto, but by denying their differences and giving themselves license to enjoy unrestrained virile pleasures, they inevitably come into conflict with one another and with their social surroundings. The possibility of transformation proposed by the film does not involve the characters renouncing the selfish desires and impulses that contradicted their shared code of honor. On the contrary, acknowledging the truth about who they are means abandoning the façade of solidarity, embracing differentiated identities, and eventually redirecting themselves toward an alternate, individualized framework of self-regulated masculine subjecthood. By critically displacing codified male values associated with nationalism yet preserving the virile core of masculinity, Cuarón's film is attempting to define gender both ways, that is, as a cultural convention sustained by a specific set of sociohistorical conditions and as an expression of the essential sameness of embodied human desires.

This equivocal understanding of masculinity grants the film's narrative trajectory credibility with its target audience of privileged-class urban consumers in Mexico (and beyond) since it coheres with the emphasis on individual ambition and self-realization that defines the dominant ethos of neoliberal cultural politics. All men are assumed to share the same basic drives and instincts, but some are considered more adept at controlling and directing themselves, which allows them to rise above others in the social hierarchy, or, at the very least, to occupy their rightful place in it. Of course, existing social inequalities play a role in determining the range of realistic possibilities for individual achievement, but it is better to recognize this reality and act according to the competitive norms of late capitalist modernity than to deceive oneself with myths of unity. From this perspective, the nationalist/collectivist model of masculinity supported and regulated by homosocial relations appears obsolete and unrealistic because it falsely presumes a state of social equilibrium in which competition takes place solely in terms of *hombría* (manhood). Individual desires are filtered through a social contract that stresses male solidarity as a means of masculine self-fulfillment, represented as the basis of shared national identity throughout much of recent Mexican history. Accordingly, it is only natural that some men continue to behave as though they can realize their selfhood and their goals in life simply by embodying virile masculinity, but this tendency puts them increasingly at odds with the neoliberal order in Mexico. These underlying attitudes, which inform and validate the boys' transformative process, reflect a fundamentally ahistorical conception of Mexican masculinity. Starting with the assumption that machismo formerly provided a stable framework for male bonding across class lines, the film mystifies the oppressive political uses of masculine gender codes. By reinscribing a fictive notion of antiquated patriarchal national unity as the point of departure for a gender-focused narrative of progressive change that leads the protagonists toward a reformed model of male subjecthood organized by neoliberal individualism, Cuarón reproduces and naturalizes the same logic that generates malformed masculinities. If legitimate masculine subjectivity in neoliberal Mexico necessarily entails a process of self-reformation, then all manner of exclusions are implicitly justified by the default classification of Mexican men as unreconstructed machos. This reasoning obscures the historical and ongoing violence of the gender system imposed on lower-class, racialized bodies.

My position does not expect that *Y tu mamá también*, or any other film, should be able to fully historicize a phenomenon as complex as Mexican gender formation, but it does argue that the reproduction of naturalized myths of machismo and the gendered logic of social exclusion undermines any potential challenge the filmmaker might seek to offer to the prevailing cultural politics of masculinity. Cuarón's attempt to represent a meaningful process of male transformation remains bound up with harmful stereotypes built on the assumption that Mexican men share a common essence and are therefore inherently prone to the same kinds of gender deficiencies. The film's focus on the experiences of white middle- and upper-class subjects does not mitigate the harm. In fact, the avoidance—or apparent impossibility—of significant engagement with

Mexico's rural, lower-class, racialized populations contributes to perpetuating the logic of malformation since it rules out any comparably credible possibility of masculine realignment. The minor character Jesús "Chuy" Carranza (Silverio Palacios) obviously does not have access to the same pathways of neoliberal integration as the more privileged urban male characters, so the film can only narrate his victimization brought about by the breakdown of the social contract and the encroachment of global capitalism into his supposedly stable, traditional fishing community. But his presumptively natural identification with conventional Mexican masculinity, as emphasized in his enthusiastic soccer-related bonding with Julio and Tenoch, reconfirms that Cuarón's project depends on the rearticulation of cultural myths invented by nationalism (fig. 1.3). It also raises the implicit question of whether Chuy's fate may be linked to the burden of his obsolescent masculinity, but the film declines to address this directly. Turning to *Rudo y Cursi*, Carlos Cuarón's highly successful follow-up to *Y tu mamá también*, my analysis reveals very similar dynamics—despite the satirical intentions—in the representation of characters situated near the bottom of the social hierarchy who are unable to overcome defective aspects of their masculine identities that are closely tied to the legacy of Golden Age machismo.

Figure 1.3. The minor character Chuy (Silverio Palacios), a local fisherman soon to be expelled from his home along with his family, cheerfully plays soccer with the protagonists (*Y tu mamá también*).

IV. The Impossibility of Masculine Transformation in *Rudo y Cursi*

The pairing of García Bernal and Luna in the lead roles of both *Rudo y Cursi* and *Y tu mamá también* is not essential to my arguments, since similar embodiments and characterizations of male gender identity could very well have been achieved by other performers. This is not to suggest that casting decisions make no meaningful contribution to the cinematic constructions of masculinity in these films. Carlos Cuarón claims in an interview that he conceived *Rudo y Cursi* as a separate project from *Y tu mamá también*, but he also describes developing the script with García Bernal and Luna in mind, consulting with them about the roles of Tato and Beto (McClanahan). The filmmaker's deployment of the celebrity images of two influential figures closely associated with transnational currents in Mexican cinema has implications related to larger structural changes in the industry,[7] but it also constitutes a directorial strategy of casting against type. Neither García Bernal nor Luna was especially known for playing straightforwardly comedic roles prior to *Rudo y Cursi*, so the film's parodic effect may have been somewhat enhanced by the implicit contrast between the conventional appeal they held as charismatic or sensitive types and their exaggerated performances as self-absorbed macho idiots. In this sense, the reappearance of these two actors does have some intertextual relevance to my claims regarding the parallels and differences with their earlier roles as Julio and Tenoch. The filmmaker's specific mode and purpose of thematizing masculinity in *Rudo y Cursi* entail the deliberate refusal to introduce any of the complex, nuanced dimensions of maleness portrayed in the earlier film. Whereas *Y tu mamá también* pivots on the pathos generated by the gradual exposure of the internal identity conflicts the main characters experience as young men at a turning point in their lives, *Rudo y Cursi* is structured around static formulas of Mexican masculinity intended as parody.

Narration is another contrastive factor relevant to my analysis. While the disembodied voice-over in *Y tu mamá también* offers neutral, objective observations and plot information understood to be diegetically factual, the role of the narrator in *Rudo y Cursi* is given to the character known as Batuta (Guillermo Francella), a crooked Argentine talent agent who recruits Tato and Beto out of their remote rural village to play soccer for professional teams in Mexico City. His offscreen commentaries, constructed as the soccer-themed musings of a jovial fraudster, are designed to generate comic disparity with the actions depicted onscreen. During one of the film's first sequences, he delivers the following risible discourse on teamwork: "En el juego, como en la vida, el esfuerzo individual no es nada si no es parte del esfuerzo colectivo. La colaboración no se entiende sin el principio básico de la generosidad. Todos nos brindamos por una misma causa. Esa actitud nos une y nos hace hermanos" (In sport, as in life, individual effort amounts to nothing if it is not part of a collective effort. Collaboration is meaningless without the basic principle of generosity. We all give ourselves to one cause. That attitude unites us and makes us brothers). As Batuta speaks these lines in the voice-over, we see shots of Tato and Beto making their way home from the banana plantation where they work, with Tato extending a wooden rod from the back of a moving cargo truck so that Beto can be pulled along the road on his bicycle, as if to confirm the ideal of mutual support expressed in the narration. But the very next sequence breaks the illusion when we encounter Beto at home explaining to his wife, Toña (Adriana Paz), that he lost her blender gambling at cards in the local cantina. The running joke in Batuta's commentary throughout the film is that his cliché metaphors about the spirit of sacrifice and fraternalism embodied by soccer are always contradicted by the self-interested behaviors of everyone involved in the sport, including himself.

Sánchez Prado suggests that much of *Rudo y Cursi*'s satire is directed at the sports film genre as a transnational cinematic paradigm that devolves into farce when applied in the context of neoliberal Mexico (*Screening* 193). This argument is supported by the central role given to Batuta since his schemes and machinations drive the narrative far more than the purported skill and talent of Beto and Tato, whose actual games of soccer are mostly relegated to off-screen space. The film certainly undercuts the ideals of cinematic sports heroism by representing the professional league as a system rife with corruption, fraud, and self-dealing, in which the athletes on the field are reduced to pawns whose actions are controlled by an array of exploitative stakeholders. But the players themselves are also implicated in the systemic breakdown of sportsmanship, as Beto's and Tato's self-indulgent conduct conveys their complete disregard for values such as teamwork, discipline, and fair play.[8] They enjoy only a brief interval of fame and success as soccer stars before losing everything and ending up worse off than they were before their recruitment. Even if Carlos Cuarón's intention is to mock the uplifting formulas of generic sports movies, his approach depends on representing the gender performances of the main characters as essentially deficient. Conventional narrative patterns of athletic triumph become absurd not only due to the fraudulent manipulations and cynical profiteering of Batuta and others but also because of the malformed masculinities embodied by Tato and Beto. Just as *Y tu mamá también* invokes the road movie as a genre template in which the protagonists' embodiments of Mexican masculinity cannot ultimately be sustained, *Rudo y Cursi* similarly emphasizes the incompatibility between the codes of the sports movie and the archetypal model of maleness derived from Golden Age cinema. The important difference, however, is that Julio and Tenoch eventually adapt and begin integrating themselves into a modern, neoliberal framework of normative masculine subjectivity, while Tato and Beto are condemned to remain on its margins.

Understanding the rationale that informs the distinct narrative consequences of the Mexican masculinity performed in each film is the focus of my comparative analysis, but before arriving at the main points I wish to make on this question, I must mention some of the tropes of mexicanidad and machismo incorporated into Carlos Cuarón's film. Classic Mexican buddy movies still serve as the main referents in my reading of the patterns of homosociality enacted by Tato and Beto, but the allusions are not identical to those in *Y tu mamá también*. For example, while Julio and Tenoch formulate a misogynistic friendship pact to enshrine their commitment to one another and to regulate their hedonistic sexual rivalry, Tato and Beto are intimately bound together as members of the same family and their macho competitions are ostensibly organized around the desire to earn maternal recognition. Just as the manly prestige of the cousins in *Los tres García* depends on winning approbations from their grandmother, Beto and Tato are engaged in a perpetual dispute over who can claim to be doing the most to honor their mother (Dolores Heredia). Their characteristic way of asserting filial devotion is to boast about the house they each plan to build for her on the beach near their village. The ties between the brothers are configured by conventional family values, and they each attempt to uphold traditional roles in the patriarchal structure. Whereas Julio and Tenoch define themselves as unrepentant womanizers, Tato and Beto pursue masculine dominance in the domestic sphere by venerating their mother, as well as by asserting authority over their younger sister, Nadia (Tania Esmerelda Aguilar). For Beto, this also entails being a provider for his own wife and children. Tato is single at the outset, but his storyline involves a romance with a television presenter named Maya Vega (Jessica Mas), to whom he eventually proposes marriage.

As in *Y tu mamá también*, the emphasis in *Rudo y Cursi*'s treatment of Mexican masculinity falls on the contradictions and self-deceptions that define the protagonists' formulaic gender performances, but in contrast to the gradual narrative exposition of Julio and Tenoch's hollow solidarity, the macho posturing of Beto and Tato is immediately discredited under the film's satirical framework. Signs of the brothers' deficiencies come to the fore in the artificial and vain enactments of their familial roles. The house promised for their mother is obviously well beyond the family's economic reach, so Tato's and Beto's empty rhetoric is merely a way of masking their own inadequacies and selfishness. Beto vows to save enough money to buy the house, but because of his uncontrolled gambling, he cannot even properly administer the meager amount he earns as the foreman of a banana packing crew. Toña turns out to be a far more effective household provider than her husband, as she steadily climbs the ranks of a multilevel marketing company throughout the film. Tato obsessively harbors dreams of achieving fame as a *grupera* singer, a rather far-fetched ambition given his hopelessly unrefined voice. This constitutes another parodic reference to Golden Age cinema's male archetypes, who almost always possessed inexplicably melodious, well-trained singing voices, even if they were supposed to have come from humble circumstances. Tato's delusional desire reflects his own passionate egocentrism, which is plainly apparent despite his pledge to use his future stardom as a means of attaining a new house for his mother. Batuta's ironic voice-over underscores how the portrayal of the brothers' self-serving maternal reverence coalesces with the overall parody of masculine fraternalism associated with sport: "El amor a la madre y el amor a la camiseta son la misma cosa. Es que la vieja es nuestra primera identidad. Por su amor, se lucha como por la vida. Toda hincha quiere demonstrar que nadie ama la camiseta como él, y todo hijo sabe que nadie ama a la vieja como él" (Love for our mother and love for our team's jersey are one and the same. Our mother is our first identity. For her love, we would struggle as though for life itself. Every fan wants to show that no one loves the team more than he does, just as every son knows that no one loves his mom more than him).

Both Beto and Tato happen to possess enough raw athletic ability for Batuta to decide that he can turn a profit by contracting them to professional soccer clubs. Beto has more serious interest in the game, but Tato is the first to be recruited, although he agrees to play only on the condition that Batuta help him with his singing career. Using his powers of persuasion and a few well-placed bribes, Batuta eventually manages to help both brothers gain recognition as rising stars in the national soccer league, and he even secures a recording opportunity for Tato. Yet the brothers' success on the field is persistently undermined by the same patterns of self-indulgent behavior they exhibited from the outset. Tato's futile fixation on musical stardom diverts his attention away from soccer, and he becomes even more distracted by his relationship with Maya, a media figure whose sexy image reflects his own narcissism, as he brags to his friends about having conquered her. When Maya eventually loses interest in him and becomes romantically involved with another soccer player, Tato flies into a misogynist rage and attacks his own teammates. Beto, for his part, allows his gambling habit to get even further out of control, going deeply into debt with a group of threatening criminals who induce him to play poker at their exclusive high-stakes casino. Predictably, neither of the brothers comes close to fulfilling the promise of buying a house for their mother. In a significant subplot, their younger sister Nadia is courted by a wealthy drug trafficker named Don Casimiro (Alfredo Alfonso) who has taken over the territory surrounding their village. When Nadia eventually marries Casimiro, he agrees to construct a house for his mother-in-law and actually follows through on the commitment.

The film culminates with the sports genre trope of the "big game," in which the brothers have one last chance to redeem themselves by cooperating with one another. The terms of the trope are parodically altered by the fact that Beto, who plays goaltender, has decided to throw the match under pressure to pay off his massive gambling debts. For Tato, a striker on the opposing team, scoring a winning goal would mean salvaging his athletic reputation, which steeply declined during his failed romance with Maya. However, the brothers botch the effort to coordinate their plans on the field, resulting in an abrupt end to both of their soccer careers. Tato is cut from the team and goes to work in a karaoke bar owned by Casimiro. For Beto, the consequences are even more severe, as the unpaid debts lead to a violent retribution that causes him to lose his leg. A closing sequence shows the brothers standing together on the beach (with Beto on crutches) in front of their mother's new home (fig. 1.4), where they sing one of Tato's preferred musical numbers, a Spanish-language version of Cheap Trick's "I Want You to Want Me," whose lyrics suitably complement their self-absorbed macho attitudes.

Critical responses to *Rudo y Cursi* by both Schaefer and Wood recognize the film's engagement with traditional models of masculinity linked to nationalist cinema, but neither of these authors seriously questions the mythology of the masculinist social contract articulated by Mexican cultural politics. For them, fraternalism rooted in shared macho sensibilities

Figure 1.4. Beto (left; Luna) and Tato (right; García) return home to their rural community much the worse for wear after their disastrous foray into the transnational world of professional soccer (*Rudo y Cursi*, 2008, dir. Carlos Cuarón).

remains a naturalized component of Mexican cultural identity that goes mostly unchallenged by *Rudo y Cursi*'s lightly critical satire of male gender roles. By contrast, Sánchez Prado associates the film with the same postnational framework epitomized by *Y tu mamá también*, arguing that both movies "exhibit the ability of commercial Mexican film to operate in forms that no longer seek any identitary claim over its spectatorship" (*Screening* 194). While I generally agree with his view that the Cuaróns' filmmaking practice aims to disengage from the homogenizing nationalist paradigm of cultural representation, I also find that their work seemingly cannot avoid returning to the cultural archive of Mexican masculinity as a means of articulating the process of detachment. As shown in my discussion of *Y tu mamá también*, the narrative trajectory configures Julio and Tenoch's masculinity as an illusory vestige of a nationalist model of fraternal unity that must eventually be abandoned and disavowed. I argued that by taking machismo for granted as the common ground on which the protagonists' story of male transformation naturally begins, the film not only distorts the historical function of gendered ideology in Mexico but also re-creates elements of the same cultural essentialism that it ostensibly sets out to displace. Furthermore, I suggested that by situating a lower-class, rural male character such as Chuy on the same naturalized common ground of national masculinity, *Y tu mamá también* opens the door to an implicit affirmation and acceptance of the neoliberal state's approach to managing capitalist penetration into impoverished regions of the country. Since the defective, outdated gender identities embodied by rural peasants cannot typically be reformed by the same integrative processes available to urban privileged-class subjects, the existing socioeconomic hierarchy can appear legitimate or even preordained, just as it did in the dominant representational regime of postrevolutionary cinema. *Rudo y Cursi* passes through the door left open by *Y tu mamá también* by explicitly representing the identities of lower-class, rural men as being fully constituted by unreformed—or rather, unreformable—Mexican machismo, portraying the protagonists as hopelessly ill-prepared to compete as individuals in the prevailing terms of transnational neoliberalism. In this sense, Wood and Schaefer are correct in observing that *Rudo y Cursi*'s satirical treatment of masculinity does not fully supplant nationalist codes of fraternalism, but they overlook the problems arising from the film's class-specific deployment of these codes and its uncritical reproduction of the same exclusionary logic inscribed into the originary representational formulas that mythologized machismo as a structure of collective identity.

Schaefer's claim regarding the film's affirmation of "the continued support of men by men" (52) may be reconsidered in relation to the transformed cultural politics of neoliberalism that have altered the meanings of the postrevolutionary ideal of machismo and its malformed underside. The nationalist model of masculine homosociality was assembled in conjunction with the myth of an equitable and inclusive social order. Golden Age films such as *Los tres García* celebrated fraternalism and the strengthening of male bonds through competition within a well-regulated patriarchal framework (supported by maternal morality), while also establishing categories of malformed men located outside the bounds of this framework. Classic cinema's construction of fictive differences between masculine and submasculine subjects naturalized the value of mutual support epitomized by the modern paternalist nation-state at the same time as it demarcated the limits of national belonging. Contemporary commercial cinema, according to Sánchez Prado, dissociates itself from the cultural politics of nationalism by refusing to posit any shared identification with Mexicanness, or, as Lahr-Vivaz suggests, by creating deliberate contrasts with the archive of national film culture. For cinema audiences in neoliberal Mexico, narratives and images of men supporting men aligned with outmoded and fallacious codes of homosocial collectivism tend to signify an undesirable mode of masculine identity and illegitimate authority, an object to be criticized, satirized, rejected, or even feared. In this regard, I suggest that such filmic imagery remains meaningful to the extent that it defines legitimate exclusions. To be sure, neoliberalism validates its own patriarchal mechanisms to enable certain classes of men to benefit from the support of other men, but these relations are structured in social and economic agendas that necessarily transcend the cultural politics of nationalism.[9]

Carlos Cuarón's strategy for severing cultural and ideological ties with Mexicanness involves making a mockery of the tropes of masculinity closely associated with the Golden Age cinematic tradition, particularly men who support other men—or rather, men who claim to support others while in fact thinking only of themselves. A major shortcoming of this approach lies in the failure to register the artificiality of the macho constructs summoned in his film. While *Y tu mamá también* also naturalizes the performance of Mexican masculinity in significant ways, the device of the Charolastra manifesto provides at least some implicit acknowledgment of the contrived basis for the main characters' behaviors, facilitating the film's representation of the inevitable collapse of their imagined solidarity and their turn toward a new, more realistic pathway of self-realization. *Rudo y Cursi* contains no comparable mechanism to mark the invented, ideological origins of machismo. Even more so than in the earlier film, the portrayal of the protagonists' masculine identities purports to reflect an organic expression of Mexican masculinity rather than an imposed framework. Of course, the satirical objectives of the film allow the audience to infer that Tato and Beto are intended to be caricatures as opposed to fully authentic portraits of Mexican men, but even the most exaggerated caricature usually has an implied real-world referent. If Carlos Cuarón's intention is to critique Mexican masculinity only as an abstraction that became concretized in stereotyped cultural imagery, his method is flawed from the outset since *Rudo y Cursi* clearly emphasizes the main characters' embodied realization and internalization of the codes of machismo. Furthermore, the film declines to remain strictly within the boundaries of farce, as it uses a realistic film language to depict rural and urban scenarios, and also introduces the theme of narco violence that unavoidably evokes real social problems in Mexico (albeit certainly not with any accuracy). The film's pretensions to realism and its lack of self-reflexivity suggest that Carlos Cuarón is making at least some claim about the actual existence of macho identities akin to those of his protagonists. Since the film's implied audience does not extend beyond urban privileged-class consumers, these claims do not run the risk of alienating spectators. To the contrary, the reiteration of prevailing cultural stereotypes about lower-class Mexican men is so thoroughly accepted that it is effectively invisible.

I suggest that this representational pattern of naturalizing, dehistoricizing, and rearticulating Mexican machismo in order to narrativize dissociations and disavowals intended to resonate with privileged-class Mexican and transnational audiences has become paradigmatic in current Mexican commercial cinema. The Cuaróns were already experimenting with basic elements of this formula in *Sólo con tu pareja*, but with *Rudo y Cursi* they achieved its definitive expression by taking full advantage of the altered sphere of spectatorship for Mexican cinema, which has been reshaped along racialized class lines and extended more strategically beyond national borders. At the present stage, Mexican films may still invoke malformed masculinity as a problematic cultural legacy to be overcome through individualized processes of male self-reformation, as it was for the middle- and upper-class characters in *Y tu mamá también*, but it is perhaps even more commonly and readily deployed as a static sign of essentialized difference affixed to men from Mexico's mostly brown and mostly impoverished masses, thereby confirming the inevitability and legitimacy of ongoing arrangements of social segregation and intensified forms of state-organized violence. I discuss some more recent examples of this pervasive pattern in this book's afterword. Next, I turn to the work of Carlos Reygadas, who offers an alternate response to Mexico's transhistorical myths of masculinity.

Chapter Two

Demystifying Machismo in *Batalla en el cielo* and *Post tenebras lux*

I. Carlos Reygadas: A Realism of Mexican Unreality

Carlos Reygadas's distinctive mode of auteurist cinema has often been defined in terms of an experimental realist aesthetic intended to provoke discomforting visceral responses in the viewer. While foregrounding questions related to embodied spectatorship could risk sidestepping the director's sustained sociopolitical critique aimed at unsettling naturalized hierarchies of class, race, and gender in modern Mexico, several studies have turned attention to the conjunction of these dimensions of his cinema. For example, in his discussion of Reygadas's "realism of the senses," Tiago de Luca draws from Jacques Rancière's theorizations of political aesthetics to posit that the director "aims to rearrange and reframe the self-evidently real through sensory experiences that disrupt the 'consensual' social order legitimated by the status quo" (*Realism* 27). By engaging the senses directly, often at the expense of narrative coherence, Reygadas's cinema exposes "pressing social realities" in ways that, according to de Luca, "enable us to see, hear and feel them afresh" (*Realism* 28). Troy Bordun takes a related position that regards Reygadas's films as pushing established genre formations into new sensory extremes, thereby opening alternate sociopolitical possibilities: "Transforming sense-experience . . . transforms social, cultural, ethical, and political engagements" (4). Both of these scholars account for the transformative effects of the sensual in Reygadas's work by addressing the director's paradoxical strategy of combining minutely planned cinematic formalism with an intense focus on the sensual experience generated from the material presence and spontaneous reality of the profilmic event. They each locate political moments in Reygadas's work at junctures between aspects of Mexican reality captured with documentary-like verisimilitude and the meticulously composed metacinematic framings surrounding them.

Such an approach has proved fruitful for these and other critics, but even circumspect readings of the ostensibly ethnographic or documentary elements in Reygadas's filmmaking have sometimes puzzlingly reaffirmed status quo representations of the self-evidently "real" existence of subjects defined by mythic social categories rather than fully registering the denaturalizing effects of the director's self-reflexive approach. To cite briefly an example that will be addressed again later in this chapter, de Luca emphasizes how sexual acts performed by "unlikely couples," depicted in Reygadas's films with "documentary authenticity," constitute radical rearrangements of existing politico-aesthetic frameworks (*Realism* 80–81). In his reading, the "shock" produced by these "impossible fictions authenticated and indeed made possible in reality" offers provocative challenges to the established myths of national identity constructed and normalized by state ideology (*Realism* 87–88). Yet de Luca's analysis engages minimally with the politics of representation specific to Mexico's modern cultural nationalism, bypassing national cinema's historical role in making intelligible the fictive social and racial differences between the characters who form Reygadas's "implausible" couplings (*Realism* 28). In contrast, I will argue that the images of onscreen sexual partners that de Luca understands in terms of manifestly real categorial distinctions are rather designed to reflect a gaze aligned with hierarchical and disciplinary parameters, constructed to a significant extent by Mexican national cinema. Bordun, for his part, likewise affirms the politically disruptive potential of the "confusion of fiction and reality" in Reygadas's filmmaking (73). However, even as he approaches the films as "performative documentaries" that "are less indexical than iconic," Bordun readily associates particular images, such as that of the "poor drunk man" in *Post tenebras lux*, with Reygadas's effort to create an ethnographic "document of Mexico" (74–75). According to Bordun, the mediating apparatus of Reygadas's cinematic frame is permeable enough for such "traces of the real" to filter through, enabling "class and race divisions to be clearly present" (75). Once again, the real presence of social difference is taken to stand incontrovertibly on its own rather than in relation to the classificatory representational logic that has historically configured the intersected meanings and perceptibility of inebriation, poverty, masculinity, and racial difference in Mexico.

By calling attention to these insufficiently problematized references to "real" distinctions among "authentic" Mexican subjects that underpin the analyses by de Luca and Bordun, I do not intend to detract from these authors' otherwise insightful contributions. However, one of my contentions is that to develop deeper understandings of Reygadas's oppositional transformations of dominant representational regimes in Mexico, critical discussions can engage more fluently with the hegemonic political culture specific to Mexico's development as a modern nation. De Luca's observation that Reygadas aims to "defy and subvert the expectations generally brought to the national image of Mexico" (*Realism* 86) remains valid and corresponds with much recent scholarship highlighting contemporary Mexican filmmakers' challenges to an array of outmoded and illusory nationalist cultural ideals. Nevertheless, while an aesthetics defined by a provocative, unconstrained realism may be assumed to offer a corrective antidote to stagnant, traditional cinematic imagery aligned with mexicanidad, I suggest that Reygadas's work complicates this formula by critically illustrating how contemporary representational languages, including those labeled as realist, can reproduce patterns of perception informed by nationalist mythologies, particularly related to the bodies and subjectivities of lower-class, racialized men. At a time when so many Mexican films continue to naturalize images of threatening, malformed masculinities, one of Reygadas's most significant contributions consists in disclosing the oppressive logical precepts and categories organizing the contemporary cultural imaginary and its dominant representational order.

This chapter considers two films, *Batalla en el cielo* and *Post tenebras lux*, in which the director reveals how cultural discourses and cinematic codes of Mexican masculinity form a network of constraints invisibly fastened around representations of the "real" in Mexico. In dialogue with Reygadas's films, I contend that masculinity has been central to the organization of discursive and symbolic frameworks of control in Mexico, as it creates an often imperceptible, naturalized imposition of order at various social levels: embodied subjects, family structures, and the imagined national collectivity. Using self-reflexive, metacinematic techniques to mediate his realism, Reygadas exposes the regulatory functions of masculinity as a classificatory system designed to uphold uneven power relations, and of cinema as one of the principal representational mechanisms through which this system is deployed and reproduced. My analyses demonstrate how Reygadas's films expose transhistorical patterns of cinematic signification that have sustained mythic perceptions of reality that legitimate violent forms of domination and exploitation.

My reading of *Batalla en el cielo* builds upon earlier discussions of the symbolic prominence of masculine icons of cinema, such as Pedro Infante, whose images were constitutive of modern subjectivity in Mexico's cultural politics of nationalism. In dialogue with de la Mora and others, I have suggested that these figures were used not only to help establish the patriarchal myth of the mestizo male's social dominance but also to delineate the external boundaries of full masculine subjecthood. I show that Reygadas uses carefully planned camerawork and other creative strategies to reveal the historical continuities of an underlying perceptual schema rooted in nationalist categories of machismo and mestizaje. According to my analysis, the film discloses how the cultural logic at work in originary cinematic formations of Mexican masculinity continues to conceptually organize contemporary, neoliberal articulations of masculine malformation that rationalize diverse modes of social subjugation and labor exploitation in Mexico. Following this, my discussion of *Post tenebras lux* demonstrates how the film's protagonist enacts this classificatory logic in his quotidian relations with subordinate male subjects, marking their apparent gender deficiencies as a means of constituting and legitimating his own patriarchal masculine identity. As a member of Mexico's ruling class, the film's protagonist commands sufficient material wealth to place other men and their labor at his private disposal, but his socioeconomic power is significantly mediated and enhanced by a preexisting class-race-gender matrix—whose genealogy ultimately reaches beyond Mexican nationalism to the colonial foundations of Western modernity—that naturalizes his dominant position in terms of rational and moral superiority. I argue that the film focalizes the protagonist's subjective gaze as a critical, self-reflexive illustration of contemporary cinema's complicity in reproducing, and representing as "real," objectifying images of malformed masculinity embodied by lower-class, racialized Mexican men.

II. Unseeing Machismo

Although most often associated with the sphere of global auteurism, Reygadas's filmmaking practice exhibits a persistent interest in subverting representational structures and mechanisms assembled by Mexico's national cinematic tradition. His films invoke and rework the symbolic language of mexicanidad precisely to expose the unquestioned meanings embedded in familiar Mexican imagery. This strategy has been described by Sánchez Prado in his discussion of Reygadas's first film, *Japón* (Japan) (2002), in which the protagonist, an unnamed artist (Alejandro Ferretis), ventures from Mexico City to a remote provincial village with the intention of committing suicide. For Sánchez Prado, the director's approach to depicting landscapes and characters in this film offers a "radical reconfiguration of existing discourses of the rural in Mexican cinema, rather than an altogether new representation" (*Screening* 199). The film nullifies and transforms established cinematic paradigms of representing Mexico's hinterland regions and their inhabitants by foregrounding the "very suspension of their inherited Mexicanness" (*Screening* 201). By setting up partially recognizable visual referents and narrative scenarios only to disallow expected patterns of signification to be replicated, Reygadas not only "disrupts the continuity of nationalist film tradition" but also creates the possibility for unexpected articulations of Mexican experience to emerge in complex confluence with "global flows of art cinema" (*Screening* 201). A dialogue with transnational arthouse directors such as Andrei Tarkovsky, Carl Theodor Dreyer, and Yasujirō Ozu is evident in the distinctive repertoire of formal techniques that Reygadas introduces in *Japón*, including the contemplative pace of the editing and camera movement, long takes, natural sound and lighting, wide angles with extensive panning, and shots with intensely subjective points of view. These elements of form have continued to define his creative practice in subsequent projects, along with his frequent recourse to nonprofessional actors and fragmentary, minimalist narrative structures. Of course, currents of auteurism and formal innovation in Mexican cinema precede Reygadas by many decades, but few directors have so self-consciously engaged with arthouse aesthetics as a means of interrogating dimensions of the national imaginary instituted and mediated by film culture.

Elena Lahr-Vivaz defines Reygadas's filmmaking in similar terms, showing how his second film, *Batalla en el cielo*, includes overtly self-aware performative and visual allusions to cinematic conventions of the Golden Age. By imbuing familiar formulaic codes and emotive signifiers of nationhood and unity with an exaggerated degree of artifice, Reygadas deliberately disables and undermines facile forms of identification and emphasizes the "limitations of the tie between spectators and screen—

and by extension, of *nosotros* as an empathetically imagined community" (122). More than references to specific films from the Mexican archive, Lahr-Vivaz finds that *Batalla en el cielo* invokes structural and thematic elements of melodrama, understood as a "metagenre" (11).[1] Drawing upon the work of Ana M. López, she observes how *Batalla en el cielo*'s main cinematographic motifs correlate closely with three "master narratives" that defined the melodramatic cinema of the postrevolutionary era: "religion, nationalism, and modernization" (Lahr-Vivaz 123; López "Tears and Desire" 256). Reygadas's film intensifies melodrama's characteristic aesthetics of "excess" in order to produce an "overload of images of Mexico" (125). The strategy for breaking out of the constraints of representational determinism instituted by cinematic traditions of Mexicanness involves closing the gap "between filmic fiction and lived reality" (127). To dismantle the mythic nation imagined by classic melodramas, Reygadas's film pays artificially excessive attention to unglamorous aspects of everyday life, especially physical spaces and bodily flesh. Lahr-Vivaz underscores how the corporeal discrepancies between the male protagonist of *Batalla en el cielo*, Marcos (Marcos Hernández), and the idealized gender identities performed by the stars of classic Mexican film, such as Infante, facilitate Reygadas's portrayal of "Mexico as a fragmentary assemblage of all-too-ordinary bodies" (123).

Lahr-Vivaz positions Reygadas's work as part of what she sees as a wider development in recent filmmaking to destabilize the optimistic narratives created by national cinema to represent Mexico as a culturally cohesive social whole. She argues that directors of current Mexican cinema, including Reygadas, lay emphasis on the idea that "we are *nosotros* no more, and indeed, that we never were" (32). While not necessarily opposed to this outlook, my approach to *Batalla en el cielo* posits a distinct relation between the representational matrix constructed around embodiments of masculinity in national cinema and the critical reappraisals offered by Reygadas. The symbolic fictions tied to the masculine spectacles performed by Infante and others like him, I argue, must be understood as part of a system of domination that has operated not by simply by inducing desire for a harmonious national community, but by establishing a mythic conception of gender malformity, underwritten by the patriarchal state, to legitimate disciplinary, social violence against mestizo men deemed unruly, irrational, and racially inferior. In *Batalla en el cielo*, this violence becomes apparent not only in the brown male protagonist's contradictory experiences of his own body but also through a cinematic gaze that reveals the terms of malformation governing his subjectivity. These corporeal contradictions reveal how myths of masculinity originated by national cinema's representational regime continue to be rearticulated, giving rise to new rationalizations for controlling, subjugating, and exploiting the labor of brown male bodies.

Although I agree with Lahr-Vivaz regarding the implicit juxtaposition of Marcos's "all-too-ordinary" male body and the idealized corporeal image of Golden Age celebrities such as Infante, my argument also shows the relevance of the contrastive masculine imagery *within* classic films themselves. As I discussed in the previous chapter, iconic portraits of cinematic machismo tended to be codified in contradistinction to male figures defined by submasculine characteristics. De la Mora demonstrates that Golden Age films delineated the archetypal hypermasculine macho as "virile, brave, proud, sexually potent, and physically aggressive" (7), qualities often articulated in paradoxical conjunction with signs of homosexuality. While he contends "machismo needs the *joto* to define and affirm itself as much as it needs a clingy woman" (5), I have suggested that another dimension of the macho persona's underside is constituted by men whose gender identities register as deficient without necessarily implying effeminacy or contravening normative sexuality. These malformed masculinities, as I have described them, are formulated in terms of an array of social vices, moral defects, and signs of irrationality, usually correlated to fictive categorial conceptions of class, race, and modernity. Although his study emphasizes codified cinematic expressions of male sexuality, de la Mora also recognizes the spectrum of signs associated with differentiated categories of heterosexual Mexican men. At the most extreme limit of the undesirable side of masculinity, one finds "men from the popular sectors, often mestizo, [who] are negatively coded as promiscuous, hard-drinking, and irresponsible; they are often not good family providers" (80). These roles typically were assigned to less famous actors, often with darker complexions. The opposite extreme is occupied by "the dominant image of the aggressive, arrogant, *criollo*," often portrayed by a white actor like Jorge Negrete, who readily embodied pride and virility but could appear somewhat cold and distant from everyday people (80). Pedro Infante stands on the middle ground, as he was especially successful at articulating Mexican masculinity as a desirable, accessible identity. Even though he was white, he excelled at portraying a positive image of the working-class mestizo, a common man who was "kind, humble, approachable, human, imperfect, rarely violent, playful, and emotionally expressive" (80).

This basic matrix outlined by de la Mora suggests how the dominant meanings of machismo were consolidated through promulgations of both positive and negative imagery. My interest lies with uncovering to a fuller extent the cultural logic that comprised the classificatory system enabling the reproduction of malformed masculinities. Part of my contention is that signifying practices established in national cinema offered an idealized spectacle of masculine superiority while simultaneously codifying corporeal signifiers to delimit categories of men deemed justifiably excludable. Implicit in this exclusionary reasoning is the fictive barrier of race. De la Mora correctly emphasizes the ideological significance of male figures situated around the midpoint of the spectrum between dominant and dysfunctional masculinities. These characterizations correspond to the statist agenda of mestizaje, which represented itself as an evolutionary process that ostensibly offered a progressive pathway toward citizenship and recognition for parts of the population who had historically been excluded from the nation. Because "indios" were understood to belong to the past, approaching modern masculinity necessarily involved mestizaje, but the positive side of the masculine spectrum was not represented as accessible to every mestizo-in-the-making. De la Mora describes how, in several prominent film roles, Infante successfully conveys the narrative trajectory of a male mestizo at an embryonic stage—not yet a fully formed Mexican macho—who must undergo a socially redemptive process of self-reformation, domestication, and integration. For example, in *La vida no vale nada* (Life Is Worthless) (1954, dir. Rogelio A. González), Infante "portrays a philandering, alcoholic womanizer in need of domestication through marriage and monogamy" (80). This formula is indeed illustrative of the salvational ideology of modernity inscribed into the paternalist discourses of statehood and citizenship. However, it should also be acknowledged that it was far more common for negatively coded masculine features to be represented as insurmountable. In many cases, especially when embodied by browner mestizos, they signified permanent, intrinsic defects. The distinction is evident in a film such as *Nosotros los pobres*, in which Infante's working-class protagonist, Pepe el Toro, stands apart from both the upper-class figures and those comprising the violent, criminal underclass. The Manichaean moral structure of traditional melodrama is somewhat destabilized in this film (and its sequels) since the story is predicated on the idea that members of the poorest, most marginalized sectors of society embody ethical values that are lacking among the wealthy. Pepe el Toro is by no means morally perfect, but he suffers far more than he deserves, and by enduring hardship with masculine fortitude, he eventually redeems himself. The most important contrast to Pepe's positive, working-class masculinity is not the devious upper-class attorney, Montes (Rafael Alcayde), who aggressively accuses Pepe of theft and murder, but rather the criminal gang leader, Ledo (Jorge Arriaga), who actually committed the murder that leads to Pepe's unjust imprisonment. Another significant disparity is with Don Pilar (Miguel Inclán), Pepe's neighbor who steals money and violently thrashes the only witness to his crime, Pepe's paralyzed mother (María Gentil Arcos). Both of these men must eventually pay for their crimes, but neither one of them is portrayed as morally redeemable.

The existence of unequivocally immoral characters in a melodramatic film is unsurprising, but the particular performative and corporeal expression of these criminal subjectivities has significant consequences for the codification of malformed masculinity. The programmatic correlation between brownness and masculine malformation can be observed even amid other fictive signs of racial differentiation. There are wealthy, white male characters in *Nosotros los pobres,* such as Montes, who embody selfish and corrupt behaviors, but the most palpable social threats come from lower-class, brown mestizo figures such as Ledo and Don Pilar. De la Mora, like most other scholars who comment on gender norms in these films, emphasizes that Infante's performances fostered male spectators' self-recognition as mestizos imbued with the potential to approach modern masculinity, offering a vision of the advantages associated with occupying a privileged position as Mexican male citizens incorporated into a patriarchal social structure. I suggest that his whiteness encodes an imaginary threshold that barred full access to masculine subjecthood for the majority of Mexican men. The hypothetical social benefits afforded to mestizo male subjects by the Mexican state depended on their successful performance of positive forms of modern masculinity associated with whiteness. Without being able to approach gender ideals, as modeled onscreen by white actors such as Infante, real men, especially poor brown ones, were always potentially perceptible as not quite fully developed modern male subjects, as malformed, criminal mestizos or inferior primitives. The cultural logic embedded in Golden Age cinema may have encouraged some degree of assimilative identification with modern Mexican masculinity, but it simultaneously reinforced a dominant discursive order that justified and concealed violent and coercive forms of subjugation carried out upon real men whose embodiments of gendered mestizaje were symbolically encoded as racial deficiencies.

The oppressive, ordering function of male mestizo identity comes visually and thematically into the foreground in Reygadas's *Batalla en el cielo* through the director's emphasis on the subjection of the male protagonist to a representational regime composed of untenable gender ideals. Reygadas uses direct and indirect references to Mexico's national cinema tradition to visually configure the body of the main character, Marcos, in terms that accentuate his discrepancies with the dominant masculine mestizo, but the contradictions are meaningfully rearticulated to reflect the prevailing regime of neoliberal cultural politics. Reygadas often frames Marcos and the modern cityscape using the cinematic language of realism to situate his corporeal presence within the concrete precarities of contemporary socioeconomic conditions. A common premise regarding neoliberalism is that it is defined by the weakening of the state's capacity to exert authority over bodies and subjectivities,[2] but my discussion of the film will suggest that neoliberal policies actually operate in concert with the state's nationalist discourses, especially those related to masculinity, which results in even tighter constraints on selfhood and corporeal integrity. In particular, the film shows how the current configuration of elite power justifies its coercive disciplining of brown Mexican males, converting their bodies more effectively and wholly into a commodity, that is, labor to be consumed in a privatized marketplace. While the film confounds narrative logic, its cinematographic composition draws attention to correlations between Marcos's marginal, subjugated position in the contemporary social order and the perceptual paradigms that make mestizo males intelligible as malformed. Reygadas reveals the contradictory construction of modern masculinity, wherein the hollow myth of male dominance is inscribed onto bodies whose gender performance is condemned to fail as a consequence of racial inferiority, effectively rationalizing their ongoing subjugation. The oppressive effect of Mexican masculinity for brown males lies precisely with this permanent condemnation that posits the enduring need for a modern social order to lift the racialized subject to the level of man.

III. Masculine Malformation in *Batalla en el cielo*

Batalla en el cielo's main narrative thread is deliberately elusive and fragmentary but can be pieced together as follows: the principal character in the picture is Marcos, who works as a driver and private security guard for a military general in Mexico City. Part of his job includes chauffeuring the general's adult daughter, Ana (Anapola Mushkadiz), who secretly prostitutes herself at a brothel known as the "Boutique." Early in the film, it is revealed that Marcos and his wife (Berta Ruiz) recently abducted a baby belonging to one of their relatives in hopes of collecting a ransom payment, but the infant died of unknown causes soon afterward. Marcos confesses the crime to Ana, who advises him to give himself up to the police, while his wife tells him instead to join her on a pilgrimage to the Basilica of the Virgin of Guadalupe in order to receive divine forgiveness. Marcos has a sexual encounter with Ana, and after a period of reflection he seemingly appears ready to accept punishment for his crime, but on his final visit to Ana he unexpectedly murders her with a kitchen knife. The conclusion is composed of a lengthy pilgrimage sequence leading up to Marcos's enigmatic death inside the Basilica.

As depicted in the film, Marcos's daily experience mostly consists of activities associated with his job, which requires him to traverse long distances in and around the sprawling metropolis of Mexico City behind the wheel of the SUV belonging to his employers. The evidently long workdays oblige him to remain seated and often physically immobile, given the extreme traffic congestion affecting Mexico City and the immense distances to be covered. An aerial shot midway through the film shows an intersection of three busy urban highways barely contained within the frame, signaling the excesses to which the city's inhabitants are subjected in their daily lives. This type of shot mirrors the extreme close-ups of the characters in which their bodies exceed the limits of the camera's perspective. *Batalla en el cielo* suggests a close correlation between the materiality of the metropolitan environment and the corporeal conditions of its inhabitants. The entire film is characterized by a distinct scarcity of action and lack of a temporal framework signaling a clear succession of narrative events. This uncertainty of time captures Marcos's experience of being subjected to an unregulated and exploitative schedule that robs him of consistent opportunities for rest and recovery. Marcos is apparently on call throughout the day and night, a regimen that limits opportunities for social interaction. As an isolated, exploited worker, Marcos reveals the difficulties of forming a working-class identity or partaking in any kind of homosocial bonding in neoliberal Mexico. Moreover, the fact that Marcos's wife works as a vendor in a subway station suggests that Marcos's salary is insufficient to support his family. The culmination of this precarious economic position is marked by the couple's act of kidnapping, which occurs outside the diegetic frame but nonetheless suggests their willingness to cross the threshold from the legal to the illegal side of Mexico's ruthless neoliberal economy.

The emphasis on the materiality of Marcos's lived condition stands in productive tension with the filmmaker's efforts to disclose the perpetuation of a normative, disciplinary configuration of masculine gender identity and its correlative racializing discourse. Through an array of compositional strategies and careful deployments and withholdings of the diegetic framework, Reygadas deliberately destabilizes his own realist aesthetic in order to raise doubts about current cinema's capacity to register a "real" referent beyond the established representational regime of Mexican masculinity. This is particularly apparent in sequences depicting Marcos's relationship with Ana, played by a nonprofessional actress identifiable as white. In my reading of several interactions between them, I suggest that Ana's perception of Marcos reflects and reinscribes Mexico's hegemonic codes of masculinity interwoven with discourses of malformation. This pervasive categorial framework, in which Marcos is visually configured as a defective macho and denied the full status of modern gendered subjecthood, subverts the film's apparent gestures toward an unfettered cinematic approach to his "real" being.

To draw the viewer's attention to these naturalized dynamics of objectification, Reygadas uses subtle forms of aesthetic defamiliarization. In one lengthy sequence that shows Marcos driving Ana from the airport to the Boutique, the camera remains static and centrally situated inside the vehicle, providing a perspective of the city's roadways passing through various commercial and residential districts, framed by the front windshield with Marcos's eyes appearing in the rearview mirror. In this apparently neutral, observational mode of cinematic realism, with the narrative suspended for a significant interval, the viewing subject is seemingly invited to take in the spontaneous, nondiegetic happenings of the urban environment. Yet, with some strategic destabilizations, Reygadas makes visible the highly mediated construction of the imagery, alerting the spectator to the operations of the cinematic apparatus as a preestablished symbolic system. Almost imperceptibly at first, significant disjunctures appear between the audio track and the imagery, as we hear Ana's telephone conversation with her boyfriend, Jaime (David Bornstein), and her few remarks to Marcos carry on unbroken through a series of jump cuts showing the vehicle's advancement along its route. Through careful editing, Reygadas self-reflexively demonstrates how filmic language enables the illusion of continuity in which the viewer instinctively fills in the spatiotemporal gaps. The effect of observing this understated crack in the realist surface is to become self-aware of our immersion in an artfully deceptive world of appearances and our own automatic processes of responding to representational cues.³

Reygadas's overall approach to filmmaking marks an obvious rupture with conventional form, but his aesthetic holds up a mirror to the structure of cinematic representation itself, suggesting its centrality in dominant symbolic orders and its profound influence in the constitution of the modern gaze. He registers continuities that persist within the language of cinema, which provide ready-made significations that attach seamlessly and systematically to certain arrangements of filmic imagery. In *Batalla en el cielo*, the director calls particular attention to the meanings of masculinity that adhere to the body of Marcos, especially as he is gazed upon by Ana, who authoritatively articulates the gender dimensions of the nationalist symbolic framework that originated in the formative period of modern Mexican cinema. About midway through the lengthy driving sequence, the static camera shifts into a more dynamic mode, situating Marcos within a cinematically codified relay of gazes designed to delineate the predetermined possibilities of his gendered subjectivity from a hegemonic perspective. Marcos brings the vehicle to a stop at a traffic signal, but when the light changes to green, he does not advance through the intersection, causing another motorist to shout a racially charged insult and spit at Marcos while maneuvering past the immobile SUV: "¡Despiértate pinche negro de mierda!" (Wake up, you damned black shit!). The camera captures Marcos's nonreaction to the violent outburst with a close-up of his expressionless visage, then pans to Ana in the rear seat who is staring uneasily at Marcos (figs. 2.1 and 2.2). Aligned with Ana's point of view, the shot frames Marcos in profile, which may be understood as visual citation of an established pattern of cinematic composition designed to accentuate a physiognomic conception of racial difference.⁴ The concurrence of racializing responses to Marcos's behavior is significantly interwoven with both subtextual and overt allusions to his malformed gender identity.

Marcos's passive, unresponsive acceptance of verbal abuse along with his physical motionlessness set him at odds with the naturalized performance of masculine dominance as defined in national cinema.⁵ By implication, Marcos's masculinity becomes coded as deficient through his failure to drive the narrative by answering the aggressor with his own display of masculine bravado or by otherwise counteracting the intimidation.

Figure 2.1. Ana (Ana Mushkadiz) gazes at her chauffeur, Marcos (Marcos Hernández), from the rear seat of the stationary vehicle (*Batalla en el cielo,* 2005, dir. Carlos Reygadas).

Figure 2.2. Close-up shot of Marcos's face in profile from a perspective implicitly aligned with Ana's gaze (*Batalla en el cielo*).

The deficiency is brought more clearly into relief with the visual rendering that represents him through Ana's subjective gaze as an archaic object, inadequate to modernity. Ana's comments bring a significant dimension of this mostly tacit process to the surface when she presumptively ascribes his distracted behavior to unfulfilled sexual desire. She invites him to the Boutique, and when he refuses, she taunts him with emasculating intimations: "¿No me vas a decir que le eres fiel a tu mujer?" (Don't tell me you're loyal to your wife?). In response, Marcos can only sputter a few words of meek compliance. This is a revealing moment, as it not only affirms that dominant codes of Mexican masculinity continue to be affixed to biologically male bodies but also that they remain a useful and effective tool of subjugation. More than a mere spectator, Ana discloses herself as the author (or authoritative enforcer) of a hegemonic narrative about Marcos's defective masculinity. Her gaze positions her employee as a failed macho, morally weak yet desperate to prove his manhood, and therefore thoroughly dependent on the patronage of those who can afford to offer him such an opportunity. Despite the dimensions of realism within the sequence, Reygadas stages this exchange in a very deliberate way by minimizing as much as possible the diegetic explanations for Marcos's behavior and by emphasizing the complicity of established cinematic language in reproducing the denigrating image of Marcos that Ana projects.

A similar effect is achieved through the refusal to provide a narrative account of why Ana works in the Boutique, a move that helps to foreground the operative ideological designs associated with the brothel as a frequently used and highly coded filmic topos in Mexican national cinema. De la Mora argues that the cabaret-brothel, as portrayed in Golden Age films, is an ambivalent site that can "safeguard patriarchal privileges" while also foregrounding "women's sexual agency" (15). Addressing such films as *La mujer del puerto* (Woman of the Port) (1933), *Las abandonadas* (The Abandoned Women) (1944), and *Víctimas del pecado* (Victims of Sin) (1950), he shows how the prostitute is always a "contradictory" figure, an "unattainable revered object of erotic desire who is paradoxically both pure and corrupt, sacred and secular" (23). While asserting that prostitution melodramas became a "pedagogical tool for teaching Mexicans how to adapt to the social changes introduced by the Revolution and modernity" (50), de la Mora's analysis does not discuss one of the most significant visual patterns that enables these incongruous elements to stabilize into a coherent and socially functional symbolic system—that is, the whiteness of the actresses who played these roles. Being white was an essential part of what allowed performers like Ninón Sevilla, Andrea Palma, and Dolores del Río to didactically convey both saintliness and eroticism. They could play archetypal fallen women without compromising the redemptive cinematic narratives. Reygadas appropriates the instructive yet unreal cinematic image of the prostitute as a collection of contradictory filmic signifiers pointedly crystallized in Ana's whiteness, and unveils its centrality in reproducing the unreal representation of Marcos as a defective macho.

At the Boutique, Ana reiterates her authoritative discourse on Marcos's out-of-control appetite for sex. She insists that her disciplinary gaze captured him expressing inappropriate and misplaced sexual desire: "¿Qué crees que no me di cuenta con la cara que me veías en el aeropuerto, Marcos?" (Do you think I didn't notice how you were checking me out in the airport, Marcos?). Despite Ana's accusation, Reygadas cinematographically registers that her own imposing gaze is the active one in this relationship. In an earlier sequence when Marcos enters a crowded metro train, his glasses fall to the floor and are crushed under the feet of the passengers. At the airport, he appears without any glasses, and an out-of-focus, point-of-view shot showing Ana from Marcos's perspective suggests his inability to see her, or anything else, very clearly. Interestingly, as she walks ahead of him and looks back, setting up the reverse point-of-view shot, Marcos appears similarly blurred from her standpoint. Although her vision is unimpaired, Ana does not have an unobstructed view of Marcos, but rather recognizes him principally through a distortive representational regime in which he signifies deficient masculinity. In the Boutique, after Marcos confesses to Ana the fragmentary story of his involvement in the failed kidnapping scheme, she stares at him once more, and the cinematic language corresponds to her perception of his essential inferiority. The camera again shows point-of-view shots from her perspective accentuating Marcos's defects, his excessively corpulent build and his sweaty back covered by a tattered undershirt (fig. 2.3). The sequence concludes when Ana dispatches Marcos with a concise set of specific instructions for what to do with her baggage and when next to pick her up.

Ana's direct control over Marcos as his employer overlaps with her conceptual command of the meanings attached to his body. In a somewhat paradoxical manner, the exercise of her authority culminates in the scene of their sexual encounter. The disciplinary dimensions of their coupling do not manifest in acts of physical domination, but rather the sex serves to corroborate the perspective of Marcos as an immoral, malformed macho whose inability to regulate his own appetites excludes him from full recognition as a man. Ana literally speaks for Marcos, articulating once again the conviction that he *must* be driven by sexual urges. She states matter-of-factly, "Tú, lo que quieres es cogerme, ¿verdad, Marcos?" (What

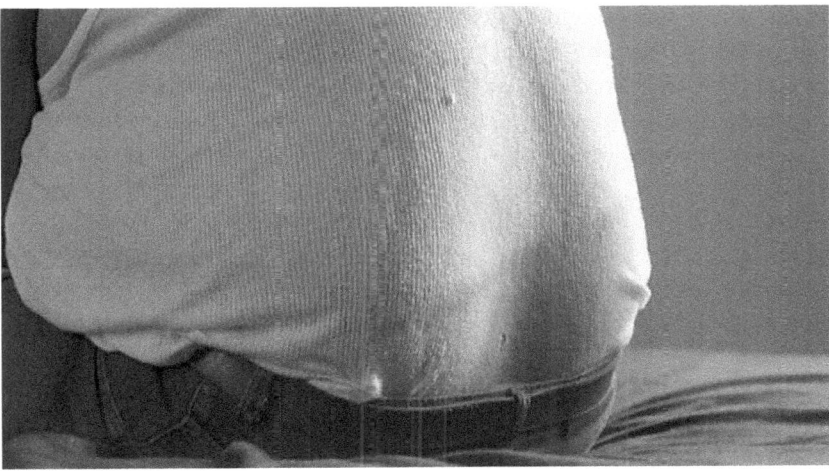

Figure 2.3. Another subjective shot from Ana's point of view emphasizes Marcos's corpulence and unkempt appearance with a close-up of his frayed, sweat-stained undershirt (*Batalla en el cielo*).

you want is to fuck me, right, Marcos?). Reygadas then conveys Marcos's emasculation through a cinematic role reversal, as Ana takes his position behind the wheel of the SUV and drives him to their tryst. By treating Marcos as an animal who must be tamed, reproachfully telling him to calm down during intercourse, Ana inscribes her own sexual performance with a didactic purpose, reprising a significant aspect of the role established for the white prostitute in Mexican national cinema. In this framing, the lengthy 360-degree traveling shot that notably interrupts the sequence forms part of Reygadas's strategy to provoke critical awareness in the spectator. The camera movement distances the viewer from the fictive space of the bedroom where, even if Anapola Mushkadiz and Marcos Hernández are engaged in real sex, the meaning of the act cannot arrive but through the mediation of a preestablished representational framework. Reygadas works to divulge the highly orchestrated and coded performances of the nonprofessional actors precisely by juxtaposing them with the world outside the filmic sequence. After this detour beyond the frame, the director marks the return to the bedroom by introducing extradiegetic music, defamiliarizing camera angles, and more frequent cuts, all elements denoting filmic construction. While the music evokes a funeral procession, Marcos's naked brown body appears rigid and corpse-like, prefiguring his imminent death and conveying the absence of masculine virility (fig. 2.4). Tellingly, Ana chooses this moment to insist that he must leave and submit himself to the authorities for his crimes.

Marcos's final encounter with Ana reaffirms the role of representational mediation in the reproduction of uneven relations of power. By referencing other mediums of cultural signification, namely European oil painting, the film adds more transhistorical layers to the modern Western imaginary that configures the subjugation experienced by Marcos. While he is waiting for Ana in her boyfriend's apartment, Marcos stares up at a framed print of *A Horse Frightened by Lightning* (1813–14) by Théodore Géricault, which depicts a stallion standing by a stormy seashore (fig. 2.5). The artist illustrates the horse's fearful corporeal reaction to the storm by highlighting its strained muscles and foaming mouth. The visual link between Marcos and the horse serves to reconfirm the hegemonic disciplinary mode of perceiving the male protagonist as an aggressive male with naturally strong and uncontrollable sexual virility. The horse's response to its unsettled environment needs to be tempered if it is going to provide useful service to a rider. It is also worth considering how the painting of the horse has been framed within the context of discourses on the modern values of liberalism. According to Stephen Eisenman,

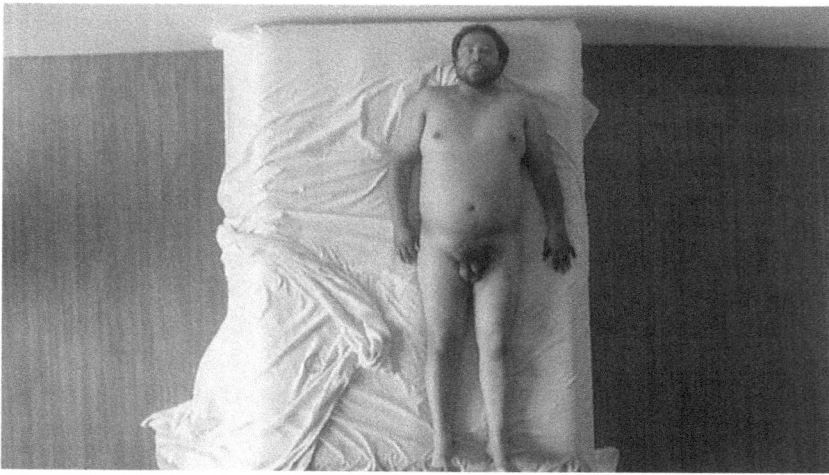

Figure 2.4. Marcos lies motionless in a cadaverous posture after his sexual encounter with Ana (*Batalla en el cielo*).

the horse's reaction to the storm in Géricault's painting represents "the 'turbulent state of liberty' chafing against slavery" (149).⁶ In other words, from the perspective associated with Géricault's romanticism, the horse may be read as an allegory of a natural desire for freedom supposedly inherent to those not yet tamed by civilization. At the same time, however, another aspect of the painting that has important relevance to my understanding of its place in the film has to do with the focus on a subject that was considered an important commodity, an item that could be bought and sold as private property. Indeed, animals such as horses appear frequently in European oil paintings throughout the centuries following the Renaissance, a tendency that John Berger associates with the general shift toward a capitalist worldview: "Oil painting did to appearances what capital did to social relations. It reduced everything to the equality of objects. Everything became exchangeable because everything became a commodity" (87).⁷ In this sense, the visual comparisons of Ana and Marcos situate them in a relationship of exploitation that has continued throughout the visual history of representing Mexico and its subjects, where white, upper-class subjects have used brown bodies to perpetuate their own privilege by positioning them as a racially deficient, malformed, bestial species of males who can be made to produce useful labor via disciplinary processes.⁸ Reygadas's cinematography suggests how Mexican

Figure 2.5. A print of Théodore Géricault's *A Horse Frightened by Lightning* (1813–14, oil on canvas) from Marcos's perspective (*Batalla en el cielo*).

filmmaking has comprised a representational regime that has evolved in accordance with the needs of the ruling class through various stages of capitalist domination, but which continues to rely on images of malformed Mexican men to sustain asymmetrical power relations.

The visual focus on the painting just before Marcos fatally stabs Ana with a knife helps to imbue the violence with contradictory meanings. Ana kisses him passionately before casually dismissing him, believing that he will accept lawful punishment for the kidnapping. To her, Marcos remains unrecognizable except as a morally deficient mestizo in need of control and order. When he begins his assault, it both reinforces and subverts her expectations. On the one hand, the murder is consistent with Ana's perceptual configuration of Marcos as a bestial being, unable to fully assume the masculine identity that would raise him to the status of modern man. The paradoxical reconfirmation of the fictive malformation coheres with other dimensions of the film designed to denaturalize the dominant codified imagery of Mexicanness by pushing it to excess. At the same time, a viewer may be tempted to assign a certain resistant agency to Marcos's attack on his employer. Breaking with his submissive pattern of behavior, Marcos perhaps releases repressed aspects of his own agency. While Reygadas's indeterminate narrative allows for such a reading, there are also compelling reasons to question it. For example, almost immediately after the murder, Marcos joins a large group of religious pilgrims making their way to the Basilica of Guadalupe, the most venerated shrine in Mexico. As though entranced, Marcos literally drops to his knees and allows his head to be covered by a penitent hood, as an evangelist screams into a bullhorn about the particular social and moral vices attributable to deficient men: "¡No mas drogas! ¡No mas alcohol! ¡No mas mujeres! ¡No mas tetas!" (No more drugs! No more alcohol! No more women! No more tits!). Despite the suggestive indication of Marcos's potentially defiant consciousness, there is no alternate social or cultural model of masculinity that would give new meaning to his experience, no other trajectory of self-realization. His body is too thoroughly codified by centuries of distortive misperception. Furthermore, his act of violence contains no hint of redemption, unlike the finale of *Nosotros los pobres*. At the conclusion of this classic film, Pepe el Toro engages in a brutal prison fight with members of the gang who committed the murder that led to his wrongful conviction. In the dramatic climax, Pepe stabs the gang leader, Ledo, in the eye and forces him to confess to the crime, allowing Pepe to be exculpated. *Batalla en el cielo* obviously disdains this type of emancipatory narrative, but the implicit contrast raises the question of what possibilities inhere within Reygadas's cinematic realism to recognize Marcos outside of the prescribed models of male subjectivity.

As critics often point out, the director's choice of Marcos Hernández, who has actually worked as a chauffeur in Mexico City, to perform in the lead role forms part of an aesthetic strategy that involves blurring the lines between fiction and reality. However, the social reality to which Hernández belongs has been constitutively distorted by powerful symbolic regimes and mythic narratives designed to render his body a potentially useful but inherently dangerous and disorderly object. De Luca suggests that the political weight of Reygadas's *Batalla en el cielo* lies in its staging of "impossible fictions," which take shape as an "incoherent, implausible and unlikely picture of Mexico, as epitomized by its central couple, a pairing which frontally defies representational logic" (*Realism* 89). While it may indeed strain the imagination to conceive of a plausible romance between characters such as Ana and Marcos, I suggest that the interactions between them confirm the continuity of a representational logic congruent with the longer tradition of Mexican national cinema comprised of almost *nothing but* implausible scenarios. The mestizo men depicted in Golden Age cinema as the venerable and dominant masculine social subjects of the modern Mexican nation, or as inherently malformed submasculine beings, represent at least as great an implausibility as any of the character portrayals in Reygadas's film. To be sure, the choice of Hernández to play Marcos as a "real" Mexican man helps Reygadas to illustrate the detrimental effects of nationalist myths of masculinity, but this does not mean that the film indexes his social being. I suggest instead that Reygadas is most concerned with cinema's participation in processes of producing realities, especially when that production aligns with the interests of power. This is a line of argument that I continue to take up in my analysis of *Post tenebras lux*.

IV. The Ordering Gaze of Mexican Patriarchy in *Post tenebras lux*

Mexican national cinema's representational matrix organized a complex of cultural myths that, as I argue in my analysis of *Batalla en el cielo*, continues to adversely affect how Mexican men are perceived, in films and in reality. By codifying male gender identity in terms of essentialized differences, manifested in the contradistinction between idealized, whitened images of dominant, masculine mestizos and denigrating depictions of mostly browner, malformed, morally deficient Mexican men, the films of the Golden Age fashioned an enduring perceptual framework around ordinary male subjects, which Reygadas reflects in his depiction of Marcos. Even though Mexican cinema abandoned portrayals of the unattainable ideals of mestizo masculinity enshrined in larger-than-life performances by Pedro Infante and others, Reygadas's film demonstrates that the same classificatory logic remains embedded in the currently prevailing postnational representational regime that regulates possibilities for perceiving Mexican men. Cinematic depictions of the mythic figure of the happy-go-lucky, hard-working, self-sacrificing, assertive, responsible family provider may have exhausted their usefulness as obfuscating didactic instruments, but the image of his equally mythic counterpart, the dangerous, undisciplined, irrational, racialized Mexican man, persists as a deeply entrenched symbolic construct that is continually renewed, reified, and reinscribed on male bodies, generating real-life consequences for diverse constituencies within and beyond Mexico.

In a more recent film by Reygadas, *Post tenebras lux*, we do not easily encounter allusive intertextual references to the history of Mexican national cinema or to other visual or discursive expressions of the cultural ideology of mexicanidad. However, we do not need to scratch very far beneath the surface of this richly perplexing film to find numerous significant confluences with the thematic concerns addressed in my discussion of *Batalla en el cielo*. As a starting point, *Post tenebras lux* dedicates a substantial amount of attention to the relationship between the white protagonist, Juan (Adolfo Jiménez Castro), an architect whose family evidently belongs to the upper crust of Mexican society, and his brown male employees, primarily Siete (Willebaldo Torres), but also Jarro (José Alberto Sánchez). Comparable to Ana's conduct toward Marcos, Juan's patronage of these men takes on considerable moral dimensions when he involves himself in their personal and family lives. Questions of modern Mexican masculinity arise in *Post tenebras lux* somewhat more indirectly than in the earlier project, but there is a notable common thread running through both films that ties into hegemonic narratives of the malformed mestizo's inability to overcome uncontrollable appetites and assume a socially normative gender identity.

While my reading of *Post tenebras lux* focuses on the attribution of an abject gender configuration to working-class mestizos, I also consider how masculinity organizes the self-perceptions and representational standpoints of Juan as a member of the dominant ruling class. And because of the close correspondence between Juan and Reygadas, I argue that the film's metacinematic construction constitutes a self-conscious critique of the implicitly masculine gaze that underlies the representational logic of modern Mexican cinema. Self-reflexive aesthetic strategies may be found throughout each of Reygadas's films, but these have a special resonance in *Post tenebras lux*, where the main character approximates a fictionalized likeness of the director himself. Although he did not follow through on his reported original intention of contributing his own performance in the role of the protagonist, Reygadas still lent many aspects of his personal life to the production of the film, including his own children (Rutilia and Eleazar Reygadas), his dogs, and his house in a rural area of Morelos (Lim). With an approach that continually calls attention to the director's presence, the film becomes a critical self-portrait addressed to both the modern subject and modern cinema.[9] The experimental, nonlinear, and hallucinatory aspects of the film pose challenges for a character-focused reading, but the protagonist provides a significant cinematic anchor, albeit complicated by his proximal relation to the director. While many of the film's sequences could be understood to represent Juan's experiences and perhaps his dreams and memories, even those that do not directly involve his subjective point of view often reveal his indirect presence or influence in some way. For example, in a sequence focusing on Siete's reunion with his estranged wife and children, it is explained that Juan was responsible for locating them. Reygadas's emphasis on the sometimes tacit centrality of Juan's agency and subjectivity to the organization of the film has significant implications related to this character's personal qualities, ethics, desires, and his particular enactments of power. By critically disassembling the positionality of an upper-class male protagonist, Reygadas not only implicates Mexico's ruling elite in the reproduction of lower-class masculine malformations that enable and justify social violence and exploitation, but also explores how the assumed rational and moral superiority of modern, Western patriarchal selfhood, with which the film's lead character identifies, constitutes itself in and through a subjective gaze that objectifies subordinate men in terms of racialized gender defects. As in Reygadas's earlier film, the director articulates the sociopolitical critique in *Post tenebras lux* via metacinematic strategies that reflect the role of film itself in sustaining unequal power relations in Mexico. For my purposes, the most salient commonality between these films lies with the director's disclosure of masculinity as a category of social difference that mystifies Mexican reality by naturalizing the malformed mestizo's inability to assume a normative gender identity.

Essentialized categories of desirable and undesirable Mexican masculinity originated in the nationalist ideology of mexicanidad, which, as affirmed by Bartra's interrogations of its formative intellectual metadiscourses, was designed to accomplish a specific set of sociocultural objectives, the foremost being to define the "typical Mexican" so as to legitimate his exploitation (6). The main architects and beneficiaries of such objectives were members of the country's oligarchy, along with state-sponsored cadres of artists, intellectuals, and filmmakers largely responsible for writing what Bartra identifies as "the rules that regulate and guide the legitimation of the modern Mexican state" (7) These figures claimed the epistemic authority to describe the so-called national spirit of Mexico by embracing the logic of a fundamental binary distinction separating the knower from the known: "At one end we find the dynamic, active subject, involving the idea of metamorphosis and change, the notion of the questioning Self. At the other pole is the passive and hidden Other, the melancholy and static object" (9). Bartra has little to say about the gendered dimensions of either side of this duality, so it is necessary to add some insights developed from my earlier discussion of de la Mora's work to the analysis to illustrate its relevance to my interpretation of *Post tenebras lux*.

When the definitive matrix of national masculinity was established, its designers, enacting their self-ascribed role as agents of knowledge, projected this ordering cultural logic onto the passive, static object they identified as a "typical" Mexican. The invention of a desirable mode of masculinity for lower-class Mexicans, encapsulated in Infante's performances of positive machismo, fulfilled the objective of concealing exploitation by offering an illusory, untenable model of redemptive national subjecthood. One ought to question the extent to which the Mexican, conceived as wretchedly melancholic and essentially submissive, was genuinely expected to emulate the hyperbolic imagery of positive masculinity in Golden Age films. I suggest that the negative portrayals of defective machos constituted the necessary counterweight that gave this cultural strategy its sociopolitical leverage. The naturalized modalities of social perception enabled by the invented figure of the pathologically inferior, unreformed male mestizo, especially when counterposed to that of the modern, stable wage-earner, provided powerful justifications for the imposition of politically repressive forms of control and violent disciplinary mechanisms, as I discussed above.

Absent from this representational framework was a clearly defined role for members of Mexico's upper classes. While unflattering portrayals of wealthy elites or pretentious bourgeois intellectuals were not uncommon in Golden Age cinema, direct criticism of Mexico's postrevolutionary class structure was obviously not part of the itinerary for these state-sponsored cultural productions. Ideological myths about the national character were primarily intended to conceal and legitimate the subordination of the lower classes, so the authors of this cultural agenda had every reason to leave themselves mostly out of the picture. As Bartra's commentary suggests, the self-understanding of those who comprised the intersecting circles of Mexico's intellectual, political, and socioeconomic elite crystallized in their shared identification with dynamism, rationality, and progress, the chief values claimed and monopolized by Western modernity, especially since the Enlightenment. While Bartra hesitates to approach this identity in terms of gender, other scholars, such as the philosopher Victor Seidler, have contributed to underscoring the subject of modernity's implicitly masculine definition. Tracing the historical formation of modern subjectivity, Seidler argues that the "core of this process is the emergent identification of masculinity with a particular conception of reason" (14).

Across numerous sequences in *Post tenebras lux*, Juan's routine relations with subordinate men reveal subtle forms of condescension, suggestive of his patriarchal superiority linked to Western modernity's self-ascribed rational, civilized, moral order. He embodies a masculine identity genealogically distinct from that constructed by the formative nationalist discourses of Mexicanness, but which underpins a representational regime that continues to reify the mythic malformed Mexican macho in the era of postnational, realist cinema. As Seidler argues, there exists a presumptive equivalence between rationality, ethical action, and modern masculine subjecthood, which "makes masculinity as power invisible" (4). To disclose the imperceptible workings of an oppressive logic within the normative constitution of Juan's modern masculine identity, Reygadas employs cinematic strategies designed to unsettle naturalistic modes of representation and question the realities they reproduce. Sequences focalizing Juan's perspective convey the self-deceptive proclivities of a subjectivity constrained by its own will to power to objectify and essentialize difference in terms of reductive rational and moral frameworks, especially difference ascribed to the gender defects of lower-class Mexican men.

As in much of his work, Reygadas's creative strategy in *Post tenebras lux* entails situating filmic perspectives at the seemingly paradoxical conjunction of spontaneous reality and formal cinematographic planning. Using such techniques, Reygadas makes critical self-reflexive gestures toward certain naturalized modalities of representation in modern Mexican cinema. A sequence that illustrates some aspects of this approach occurs in the depiction of the Alcoholics Anonymous meeting in the rural community near where Juan resides. The sequence is partially composed of medium shots at eye level from a fixed camera focused on a podium where several of the male AA group members deliver short speeches (figs. 2.6 and 2.7). These shots are intercut with close-ups of other group members seated in the audience, among whom we find Juan in the final shot. The group is made up of nonprofessional locals, and their speeches have the appearance of being unrehearsed, yet the shooting and editing denote a highly controlled and orderly cinematic arrangement of imagery, analogous to the formal structure governing the AA meeting itself. Despite the evocative colloquial character of the discourses, the speakers are constrained by a predefined set of rhetorical expectations. Reygadas's carefully arranged

Figure 2.6. El Siete (Willebaldo Torres) speaks from the podium at an Alcoholics Anonymous meeting (*Post tenebras lux*, 2012, dir. Carlos Reygadas).

Demystifying Machismo 99

Figure 2.7. Another AA group member, El Sapo, stands at the same podium (*Post tenebras lux*).

mise-en-scène features printed posters listing the Twelve Steps and framed portraits of the founders of Alcoholics Anonymous, Bill Wilson and Bob Smith, which serve as further reminders that any meanings contained within this cinematic situation are partially determined by a set of influential precepts regarding the role of morality in recovery from addiction. In this sense, the individuated shots of the group members closely align with the orthodox tenets of AA, which include openly admitting one's personal defects. As each speaker accounts for his own self-destructive behaviors without any reference whatsoever to a wider context of social injustice, the camera participates in framing their admissions of failure by subjecting each of them to the same depersonalized cinematic gaze, suggesting a uniform, rational standard of moral scrutiny. The unveiling of Juan's presence at the end of the sequence points to another layer of mediation in the images of these "real" Mexican men.

The differential significance of Juan's presence at the meeting gets marked by Siete, who introduces him, with a notable degree of equivocation, as "Un amigo . . . un invitado, pues . . . Es un amigo mío, bueno, era mi patrón. Lo considero mi amigo" (a friend, a guest I suppose . . . He is a friend of mine, well, he was my boss. I consider him a friend.). More than simply class distinction, Siete's remarks denote a relationship of patronage that coexists tenuously with claims of friendship. The friction surfaces in the incongruities of Siete's speech, where instead of narrativizing his struggles with addiction, he dwells on the details of the renovation work he completed at Juan's house. Another speaker, known as el Sapo, similarly reiterates his various skills as a tradesman. These conspicuous patterns in the dialogue suggest that the already constrained modalities of public perception and self-representation at the meeting undergo further pressures as a result of Juan's presence. Siete and el Sapo are compelled to submit themselves to an ordering gaze, a representational regime that objectifies them as morally defective, submasculine beings whose limited potential for social redemption depends on their provision of useful labor to the wealthy elite.

Situated at several removes from anything that could be considered a naturalistic portrait of Mexican men, the sequence instead illustrates how Reygadas's filmmaking confronts the production of dominant perspectives that become naturalized as reality. Juan's own gaze is the most prevalent lens through which the film examines these processes, and Reygadas introduces a variety of cinematic strategies to reflect the limitations and constraints created by this process of subjectification. This is most apparent in a sequence that takes place at Juan's house early in the film. It begins with Juan having a brief exchange with Jarro, who works as general caretaker on the property. Juan calls Jarro away from his work in order to ask about borrowing his camera, but their conversation gets put on hold while Juan interacts with his numerous dogs. Suddenly, Juan notices a puddle of urine on the wooden deck around the house and begins brutally punishing one of his dogs, Martita. He repeatedly batters and strangles the small dog while it squeals in pain. The beating continues until Juan's wife, Natalia (Nathalia Acevedo), yells at him several times to stop. When Juan's young son, Eleazar (Eleazar Reygadas), emerges from the house after the commotion, Juan tells the boy that he was only doing exercises with the dogs. Following this, he resumes his exchange with Jarro, complaining about the poor image quality of the camera and commenting on the pleasant sighting of several hummingbirds in the garden.

In this relatively brief sequence, Reygadas introduces a number of key elements of his critical self-reflexive cinema. The prolonged extent of

Juan's brutality toward his dog is underscored when Reygadas cuts away from the scene of violence to a shot of Jarro, who is visibly uncomfortable as he silently waits for the beating to end. While cutting or panning away from scenes of violence is somewhat of a convention in commercial and popular cinema, Reygadas's metafilmic perspective foregrounds the positioning of the camera and the subjective view. The shots of the animal abuse are carefully composed to suggest control over how the violence is perceived. From his standpoint, Jarro has a full perspective of the spectacle, but the camera does not show his point of view. Juan grapples with the dog, but the camera remains fixed at an angle that keeps most of the sight/site of actual violence just outside the frame of the shot, making it appear as though Juan himself is holding it out of view (fig. 2.8). Further signs of his intentional concealment of this violent behavior appear in the dialogue when Juan lies to his young son about what was happening. Later, more lies are revealed in a short dialogue with Natalia in which Juan describes how the veterinarian is growing suspicious and does not believe Juan's false account of his dog's injuries.

While, for some viewers, the animal abuse alone might be sufficient to discredit any moral authority claimed by Juan, I suggest that it does not amount to a straightforward condemnation, as such would be

Figure 2.8. The explicit act of violence Juan commits against his dog remains mostly unseen from the audience's perspective throughout this static shot (*Post tenebras lux*).

incongruous with the director's overall approach. Reygadas does not aim to present Juan as aberrantly cruel, but rather as a banal and normative embodiment of modern, Western masculine subjectivity. For my purposes, the cinematographic composition of this sequence and the complementary dialogues are more suggestive of the unseen constraints inherent to a purportedly realist aesthetic governed by a subjective gaze that refuses to account for its own violent, disciplinary effects. A relay of connective implications builds from the links between the careful framing that positions the dog's suffering just off-screen, Juan's attempts to exert control over how his conduct is perceived, his complaint that Jarro's camera produces blurred images, his confident judgment of aesthetic taste regarding the birds, and his ambivalence toward Jarro's point of view. Considering this sequence in conjunction with the AA meeting, in which Juan's gaze helps to configure the lower-class men in terms of gender defects that render their labor more readily available, my reading finds that the film critically reflects a construction of reality mediated by Juan's ego-driven modern masculinity. Manifested as a will to power that normatively constitutes itself in and through the perception of the naturalized inferiority of others, Juan's masculine subjectivity connotes an unacknowledged ordering principle in Mexico's current representational regime.

According to some critics, Reygadas's introduction of animals into his films forms part of his overarching aesthetic concern with realism. In these discussions, animal bodies are associated with the "real" in the sense that their contingent movement and behavior escapes the absolute control of the director and conveys a trace of indexicality, a direct reference to the world and time outside of the representational logic and narrative temporality of the film. As de Luca explains in the context of a discussion of *Japón*, the film's use of animals, when combined with the seemingly autonomous panorama shots, contributes to a sense of immersion in boundless reality and release from the determinism of an anthropocentric order: "Cinematic non-anthropocentrism is thus equated here with a quest to include the accidental, which is enabled by the movement of the camera and embodied by that of animals" ("Natural Views" 225). Representations of violence toward the nonhuman element, according to de Luca, become a useful reference point for posing questions related to power and control in Reygadas's filmmaking, especially considering that *Japón* depicts a subject who "asserts [his] human agency and power through real acts of killing perpetrated against animals" ("Natural Views" 227). On one hand, this violent form of human agency that reduces living beings to inanimate matter would seem to symbolize an antithesis to the quest for contingency that de Luca associates with the "real" and the nonhuman world. On the other hand, as de Luca explains, the killing of animals on camera can in fact ultimately reconfirm the pursuit of filmmaking that conveys an indexical reference to reality because of the radical contingency and uniqueness of the event of death itself ("Natural Views" 223).

For de Luca, it is important that *Japón* takes place in a remote, rural setting intended to highlight ethical differences in human/nonhuman relations. From this perspective, Reygadas's depictions of violence against animals contribute to his realist aesthetic by reflecting local attitudes toward nonhuman life, which tend to be much less sentimental than those that are pervasive in Western metropolitan societies: "The visibility of animal killing [in *Japón*] . . . is thus also a result of . . . adherence to the peoples and areas [it] strive[s] to depict through a realist approach which is not only open to physical nature and animal life but which is also eager, with all its ethical implications, to show and inflict death" ("Natural Views" 229). Although attentive to the ambivalent meanings of violence toward animals in cinema, de Luca's argument posits that *Japón* holds firm to the tenets of Reygadas's project to incorporate the "real" into his cinematic representations of Mexico. The reading offered by de Luca usefully raises the question of how violence against animals can reflect the power relations involved in filmmaking. The scenes of animal killing in *Japón*, however, are quite distinct in several ways from the sequence featuring Juan's punishment of his dog in *Post tenebras lux*, and therefore lead to a different set of conclusions than those drawn by de Luca in his analysis of the earlier film. Whereas de Luca links the inclusion of scenes of violence against animals to an immersive realism enhanced by unfiltered perspectives of cultural difference, the scenes that I have been discussing in *Post tenebras lux* focus on the actions of a modern masculine subject whose sensibilities and cultural identity register as thoroughly Western. Furthermore, the image of Juan's violence toward the dog is explicitly obscured, shifted off-screen and out of view. Considering the brutal form of discipline and Juan's role as a proxy of the director, this violence manifests as a critical self-reflection on the desire for control and power more so than as abdication of directorial authority.

As opposed to opening itself to unfiltered reality, the camera in *Post tenebras lux* conveys an image generated within the fixed parameters of a predetermined order. The lens *produces* reality as an object rather than unquestioningly *observing* the world and its contingencies. Again, this film has numerous features quite distinct from those that de Luca highlighted in his arguments about *Japón*. In particular, de Luca foregrounds the role of the seemingly autonomous camera and its wide-angle lens that contribute to the nonanthropocentric perspective ("Natural Views" 225). In the case of *Post tenebras lux*, Reygadas uses a squarish 4:3 screen ratio, and in many sequences a special lens filter that produces images with a pattern of diffraction around the edges. These technical features mark the film with a distinctive appearance, which I argue reflects a subjectivized camera and encourages a critical appraisal of modern cinema's capacity to represent Mexican realties. Juan's controlling attitude, his desire for order, his willingness to impose it through violence, and his power to strategically conceal it from view in order to uphold an established narrative—all of these metonymically refer to tendencies within modern filmmaking itself that lead to the perpetuation of an objectified image of Mexico.

Through Juan, Reygadas illustrates the shortcomings and self-deceptions of postnational Mexican cinema that rearticulate established frameworks of perception. Filmmaking that purports to incorporate Mexican realities without first deconstructing its own rationale of representation will run the risk of sustaining differences objectified and domesticated for the maintenance of the Western subject's centrality and power. During a sequence in which Juan is lying in what we take to be his deathbed, having been mortally wounded by Siete during a robbery, he engages in a lengthy monologue focusing on a newfound inner peace, articulated in terms that arguably resonate with an idealized notion of cinematic realism as a quest for boundless vision. Juan speaks of viewing the world as though with new eyes, unconstrained by time and preconceptions. He describes memories of sensations, experiences that allowed him to perceive reality with extreme clarity and sharpness. The things around him fully exhibited their own existence, which endowed him with a sense of the full potential of his own subjectivity: "Sólo tenía que existir" (I only had to exist).

Reading this discourse as an allusion to a cinematic ambition that would seek to incorporate otherness as part of an orderly totality with the modern subject at its center invites attention to the ways in which Reygadas forecloses Juan's idealized mode of unconstrained perception. Juan's monologue is prefaced by Natalia's performance of Neil Young's song "It's Only a Dream," to which Juan sings along. The particular dream or fantasy most clearly associated with Juan is the dangerous self-deception that he has managed to transcend his own masculine ego and will to power. When the sequence ends with Juan asking Natalia to bring him his dogs, the close-up shots of the animals in this context serve as a visual reminder of Juan's proclivity for violence and obscurity, his drive to discipline reality into an object that conforms to his preferred criteria. The possibility that Juan could see anything beyond the framework of his own domineering subjectivity seems to fade away like any other dream.

Since the 1990s, the Mexican state's retreat from direct involvement in the national film industry ostensibly created the conditions for filmmakers to generate a range of new representations of the country, casting off the symbolic restraints of mexicanidad that had ceased to be socially meaningful. Aesthetic experimentation in independent Mexican cinema of the new millennium has included a significant emphasis on realism, and Reygadas's filmmaking has been a pillar of this development. But Reygadas's critical engagement with realist techniques serves to illustrate that the new postnational auteur cinema of Mexico does not constitute an aesthetic arena freed from all constraints on representation. Perhaps paradoxically in a filmmaking style that often appears to foreground the lived experiences of nonactors, the contingency of profilmic events, and the materiality of local spaces, Reygadas repeatedly calls attention to unseen forces dominating and subduing Mexico, binding the nation to networks of power that sustain social and political hierarchies. From this angle, the premise of his realism is not to make Mexican realities more palpable and intelligible, but rather to expose relations of power and patterns of perception that violently render Mexico a "real" object defined by an unruliness that demands control and discipline. In contrast to critics and scholars who understand Reygadas's filmmaking in terms of its ethnographic portraits of "real" Mexican subjects, I posit that the lower-class Mexican men in his films are deliberately represented within the fixed parameters of a predetermined order of perception. For this reason, his characters become cinematic reference points tracing the contours of masculinity as a hidden system of power that cloaks its own violent subjugating tendencies beneath naturalized images of deficient Mexican men. *Batalla en el cielo* and *Post tenebras lux* chart the tacitly central role of masculinity in the representational regimes that still govern meanings attached to Mexican reality. In the next chapter, I discuss how Reygadas's sometime collaborator, Amat Escalante, explores a similar set of issues related to realist representations of social violence in his film *Heli*.

Chapter Three

Manufacturing Malformed Masculinities in *Heli*

I. Barbarous Geographies in Mexican Cinema

The rapidly accumulating stockpile of sociocultural imagery and discourse dealing with Mexico's so-called war on drugs, officially declared by President Felipe Calderón in 2006, abounds with categorical inscriptions of malformed masculinity. Articulations of violent male criminal subjects as "narcos" often assemble an array of gender defects that convey a sense of the uncanny by making these figures appear as fully recognizable expressions of conventional Mexican machismo and simultaneously as exceptional, alien, and singularly aberrant, especially due to their perceived association with the recent levels of carnage not seen in Mexico since the revolution. Existing cultural frameworks of gender classification identify these men in terms of long-standing essentialisms, yet they are also understood to represent an entirely novel phenomenon. They are familiar relics of the past while at the same time original products of the contemporary moment. Discourses intended to explain these figures introduce a circular paradox, making them at once the cause and the effect of Mexico's current ills. To begin redressing the ontological distortion generated by interpretations positing inherent ethno-cultural or reductive sociological links between Mexican men and narco violence, it is worth considering how these assumptions reflect existing patterns of cinematic self-referentiality that have reproduced modern myths of masculine malformation in Mexico.

That the prevailing contemporary image of the narco fixates on mostly lower-class, racialized, masculine bodies spatially correlated to desolate hinterlands and dangerous border zones evinces significant continuities and discontinuities with the archive of tropes deployed by national cinema to invent the macho as a cultural archetype of mexicanidad. As discussed in chapter 1, the *comedia ranchera* of the Golden Age offered nostalgic depictions of rural spaces occupied by happy, compliant campesinos and elite landowners who typically embodied normative national gender identities. However, in these and many other genres and categories of postrevolutionary cinema, rural geographies and their local populations frequently represented a darker side of Mexico's history through naturalized associations with premodernity, lawlessness, barbarism, and malformed masculinity. Negative gender-, class-, and race-based stereotypes characterizing inhabitants (especially males) of isolated towns and indigenous communities as primitive, childlike, and bestial recur across a wide range of Mexican films, from *María Candelaria* (1943, dir. Emilio Fernández) and *Rio escondido* (1948, dir. Fernández) to *Canoa* (1975, dir. Felipe Cazals) and *El lugar sin límites* (1978, dir. Arturo Ripstein). National cinema's repertoire of myths about the retrograde subjectivities of rural Mexicans served as counterparts to equally illusory narratives of social modernization and collective cultural identity based on mestizaje and machismo discussed in the previous chapter, but they eventually outlived the ideological agenda of state-sponsored filmmaking that placed emphasis on the urban, domesticated, whitened, working-class masculine ideal, embodied most famously by Pedro Infante.

Toward the end of the twentieth century, transformations in Mexico's political economy and corresponding shifts within the national film industry displaced celebratory masculinist fictions directed at the popular classes in favor of cinematic narratives designed to appeal to more affluent audiences, bringing an intensified focus to urban geographies, especially stylish neighborhoods in Mexico City. The new cinema has overwhelmingly promoted neoliberal models of gender identity, positioning Mexican machismo as an antiquated and reviled expression of masculinity to be transcended by privileged-class urbanites inhabiting spaces aligned with the values and ambitions of globalization. Regions outside the capital have played an ambivalent role in illustrating this transformative process in many films. According to Emily Hind, the metropolitan cultural imaginary of recent Mexican cinema often assigns emancipatory meanings to *provincia*, defining it as "a permissive space that facilitates social freedom" (26), including freer exploration of alternative sexual identities and feminist social perspectives (28–29). Certain films, however, question the liberatory potential of spaces outside the capital by using them to "illustrate not social freedom but national apathy before acts of corruption as well as gender and race based discrimination" (30). Hind's analysis focuses on a trio of films that offer more cynical views on the possibilities for individual and collective transformation in contemporary Mexico—*La ley de Herodes* (Herod's Law; dir. Luis Estrada, 1999), *Y tu mamá también*, and *El Tigre de Santa Julia* (The Tiger of Santa Julia; dir. Alejandro Gamboa, 2002)—but her conclusion finds that each of these works "suffers a debilitating contradiction with the casting of *provincia* as a soundstage for a national metaphor largely directed at the Mexico City-based audience" (43). In other words, local realities and social problems in rural Mexico are overlooked by films that articulate political critiques from the narrow *capitalino* perspectives of the ruling order.[1]

Hind's main contention is that representations of *provincia* in many recent Mexican films, including those expressing skepticism toward optimistic neoliberal visions of social change, are generally configured to align with the dominant cultural politics, values, tastes, and worldviews of affluent urban spectators. While concurring with Hind's position that commercial cinema's implicitly metropolitan gaze tends to supplant distinct local perspectives, I would add that this displacement often involves recourse to an array of mythic threats and dangers that rural regions hold in the privileged-class imagination, especially as hotbeds of violent, criminal masculinities.[2] It is worth noting that several of Hind's examples of films set in *provincia* that thematize gender liberation also feature prominent depictions of rural machos involved in drug trafficking.[3] Much like the undesirable embodiments of masculinity portrayed in the national cinema of earlier decades, these images provide the negative impetus for the positive change promoted by each film's narrative logic, now configured in accordance with contemporary gender politics endorsing the "rejection of *machismo*" by men and rebellion against "submissive roles" for women (Hind 28, 29). In more recent years, the dramatic surge in violence attributed to narcos and cartels has created new reasons for Mexican cinema to reproduce the mythos of malformed masculinities geographically situated in rural parts of the country.

In a brief discussion of four Mexican films that represent aspects of the drug trade in the context of Mexico's present-day epidemic of bloodshed,[4] Ignacio Sánchez Prado partly reaffirms Hind's argument when he suggests that these works "busca discernir la mecánica de la guerra para la percepción de las clases medias y altas, sectores que hasta la era calderonista se encontraban inmunes a los efectos materiales y simbólicos del narcotráfico" (seek to discern the mechanics of the war for the perception of the middle and upper classes, sectors that had been immune to the symbolic and material effects of the drug-trafficking until the Calderon era) ("El narco como arte y mercancía"). By framing and fictionalizing the *guerra contra el narco* in ways designed to resonate with affluent metropolitan audiences, these films repeat the generalized pattern, described by Hind, of placing social reality in rural regions under erasure.[5] Sánchez Prado argues that these representations of drug-related violence respond primarily to the "fantasías y miedos de las clases privilegiadas en México" (the fantasies and fears of the privileged classes in Mexico) ("El narco"). Although his commentary does not touch on the gendered dimensions of this class-specific cultural imaginary of the narco, I suggest it is very much entwined with existing codifications of defective masculinity. Another aspect of Sánchez Prado's remarks on this topic that should be mentioned is his claim that Mexican cinema's interest in thematizing drug violence stems from the fascination this phenomenon has generated in diverse transnational media venues. In particular, he suggests that the global art film festival circuit has opened opportunities for Mexican filmmakers to respond to the international demand for more serious and authentic engagements with narcotrafficking. The imperative to package cinematic fictions as explanatory accounts of violent Mexican realities for consumption by transnational audiences contributes to the same set of problems arising from the *capital-provincia* dynamics identified by Hind, namely that the films tend to reinforce the self-perceptions of metropolitan subjects rather than addressing the experiences of people who actually live in the rural regions and communities being represented. Sánchez Prado maintains that Mexican cinema's recent approaches to the drug war may be counted as successful only in terms of their status as "estética y mercancía" (aesthetics and merchandise), not as authentic portrayals of the social effects of the violence ("El narco").

One of the films informing Sánchez Prado's observations, Amat Escalante's *Heli*, will be the main focus of this chapter, which introduces malformed masculinity into a discussion of the filmmaker's formal and aesthetic strategies in order to rethink their relation to realism, local authenticity, and drug-related violence. For many critics, *Heli* offers a hyperrealistic representation of overlapping political, social, and economic processes that are violently reshaping the contours of everyday life in an impoverished rural zone in the state of Guanajuato. Laura Podalsky and Juan Llamas-Rodríguez both argue that the film's cinematography foregrounds the profilmic reality of bodies, objects, spaces, and actions in order to represent the adverse consequences of the drug war and other forms of structural violence for local populations whose communal, familial, and affective ties are coming undone. Unlike Sánchez Prado, who regards *Heli*'s translation of Mexico's drug wars into the language of global art cinema as an aesthetic commoditization disengaged from local perceptions of social issues in rural Mexico ("El narco"), Podalsky and Llamas-Rodríguez emphasize the film's attempts to create a sensorial connection between the viewer and the distressing experiences of violence and suffering represented on screen (Podalsky "The Aesthetics of Detachment" 251; Llamas-Rodríguez 30).[6] Although Hind's article predates *Heli* and other recent Mexican films offering fuller thematizations of narcotrafficking for national and transnational audiences, she engages with a similar set of questions, describing how the metropolitan representational paradigm treats "*provincia* as the basis of a national metaphor that does not ultimately center on rural life itself" (42). These critical discussions may be partly understood as a continuation of existing debates on formal and aesthetic approaches to violence in recent Latin American cinema, such as those which addressed whether a commercially successful film like *Cidade de Deus* (City of God) (2002, dirs. Fernando Meirelles and Kátia Lund) sacrificed political engagement and social realism for shock value, fetishized misery, and Hollywood-style thrills.[7] While taking these issues into account, I posit that *Heli* offers an alternative entry point into issues of social violence in Mexico by elucidating the enduring cultural function of myths of Mexican masculinity in the neoliberal state's systems of oppression and exploitation.

My analytic approach identifies aspects of *Heli*'s diegetic content and formal composition that expose self-referential patterns of cultural representation involved in reproducing images of monstrously violent males associated with Mexico's rural geographies. The strategies I describe in Escalante's film share commonalities with those I examined in Carlos Reygadas's *Batalla en el cielo*. Acknowledging the close collaboration between these two directors and the stylistic similarities in their work, I find some parallels in their critical practice of self-reflexive filmmaking but also considerable divergence in how they address specific articulations of malformed masculinity and illustrate their ideological effects in contemporary Mexican society. My reading of *Batalla* argued that the direct and indirect allusions to the national cinematic archive of idealized machismo and mexicanidad generate a meaningful contrast with the embodied performance of the film's main protagonist, Marcos, resulting in an illuminating portrait of the ongoing oppressive consequences of the postrevolutionary state's modernizing gender system for racialized, lower-class Mexicans. In accordance with the disciplinary function of this system, the masculine deficiencies attributed to male mestizos in Golden Age national cinema—melancholia, idleness, alcoholism, licentiousness, unmediated aggression, and so forth—were represented as surmountable via a process of internalization of modern gender norms, but always narratively and symbolically interwoven with the exclusionary logic of the country's racialized power structure. These popular screen fictions helped install persistent cultural myths of malformed masculinity that facilitated the state-mediated development of Mexico's modern capitalist economy in which high degrees of surplus labor could be legitimately exploited from the unmanned brown bodies of the urban-industrial workforce. I argued that Reygadas's realist techniques are not designed to document Marcos as a real mestizo in contemporary Mexico City, but rather to creatively insinuate how naturalized masculine malformations are implicated in the neoliberal reorganization of Mexico's cultural, political, and economic structures. Escalante's film, I suggest, is likewise not chiefly concerned with documenting violent social reality in the rural region of Guanajuato where it is set. Like Reygadas, he deploys an aesthetics of realism as part of a creative self-reflexive strategy to unsettle representational mechanisms that reproduce prevailing mythologies of Mexican males.

In *Heli*, there are no direct references to the macho ideal celebrated as intrinsic to mexicanidad in canonical national cinema. Instead, the film introduces an array of intertextual citations of more contemporary, transnational forms of audiovisual mass media, including television news broadcasts, video games, and YouTube, which have become instrumental to the reproduction and circulation of dominant sociocultural narratives about threatening men who turn to narcotrafficking after being disenfranchised by the state and excluded from legitimate participation in the neoliberal economy. In my reading, the film illustrates how such explanatory accounts are underpinned by long-standing assumptions about lower-class rural males in Mexico, placing the current proliferation of narco imagery in genealogical relation to a history of cinematic mythmaking in Mexico. Globalized mass media products readily reiterate preexisting cultural discourses about naturally violent Mexicans, and media consumption itself often figures into sociological theories as a source of the frustrations driving marginalized men to commit violent drug-related crimes.[8] By situating ostensibly realistic depictions of social violence within a cinematic scenario encompassed by an assembly of mediated images, *Heli* makes perceptible a paradoxical feedback loop that recycles distorted representations of malformed Mexican men as monstrous criminals.

My analysis will show that *mise en abyme* (put in the abyss) serves as an effective visual device illustrating the filmmaker's concern with these self-referential dynamics that generate cultural discourses on drug-related violence in rural Mexico. The mise en abyme, which is often associated with images of cascading mirrors, pictures within pictures, copies of copies, and so forth, has acquired a complex and contradictory set of conceptual meanings in contemporary aesthetic analysis.[9] For my purposes, more than a generalized postmodern sense of infinite regress or endless deferral of meaning, the term denotes conscious performances of cinematic self-reflexivity addressed to culturally specific representational codes and templates. In *Heli*, this includes compositional strategies that center the gaze-organizing presence of cameras, television screens, photographs, and frames of various kinds. My discussion shows how Escalante invokes mise en abyme to situate acts of representation and spectatorship in relation to preexisting visual and discursive structures of meaning, especially in scenarios where these function to make rural Mexican men intelligible as threats to the social order.

Heli makes the politics of representation a central focus by critically visualizing processes that mediate and manufacture perceptions of Mexican social reality, particularly in relation to the phenomenon of drug violence. In his book *Los cárteles no existen*, Oswaldo Zavala argues that official state discourses contribute to inventing and exaggerating the threat posed by organized crime in Mexico in order to advance a transnational security agenda that rationalizes and disguises violent exertions of governmental control.[10] These discursive articulations of menacing drug cartels are reproduced and recirculated in all manner of mass media and cultural productions, resulting in the proliferation of distorted myths that feed perceptions of a security crisis without any basis in reality: "No existe una materialidad histórica debajo de la representación textual que supone mostrar lo *real* del narco" (There does not exist any historical materiality beneath the textual representation that purports to show the *real* narco) (Zavala 67). Building on Zavala's insights, while also adding gender dimensions to the analytic framework, I will argue that Escalante's film offers a critical counterperspective to much of the existing visual-discursive archive related to narcotrafficking in Mexico.[11] In my reading, *Heli* shows how displacements of "real" male referents by fictionalized criminal caricatures in portrayals of rural Mexico constitute crucial discursive complements to the neoliberal state's aggressive assertion of power over peripheral territories and resources—especially laboring bodies—as part of general drive to incorporate them more fully as commodities in the transnational economy. The film registers how perceived threats to public safety in Mexico are reified by the production, dissemination, and consumption of fetishistic narco-related images, not only menacing criminals but also the tortured, mutilated flesh of lower-class rural men, thereby providing the state-corporate nexus with an ongoing justification for the militarization of law enforcement and increased public investment in the globalized private security industry. In this way, the film also raises questions about the assumptive associations between the drug war and Mexico as a "failed state."[12] Despite the outward appearance of irrelevance, ineptitude, and debilitating corruption, state institutions depicted in *Heli* exert significant authority over the bodies of local constituents, wielding gender codes as particularly effective discursive instruments. The state's ability to define, maintain, and reinforce categories of masculine malformation strengthens its allegiance with transnational capital by facilitating direct and indirect forms of control over the availability of labor, land, and raw materials, including via the selective abdication of governmental responsibilities. In these dimensions, I connect *Heli*'s visual-aesthetic strategies to a critique of the cultural politics of gender in the neoliberal state, wielded as a lever of economic control and social discipline.

II. Amat Escalante's Mediating Aesthetic

Critical and scholarly discussions of *Heli* often foreground its deliberative pacing, lapses in continuity, languid performances by nonactors, and other formal qualities linked to aesthetic currents of realism in global art house cinema. Reducing narrative content to a minimum and de-emphasizing linear cause-and-effect plot development are strategies that Escalante notably shares with Reygadas, whose "practically plotless" films have been characterized as "meditative" and "metaphysical" (Hale). Such descriptors are perhaps not readily transferrable to the unsettlingly topical themes and dark subject matter treated in *Heli*, but the two directors are commonly understood to have mutual interests in developing cinema capable of broaching the "the real" in Mexico. Tiago de Luca identifies

Reygadas's work with a widespread "materialist impetus" in world cinema, driving many filmmakers to give precedence to "the facticity of things and beings . . . over representational categories and functions" (*Realism* 12). He describes an array of strategies that global auteurs use to "assert the reality of the profilmic event at the expense of illusionism" (12). As de Luca explains, Reygadas and other directors who consistently deploy "the long take, realist techniques and oblique narratives" have come to be associated with an imprecisely defined film movement known as "slow cinema" (13). Discussions of Escalante's films frequently invoke this loose categorization and correspondingly highlight the presence of profilmic reality in his work. In analyses of *Heli*, this sometimes leads to a fixation on the film's indexical register, resulting in overstated claims regarding the perceptibility of narco violence as a distinct sociohistorical phenomenon in Mexico.

Some critics identify *Heli*'s scenes of torture and killing as realistic reflections of horrific practices associated with narcotrafficking that have become commonplace in certain parts of the country. César Albarrán-Torres, for example, describes the film as a matter-of-fact portrayal of the "disruptive effect of criminality in everyday life in rural Mexico" (20). Situating the film within an explanatory sociocultural discourse on Mexican drug cartels, Albarrán-Torres asserts that Escalante's "*cinéma vérité* style" and "quasi-clinical" depiction of death mirror real-life atrocities carried out by narco gangs, which are sometimes captured on camera and distributed online in snuff videos (20). The violent imagery in *Heli* provoked a negative reaction from the *New York Times*' reviewer Manohla Dargis, whose remarks about the director's pretentious use of art house aesthetics to depict graphic bloodshed "without discernible point or politics" then prompted Mexican critic Fernanda Solórzano to counter that the representation of the banality of death in Mexico constitutes the film's primary claim to authenticity. Solórzano is careful to note that, as a work of cinematic fiction, *Heli* remains autonomous from any real-life referent, but she nonetheless emphasizes the close correspondence between the emotional detachment conveyed in the film's scenes of violence and the ordinariness of everyday killings committed in Mexico by dangerous cretins and corrupt authorities: "Seres no solo apáticos y/o imbéciles, sino que, en casos como los militares coludidos de *Heli*, tienen la investidura para organizar al país" (Not only apathetic and/or imbecilic beings, but also, in cases such as the collusive soldiers in *Heli*, those empowered to organize the country) ("*Heli* de Amat Escalante" 91). In these discussions, the formal construction of Escalante's film is interpreted as a viscerally realistic rendering of the rampant carnage generated by Mexico's drug wars.

Along similar lines, Podalsky examines *Heli* as part of wider selection of recent films by Escalante, Reygadas, Fernando Eimbcke, and Lisandro Alonso, to elaborate her formulation of the "aesthetics of detachment" ("Aesthetics of Detachment" 239). In her view, *Heli* offers a "clinical gaze upon the pro-filmic events and promote[s] a form of detached viewing that parallels the affect-less-ness of the characters" (247). Whereas cinema conventionally seeks to create affective ties between the audience and the fictional subjects depicted onscreen by fostering emotional investment in the diegetic events, *Heli* and similar films opt for a different strategy that minimizes the circulation of feelings. With the objective of revealing "structural violence" in contemporary society, Escalante's films position spectators as "detached witnesses in ways that parallel the routinized existence of their protagonists" (247). In relation to Mexico's drug war, Podalsky claims that an aesthetic of detachment aims to reactivate sensory perception of the routinized horror precisely by foregrounding the breakdown of social and familial bonds. For example, by introducing a distant, detached mother figure as a surrogate for the viewer in a prominent torture scene, the film evinces "the extent to which violence has become another banal aspect of everyday life" (250).

In a related argument, Llamas-Rodríguez posits that *Heli* differentiates itself from mainstream depictions of narcotrafficking by adopting a perspective attuned to "slow violence," a category referring to insidious and generally invisible injuries that unfold across extensive geographies and protracted timescales (27). He explains that because drug-related violence in cinema is so often represented in terms of spectacle and excess, its far-reaching effects in the real world frequently remain hidden from view. By contrast, "*Heli*'s decentering of the narco-narrative from traffickers to regular people creates an opening to make salient the pervasive, continuous nature of violence beyond its already well-known spectacular instances within narcotrafficking" (29). By broadening, lengthening, and decelerating its visualizations of Mexico's drug war, the film attempts to "environmentalize violence," as exemplified in a sequence showing brutal military training that acknowledges how complex transnational networks of power generate widely dispersed "causal chains" that ultimately inflict pain and suffering on the bodies of local disenfranchised populations (31). Although Llamas-Rodríguez claims that his definition of the cinema of slow violence has more to do with an ethical stance adopted by filmmakers, critics, and audiences than with any specific formal techniques associated with the aesthetics of "slow cinema," he nonetheless places emphasis on film as the medium most capable of engaging the senses and "revealing the material world" (34). In this regard, he concurs with Podalsky's position that *Heli* calls upon audiences to bear witness to unperceived quotidian dimensions of the drug war. Although he shares Solórzano's recognition of Mexican spectators' "distinct sensibility for the violence depicted in the film," he argues that the slowness forces transnational audiences to reorient their perceptual and critical orientations relative to Mexico's violent reality (34).

This tendency to frame *Heli* as a realistic engagement with the phenomenon of drug violence does not necessarily imply that critics treat the film as a transparent window looking out on everyday life in a rural community overrun by narco gangs, teenage torturers, and corrupt cops. These discussions acknowledge contingent factors that shape and mediate the film's representations of social reality under the rapidly shifting cultural and economic conditions of neoliberal Mexico. They are generally informed by an understanding that, as Nilo Couret puts it, "[cinematic] realism allows us to sense history in its elusiveness rather than hold it captive for accurate depiction" (242–243). At the same time, however, aspects of these critical responses are underpinned by a shared set of assumptions about the social identities, behaviors, and motives of the subjects purportedly responsible for the kinds of violence on display in the film. In some cases, as in Albarrán-Torres's commentary, *Heli*'s hyperrealistic scenes of horror are noteworthy because they are corroborated by existing documentary and journalistic accounts of the brutality of Mexico's drug cartels (19). Solórzano's defense of the film as a mirror of Mexican reality similarly rests on claims about the legitimate social existence of monstrous figures like those depicted in the film: "personajes . . . [que] son primitivos, poco articulados y algunos [que] rondan la bestialidad" (characters who are primitive, inarticulate, and some who approach bestial brutality) (91). More circumspect analyses by Podalsky and Llamas-Rodríguez address how *Heli* enhances the perceptibility of the mundane and intangible consequences of drug-related violence, implying an acceptance of its naturalized presence in the quotidian milieu of rural Mexico. Even critical perspectives like these can unwittingly reproduce elements of state-sanctioned discourse since the very vocabulary used in this context transmits a predetermined narrative. As Zavala explains, "Escribimos *narcotraficante, sicario, plaza, guerra* y *cártel* y con esas palabras reaparece de inmediato el mismo universo de violencia, corrupción y poder que puebla por igual las páginas de una novela y las planas de un periódico, la letra de un corrido, la vestimenta de un narco actuando en una película de acción. El lenguaje para describir esa realidad está fatalmente colonizado por ese *habitus* de origen oficial que sólo en contadas ocasiones es posible fisurar" (We write *narcotraficante, sicario, plaza, guerra* and *cártel*, and with these words what immediately reappears is the same universe of violence, corruption, and power that is equally at home in the pages of a novel or the cover of a magazine, the lyrics of a *corrido*, or the costume of someone playing a narco in an action film. The language for describing that reality is fatally colonized by that *habitus* of official origins which only on rare occasions it is possible to fissure) (44).

In my reading, more than confirming or revealing violent dimensions of everyday reality, *Heli* raises doubts about film's capacity to provide truthful reflections of the problems affecting Mexican society by underscoring the role of cinema and other mass media in the reproduction of distorted sociocultural narratives about narcotrafficking, especially those that precategorize lower-class rural males as potential threats. This is not to say that the film is uninterested in the sources and consequences of real violence, only that it is more directly engaged with critically thematizing the systems of representation that make the violence intelligible in accordance with ideological justifications for the neoliberal state's ongoing transformation of the country's structures of order and control. In this sense, my approach does not wholly diverge from those of Podalsky and Llamas-Rodríguez, both of whom consider the film as a response to the dominant frameworks of cultural mediation that influence public perceptions of violent crime in Mexico. Whereas these scholars apprehend Escalante's realism as a revelatory practice that challenges habitual modes of perception by foregrounding profilmic events and objects using arresting images and detached perspectives, I view it chiefly in terms of self-reflexivity that turns the mediating apparatus of cinema back on itself in order to expose and unsettle mechanisms that perpetuate myths legitimating exploitation and oppression, particularly those constitutive of malformed masculinity.

III. The Absent Referent of Narco Violence

While my discussion moves away from prevalent understandings of the film as a reflection of quotidian reality, I recognize along with most reviewers and critics that *Heli*'s storyline, dialogue, and dramatic performances are less contributive to its overall impact than the director's cinematographic and compositional choices. Nevertheless, a summary of information contained within the plot facilitates the analysis offered in the rest of this chapter. *Heli*'s main narrative thread follows events connected to a lower-class family living in an unnamed town in the state of Guanajuato. The film's protagonist and title character, Heli Silva (Armando Espitia), is a young assembly worker in an automobile plant. He lives in a small house with his middle-aged father (Ramón Álvarez), his twelve-year-old sister Estela (Andrea Vergara), his wife Sabrina (Linda González), and their infant son. Heli and his father are employed in the same factory, though they are assigned to opposite shifts. Early scenes in the film portray normal day-to-day activities of the family, while also hinting at marital tensions arising from Sabrina's sense of separation from her relatives in Durango. Another source of friction in the household is Estela's relationship with her seventeen-year-old boyfriend Beto (Juan Eduardo Palacios), a cadet in training with a militarized police unit specializing in narcotics enforcement. Despite her family's strong disapproval, Estela pursues a romance with Beto, skipping school in order to spend time with him. They want to elope together but lack money, so Beto launches a plan to steal two packets of cocaine recovered from a recent drug bust, stashing them at Estela's house. The theft is rapidly uncovered by evidently corrupt members of the police force, who violently invade the family home, killing Heli's father. Heli and Beto are both taken to a house in a local neighborhood to be tortured by a group of adolescents, while Estela gets transported to a separate location. The torturers murder Beto by hanging him from a bridge, but Heli is released and allowed to return home alive though badly injured. The second half of the story deals with Heli and Sabrina struggling to cope with the repercussions of the violent events. Two aloof detectives (Reina Torres and Gabriel Reyes) conduct a perfunctory investigation of the crime without producing any results, and Heli begins his own fruitless search for Estela, putting up posters around the town. After being held captive for what appears to be several weeks, Estela eventually escapes her captors and returns home pregnant and traumatized into silence. Heli finds and kills a man who may or may not have been involved in the abduction and rape of his sister. The film concludes by vaguely suggesting the beginnings of a return to normalcy and spousal intimacy in the household.

Considered as a series of plot points, *Heli* appears to contain at least some conventional genre elements of a cinematic crime thriller, that is, risk-taking and suspenseful secrecy followed by violent disruption, confusion, apprehension, vengeance, and finally redemptive renewal. The visual-aesthetic realization of the underlying storyline, however, separates the film from analogous portrayals of criminality and drug violence in commercial and mainstream cinema. As explained in my overview of the existing criticism, the difference tends to be attributed to the filmmaker's attempts to register the banalized presence of violence within quotidian reality. By contrast, I suggest that aspects of the film's narrative structure, in combination with dimensions of self-reflexivity in the cinematography and mise-en-scène, contribute to Escalante's efforts to address representational templates that reinforce the neoliberal state's transformative agenda in Mexico, including those corresponding with categories of masculine malformation. From this perspective, *Heli*'s partial alignments with genre conventions may be understood as deliberate allusions to marked patterns in the construction, distribution, and consumption of images of Mexican drug violence in mass media.

Heli's opening scenes provide a useful example of how the filmmaker activates a critical perspective on the representational formulas that structure the existing cultural imaginary, which configure narcos as a dangerous manifestation of malformed masculinity in contemporary Mexico. The initial sequence offers an elliptical introduction to the narrative, providing no exposition or background information, but uses visual cues to situate the audience within a familiar array of signifiers associated with the violent criminal activities of Mexico's notorious drug cartels. At the same time, however, the imagery draws attention to its own artifice both at the diegetic level and in terms of cinematic construction. The first shot tilts slowly over the prostrate bodies of two badly injured male victims, gagged with silver duct tape and showing only the barest signs of life, who are being transported in the back of a pickup truck along a rural roadway. The truck stops underneath a pedestrian bridge and a group of men unload the bodies. Ascending the ramp to the main span of the structure, the men perform a highly recognizable practice that involves suspending one of the victims from the bridge with a rope around his neck. The shot stays centered on the now totally lifeless body dangling from the overpass while the men hurriedly descend the ramp to return to their vehicle, leaving the second victim in a heap. The camera remains positioned in the back of the truck as it drives away, keeping the gruesome display in view. These images hang unexplained over the first part of the film until the linear development of story information allows the audience to connect the sequence to the main narrative thread and identify the victims as Beto and Heli.

The selection of this fragment to commence the film in media res ostensibly functions to imbue the first half of the film with tension, portending the sudden violent disruption of the relatively ordinary lives of the characters. However, as the only instance of a deliberate rearrangement of narrative events in the film, the opening takes on additional layers of meaning as a specific and purposeful act of emplotment. By using this spectacle of death to create the film's first impressions, Escalante evokes its prevalent associations in the existing cultural imaginary and implicitly raises questions about how these types of images have become integral to narrativizations of drug-related violence in Mexico. In his comments to the *Guardian* newspaper, Escalante allows that *Heli* deals with violent aspects of Mexico's present-day reality, but he also stresses that "there are no narcos in the movie, there are only the authorities and vulnerable young people who are in trouble" (Tuckman). In light of the filmmaker's insistence on this point, it is worth considering how the opening sequence and other parts of *Heli* contribute to unsettling the fixed array of meanings attached to the display of mutilated bodies in contemporary Mexico. One might take Escalante's remark, in its most straightforward sense, to refer to the specifics of the diegetic scenario, in which members of the militarized police unit are represented as the primary perpetrators of brutal crimes, as opposed to stereotypical rural Mexican gangsters such as those who appear in Luis Estrada's semiparodic film *El infierno* or in the Netflix series *Narcos: Mexico* (2018–19). While I grant that the film's avoidance of such superficial depictions is significant on its own, *Heli*'s critique clearly moves beyond the issue of compromised or rogue elements of law enforcement agencies in Mexico, which, in any case, already constitute a fairly common trope in mainstream representations of narcos (including in *El infierno* and *Narcos*). In my view, one can begin to approach the fuller implications of the director's claim by examining how the film introduces the problem of the absent referent in images purporting to denote organized forms of violence.

One thing generally presumed about sophisticated criminal networks is that they are inclined to be secretive in their operations, which is partly why the brazenly public atrocities associated with Mexican narcotrafficking are regarded as so anomalous and alarming. Somewhat counterintuitively, the phenomenon of blatantly overexposed violence in Mexico tends to generate greater opacity and confusion regarding its causes and sources, facilitating the construction of manipulative, fear-inducing narratives, especially about extremely wealthy gangs of malformed men who are attempting to take over large swaths of the country using the most savage tactics. Albarrán-Torres gives a credulous explanatory account of the barbaric practices of exceptionally brutal cartels, and even fanatical cannibalistic "nacrocultos" (14), but like many other commentators, he also acknowledges that the theatrical violence performed in public or captured on video functions as "narco-propaganda," in which the mutilated body becomes a "discursive device" to embellish the intensity of the threat criminal groups may pose to their rivals or to the authorities (4). He describes how propagandistic videos employing "the cinematic conventions of body horror" may be produced for the purpose of intimidating specific adversaries, but they also reach much wider audiences due to internet-based distribution platforms (4). Frequently, these same gruesome images get reappropriated and recirculated by unscrupulous film, television, and news producers who use them as a reductive "narrative tool" (14). For Albarrán-Torres, the issue of media representation raises ethical questions as to whether audiences are enabled to bear witness to a "real humanitarian crisis . . . [with] a complacent or an empathetic gaze" (21). As I already suggested, he joins several other critics in applauding *Heli* for rejecting the sensationalism of the mainstream media in favor of a "quasi-clinical" approach to the kinds of violent deaths associated with Mexico's drug war (20). My reading diverges to show that what *Heli* foregrounds are precisely the many intersecting levels of mediation and self-reference that cause prevalent representations of malformed men engaged in violent narco activities to lose all meaningful relation to an external, real-world referent. To be clear, this is not to equate the phenomenon of drug-related violence in Mexico with an unreal illusion, but to posit that the limits of its intelligibility are predetermined by existing cultural narratives, discursive categories, and representational paradigms, including those related to masculine gender malformation. The fear and mystification generated from these codes and frameworks generally tends to be in the interests of the sociopolitical and economic agendas of the neoliberal state.

Returning to the opening sequence, what the audience witnesses is not simply a representation of a violent crime directly comparable to a real-world event or experience, but rather the deliberate deployment of codified signifying practices aligned with a familiar set of culturally mediated imagery. The effects of this artifice are significant both in terms of the film's formal strategies and within the diegesis. At the outset of the film, there is no story information to identify the group of men engaged in assembling the macabre display on the bridge as affiliates of a so-called cartel, but the activation of this assumption would seem to form part of their intention. Indeed, the only certainty about these figures is that they are *performing* as narcos/*sicarios* (contract killers) to create a scene intended to be recognizable in terms of established narrativizations of malformed masculinity and drug-related violence. Within the film's fiction, the distinction between "real narcos" and local teenagers coerced into doing some dirty work for a corrupt police commander may not matter much to the victims, but the uncertainty implicates the spectator in the interpretation of the violent opening spectacle. Witnessing the elaborate public exhibition of Beto's dead body does not enable the audience to better understand organized criminal brutality in the real world, as Albarrán-Torres and others would seem to imply. To the contrary, the fictional representation emphasizes the ambiguous performativity of the violence precisely to highlight the elusiveness of its referents and to cast facile truth claims into doubt. The plot development reveals how members of the special police force are involved in acts of abduction, torture, and killing, as well as illicit commerce in the confiscated supply of narcotics, yet a substantial degree of indeterminacy pervades the entire film, deferring the assignation of any categorical motive, meaning, or causality to the events. The focalization allows the happenings to be understood only in partial, fragmentary, disjointed ways, disrupting the production of a coherent narrative.

More than simply withholding plot information, Escalante illustrates a confluence of mediations that contribute to reproducing formulaic and fundamentally distortive explanations of the violence. Some of these factors originate with the crimes themselves, as the perpetrators propagandistically exploit the predetermined meanings attached to spectacles of death and the mutilated bodies of male victims presumed to be traffickers. Further distortions are introduced by state power structures, manifested in several ways but perhaps most directly in the abuses of authority by members of the special police unit as well as in the abdication of responsibility for investigative and judicial processes by the detectives assigned to Heli's case. When the investigators ask him to sign a declaration stating that his father was involved in criminal activity, Heli quickly comprehends that they will invent any pretext to absolve the state of the obligation to pursue justice. Another significant contributor to the distortion comes, of course, from systems of mass media that disseminate myths and half-truths about drug cartels.[13] For example, the police commander (Felix Alberto Pegueros Herrera) who orchestrates much of the violence in the film appears to suffer a brutal death himself, as Heli recognizes his severed head in a television news program covering what purports to be a drug-related massacre. The screen displays the gory results of the beheadings and a government official reading out an accompanying message full of clichéd threats, while the reporter describing the situation repeats the commonplace euphemism *ajuste de cuentas* (settling of accounts). This phrase is emblematic of the occlusive effects of the prevalent explanatory discourses on narcotrafficking. Even if there were some kernel of truth in the news bulletin of the commander's death, the formula "ajuste de cuentas" conveys the idea that justice has already been done and that there is little to be said or known about the causes of the crime, especially as the victims appear to fit the profile of masculine malformation. The film suggests that these mediating mechanisms work in concert to perpetuate illusory understandings of the phenomenon of drug violence, projecting referent-less images of narcos into a hall of mirrors leading to a dead end.

I suggest that many of the cinematographic strategies Escalante uses in *Heli* are designed to stimulate critical awareness of the self-referential dynamics in representations of violent realities in Mexico. Some of these techniques may be characterized as figures of mise en abyme, particularly when they reflexively invoke signifying practices and forms of spectatorship to call attention to the representational frameworks in which they are situated. The newscast described above provides one example of how the director introduces existing templates of visual-discursive mediation into the film for the purpose of destabilizing the naturalized link between image and referent. Although television screens figure prominently into the composition of many other shots and sequences throughout the film, the news program dealing with the death of the police captain is the only instance when the televisual imagery represents an approach to social violence. In this framing, the spectacle of the decapitated heads of male victims and the familiar language of organized crime may be more readily detached from their purported meanings, not because the film gives us privileged knowledge of the matter, but rather because we are positioned to perceive the barriers to knowability.

There is an indirect mirroring between the images in the news report and those comprising the opening sequence of the film. In both cases, we witness scenes of horror carefully constructed to correspond with the existing sets of signifiers associated with narco violence. On the surface, there appears to be a contrasting juxtaposition, as the opening sequence is filmed in realistic style with few cuts, minimal camera movements, natural lighting, and without narration, music, or sound effects. The newscast, on the other hand, offers a filtered and highly composed representation of violence packaged to conform to prevailing official accounts of the drug war (fig. 3.1). In my view, contrary to what other critics have suggested, the implicit comparison does not amount to a straightforward privileging of cinematic realism as the more faithful mode of bearing witness to violence in Mexico. In its cinematographic form, the opening sequence calls attention to itself as a deliberate selection, framing, and deployment of profilmic "reality," as the director makes a visual gesture correlating the frame of the shot with the rectangular structure of the bridge. The composition creates a mise en abyme via the reflective transposition of the space of the movie screen with the space under the bridge, where the figure of Beto's mutilated body can be seen swaying on a rope (fig. 3.2). A related doubling effect is achieved through the repetition of the same images that comprise the opening sequence from different vantage points about halfway through the film. The second time we are shown Heli and Beto lying semiconscious in the back of the pickup truck, it is literally the mirror image of the first shot (figs. 3.3 and 3.4), and the camera's second

Figure 3.1. The image of decapitated heads is included as a banalized visual element of generic television news coverage of drug violence (*Heli*, 2013, dir. Amat Escalante).

Figure 3.2. The brutalized body of Beto (Juan Eduardo Palacios) hangs from a pedestrian bridge whose rectangular structure subtly mirrors the shape of a cinema screen (*Heli*).

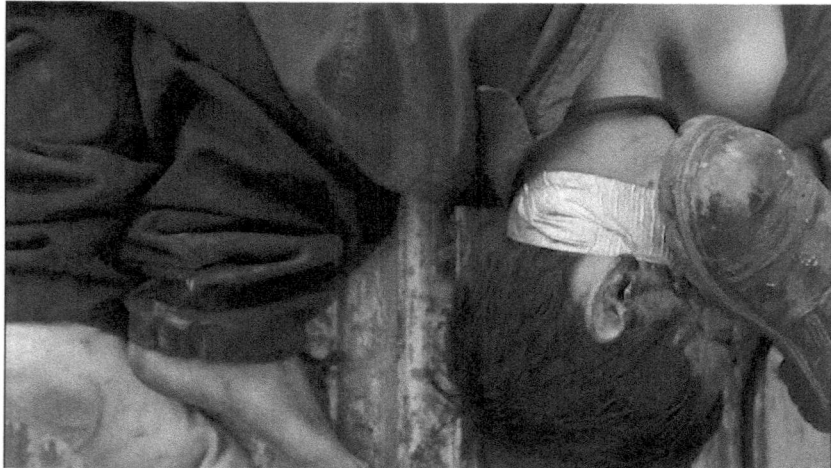

Figure 3.3. The protagonist (Armando Espitia) appears bound and gagged with his captor's boot pressed on his head in the opening shot (*Heli*).

perspective on Beto's hanging is repositioned behind his body, a reversal of the initial standpoint. The reconstructions and redeployments of these images, and their reinsertion into the narrative in chronological order, signal their status as products of the grammar of cinema necessarily shaped by postproduction processes of selection, editing, and arrangement. To mark

MANUFACTURING MALFORMED MASCULINITIES IN *HELI*   127

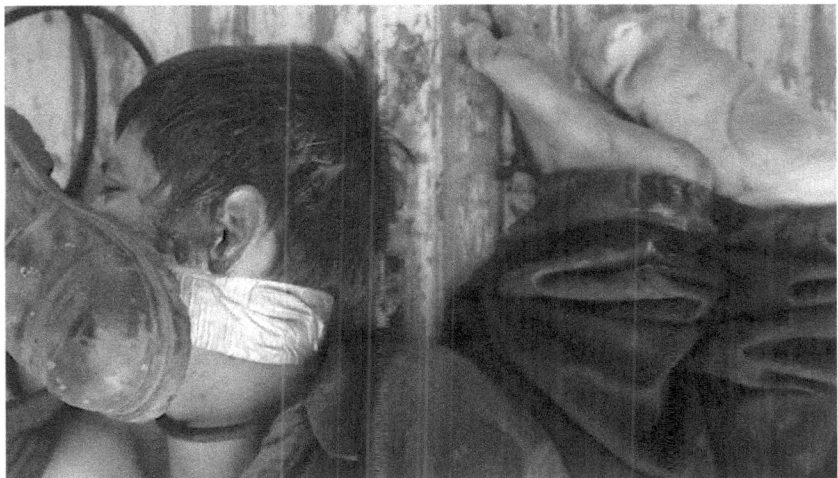

Figure 3.4. An inverted mirror image of the opening shot reappears approximately midway through the film (*Heli*).

these signs of filmic construction is not to posit a simplistic equivalence between news programs and arthouse films in terms of their approach to representing violent realities. It is only to assert that, although each medium relies on a distinct formal language, both equally confront the fugacity of the referent and its irrevocable replacement by interpolated images.

In an interview with film critic Fernanda Solórzano, the director offers illuminating though somewhat equivocal remarks about the graphic, hyperrealistic violence in the film, including the hanging of Beto in the opening sequence. Escalante comments on his choice of subject matter in *Heli*, suggesting that it was indeed motivated by the sensation of the proximity of violence one feels in Mexico: "Habla de cosas que ves en la calle o que le están pasando a gente cada vez más cercana a ti" (It speaks of things you see in the street or that are happening to people who are closer and closer to you) (Solórzano "Retratos" 32). However, when asked whether this means that non-Mexican audiences might reasonably find the film's treatment of violence too excessive to be realistic, particularly the hanging scene, Escalante demurs. He affirms that images of bodies strung from bridges have become a familiar part of Mexican social reality, but adds that the spectacle of violent death remains a phenomenon perceived mostly through the media: "siempre la vemos en foto" (we always see it in photographs) (32). In other words, as pervasive as the problem of violence may be in contemporary Mexico, most people do not have firsthand experience of gruesome killings, let alone as an ordinary part of their daily life. Rather, knowledge of these horrific dimensions of social reality generally circulates in fragmentary form severed from an immediate context. These disjointed visual-discursive fragments are all too readily assembled into influential social narratives serving the interests of power.[14] While Escalante does confirm his interest in creating unadorned representations of violence, he also makes some ambiguous comments about the possibilities for achieving this within the limits of film as a medium: "Siempre me ha interesado mostrar el lado de las cosas que no solemos ver, sin editarlo. De ser posible, que los únicos cortes sean los parpadeos" (I have always been interested in showing the side of things we do not tend to see, without editing it. And with blinks being the only cuts, if at all possible) (32). By seeming to endorse a version of direct cinema to reveal aspects of violent phenomena not normally seeable while at the same time implicitly admitting the infeasibility of such an approach, Escalante defines his own filmmaking practice in what I suggest are knowingly ambivalent terms. As I have shown, editing, selection, arrangement, and other aspects of postproduction are indispensable elements of his work. Adding to this contradiction, he openly emphasizes the importance of digital special effects in producing the desired imagery of brutal acts of cruelty in *Heli*, even likening his techniques to those used by Steven Spielberg to bring monstrous dinosaurs to life in *Jurassic Park* (1994) (32). Far from immersing us in unvarnished social reality, *Heli* situates the audience within a virtual space composed of mirage-like imagery that recedes and dissipates the moment we attempt to concretely connect it to the facticity of the material world.

Marking the indeterminate status of "the real" in *Heli*'s cinematic realism does not reduce its portrait of contemporary Mexico to pure spectral surfaces. What Escalante's approach enables, I argue, is a clearer perception of the variable interplay of real bodies and the dominant cultural images projected onto them, unsettling the naturalized meanings they acquire in the prevailing social discourse. This is particularly evident in how the film configures representations of young men in rural Mexico who brutalize one another in the most dehumanizing ways possible. In the film's most harrowing sequence, Heli and Beto are subjected to physical torture by a group of six young males, although two of them do not participate actively. Ranging in age roughly between twelve and twenty, the boys are gathered in a room with few furnishings apart from a large television connected to a videogame console. The sequence is composed of static medium shots focused on the bodies being inflicted with punishment alternating with somewhat closer shots and slow pans showing the boys vacantly watching the violence take place in front of them. Bearing in mind Escalante's refusal to classify these figures as narcos or any other kind of villainous stock character, I suggest the film purposefully raises, without pretending to resolve, the question of what makes these subjects capable of committing such atrocities. Because their identities and motives are never conclusively established at the diegetic level, the torturers become a kind of blank slate to be inscribed with assumptive meanings originating from outside the film's representational field. The parameters within which they are perceived therefore tell us more about existing social narratives that ascribe violent proclivities to young lower-class men in rural Mexico. For example, their extreme cruelty may be explained in terms of pathological malformations, as in Solórzano's account, which describes the torturers as deranged, bestial beings likely affected by mental illness ("*Heli* de Amat Escalante" 91). Other critical readings offer more elaborate sociocultural explanations attributing their nihilistic apathy to the unraveling of the broader communal fabric. Attending to the detail of the mother figure who observes the torture from the background but does nothing to intervene, Podalsky contends that the spectatorial detachment of the characters signals the "weakening of sensorial bonds between subjects that, once upon a time, lent density and depth to the human experience" ("Aesthetics" 251). In my understanding, the incongruous array of mostly empty signifiers in which the nonactors are situated is designed to preclude sociological rationalizations of how and why lower-class youths in Mexico get recruited or coerced into participating in appalling acts of real-life violence. Instead, I argue, the composition of this sequence functions to critically address how threatening images of rural males circulating in the cultural economy overdetermine the possible interpretations of real social subjects.

From this perspective, the most meaningful elements of the sequence are the violent videogame displayed on the television screen and the smartphone used by one of the young men to make a recording of the torture to be uploaded to the internet, not because they help to explain the actions of the characters within the story, but because they self-reflexively allude to the mechanisms involved in the transposition of adolescent males into the image of a social threat. In one sense, the videogame console may be understood as a reference to the familiar sociocultural logic that considers violent images in popular forms of entertainment to be causal factors in extraordinary acts of cruelty committed by disaffected youths in the real world. Although such arguments have been thoroughly and repeatedly debunked, they continually resurface even in serious intellectual discourse dealing with social violence in Mexico.[15] The framing constructed by *Heli* challenges such gross oversimplifications by drawing awareness to the contrivances involved in establishing any definitive account of what drives these young men to torture their peers almost to the point of death. A related aspect of the videogame's presence in the sequence is the way it alludes to control over the correlation between physical and virtual reality, particularly as it pertains to the bodies of young men in rural Mexico. An important detail about this console is that it allows players to control the digitized onscreen avatars via corporeal movements in three-dimensional space. In other words, ordinary hand gestures are translated into the virtual acts of violence represented in the game. Escalante creates a subtle analogy to suggest how real bodies are transposed into virtual systems of meaning via powerful social narratives, cultural codes, and categories of malformation. While they can stop playing the videogame whenever they wish, there is no equivalent way to easily extricate themselves from the codes of defective masculinity implicitly affixed to their bodies in social reality.

The analogy extends into a self-reflexive allusion to filmmaking practice, particularly because of the mise en abyme between the virtual images of the videogame screen and the computer-generated graphics used to simulate the fire applied to Beto's genitals. Both within and beyond the diegesis, his body becomes the canvas for the projection of a violent narrative reflecting the centrality of mutilated flesh in the image-based repertoire of narco violence. The physical signs of torture serve to codify Beto's corpse, making it socially legible only in terms of the threat posed by other young rural males, thus reifying the reductive "ajuste de cuentes" formula. The video recording made by one of the boys in the room becomes a further extension of this self-reflexive device (fig. 3.5). While referencing the real-life practice of using video to amplify the intimidatory effects of brutal violence, it also reemphasizes the independence of reproducible images from the real existence of the specific bodies and events they purport to represent. The dialogue makes clear that the boys making the video have no knowledge of who is being tortured or why, which suggests that the recorded images they upload to YouTube will become yet another set of free-floating signifiers whose meanings will

Figure 3.5. One of the anonymous boys observing the torture records the scene on his cellphone camera with the intention of posting it online (*Heli*).

be derived from the preexisting archive of narco narratives populated by malformed men.

Another instance in which *Heli* uses a metafilmic approach to critically address prevalent visual-discursive narrativizations of Mexican drug violence is the sequence showing a government-organized press conference. Standing at a podium in front of a huge bonfire of contraband, a high-ranking military officer reads out a statement expressing the federal government's commitment to public security. With its careful scripting and theatrical choreography of soldiers standing in formation while others busily destroy hundreds of packets of narcotics, the event has the familiar flavor of many similar real-life public spectacles staged for television cameras in contemporary Mexico. The presence of an assembled audience as well as a film crew and television news van clearly mark the purposeful construction of the imagery within the fiction, but the sequence also makes self-reflexive gestures toward the cinematic frame. In a static shot showing the empty podium after the main event has ended and the flames have died down to a smoldering pile of ashes, a child approaches the microphone and looks directly into the camera lens without speaking. This kind of composition once again implicates the viewer in the assignation of meaning to imagery transparently composed of props and performances, smoke and mirrors. A state security spectacle appears at once more discursively authoritative and more contrived than raw videos of torture and public displays of mutilated corpses, yet *Heli* allows us to view each of them as co-constitutive components within a self-referential system of signifying practices that fundamentally distorts the reality of Mexico's so-called drug war.

The interdependency of images designed to project state power and those intended to spread fear and confusion is not difficult to apprehend, as this dynamic organizes articulations of conflict involving governments and national public interests in many other contexts, but *Heli* shows how the representational templates and narrativizations surrounding the drug war have particular consequences for lower-class subjects inhabiting rural spaces in Mexico. Because the male body is such a central visual element in the prevailing cultural imaginary of narcotrafficking and the state's efforts to combat it, there is an intensified exertion of control over signs of masculinity, which leaves ordinary men with even less agency over their own corporeal being. A key demonstration of this in the film may be found in the sequence showing the humiliating punishments to which Beto is subjected as part of his training regimen with the militarized police force. Physically exhausted from a lengthy exercise drill, Beto is seen kneeling on the ground near a puddle of fresh vomit, while two trainers stand over him, one of whom gives commands spoken in English with an American accent. After making Beto roll into the puke and lie face down on top of it, the American trainer grabs him by the legs and drags his limp body along the ground, ensuring that he is thoroughly coated in filth. Following this, two cadets blindfold Beto and hold him above an open latrine while a commanding officer sprays carbonated water into his nose as he gasps for breath. What is most notable about these shots is that they are carefully composed reenactments of actual videos documenting harsh training techniques used by the Special Tactics Group of the Guanajuato state police force. The original videos became the subject of national and international attention in 2008 after they were leaked to a local newspaper in Leon, Guanajuato, and posted online. In response to accusations from human rights critics that the methods amounted to torture, the mayor of Leon defended the police by saying that such aggressive training was necessary to confront the threat posed by drug cartels (Roig-Franzia). Escalante's reconstruction of these videos in this sequence of *Heli* incorporates many details from the originals, including the presence of an English-speaking instructor who, according to reports, was contracted from a U.S.-based private security firm.

While the director may have had ambiguous reasons for choosing to appropriate these specific images to be re-created in *Heli*, I posit that the strategy coheres with other aspects of the film exemplifying the transfiguration of the bodies of lower-class rural men into detachable signifiers used to manufacture the "reality" of the drug war. Separating the leaked video imagery from its original context and weaving it seamlessly into the fiction produces effects similar to the self-reflexive devices and figures of mise en abyme already discussed. Even if the spectator is not familiar with the original materials, the scenario still illustrates how Beto's body is being stripped of individual subjectivity and conscripted into the designs of the state-corporate nexus. Having been degraded to the point of dehumanization, Beto becomes proof of his own defective masculinity, creating a legitimate need for military discipline and control to be imposed on him. Being aware of this sequence's relation to the real-life recordings facilitates an understanding of how video evidence implicating the state in abuses of power failed to produce any effective criticism or policy change since the meaning of the referent is overdetermined by existing narratives about threatening rural men. Images of tortured male bodies provide both the impetus for more expansive and forceful state interventions and confirmation that the problem of organized crime is being taken seriously. Real experiences of suffering in the rural regions of Mexico most afflicted by violence are thoroughly displaced by preconfigured arrangements of signs and meanings articulated in the prevailing cultural politics of the neoliberal order.

IV. Futile Forms of Masculine Empowerment

Heli not only addresses how the visual-discursive mechanisms that attribute violent tendencies to lower-class rural men serve to legitimate the state's war on drugs, but also how they interlock with related definitions of malformed masculinity to facilitate the aggressive expansion of the neoliberal state's agendas in Mexico. In the film, we can observe numerous discrepancies, contradictions, and fissures between the principal characters' embodiments of masculinity and the dominant gendered constructions of affective and economic subjecthood. Escalante alludes to prevailing sociocultural frameworks of modern romance and domesticity that configure lower-class rural men as aberrant defectives who fail to live up to the standards of modernity and are justifiably excluded from the protections of the neoliberal state, as well as from its model of economic prosperity and progress. Not only are their bodies readily identifiable as potential threats to the social order, but they are also inscribed into preexisting gender narratives of romance and the patriarchal family designed to mark them as malformed, defective embodiments of manliness.

Beto's peculiar performance of courtship illustrates how cultural discourses of intimacy and affect participate in reinforcing his symbolic exclusion from manhood. The fact that he actively expresses desire for a pubescent girl is an obvious factor that determines his defectiveness, at least from the audience's perspective, but this is not necessarily definitive since children of Estela's age are routinely sexualized in metropolitan and privileged-class contexts without diminishing the masculinity of the men who may objectify them. More significant, in my view, is the way the film emphasizes Beto's failure to cohere with the contemporary language of love, as articulated in romantic comedies and similar cultural productions that tend to be exclusively concerned with the emotional lives of privileged-class subjects inhabiting affluent urban spaces.[16] Instead of expressing his romantic feelings in terms compatible with neoliberal consumption patterns, which are far out of his reach, he engages in antiquated demonstrations of sentimentality, for example, in his choices of music, gifts, and excursions, along with his somewhat amusing show of masculine physical prowess that involves lifting Estela as though she were a set of barbell weights. His recourse to this set of obsolete signifiers accentuates his illegibility as an affective subject, marking his gender performance as incompatible with contemporary codes of desire. The formulaic way in which he lays out his ill-planned scheme to use profits from selling stolen drugs to finance his elopement with Estela emphasizes his divergence from current cinematic paradigms of romantic love and the absence of equivalent narratives centered on rural and lower-class characters. Beto's attempt to initiate a romantic adventure in this way appears ludicrous not simply because of the immense risk involved but because nothing in this scenario corresponds to the cultural norms of affective desire and gendered subjecthood articulated predominantly from metropolitan privileged-class standpoints. As the film makes clear the artificiality of his aberrant performance, Beto's irregular approach to love says less about him as an individual character than it does about the gulf within dominant representational templates separating lower-class rural males from normative masculine expressions of intimacy, passion, and romance.

Discrepancies with determinant codifications of maleness are also apparent in the film's portrayal of Heli, though in his case the contradictions arise not from prevailing cultural paradigms of romantic sensibility but rather primarily from patriarchal definitions of citizenship based on criteria of domesticity and economic autonomy. The film introduces Heli as the protagonist in a sequence showing him at the doorway of his home responding to a government census taker who is collecting data about the family's domestic situation by enquiring about the number of household members, their levels of education, employment status, and standard of living, for example, whether they have running water and certain types of appliances. At the same time as this brief interview functions as an efficient expository device to situate the audience in relation to the characters and setting, it also serves to signal that, despite outward appearances of lawlessness and impunity, the authority of the state remains in effect in maintaining the underlying structure of social categories that organize everyday life and regulate access to the neoliberal economy. The census questionnaire articulates the abstract norms and standards against which all members of the society are measured, establishing the terms of social equivalence that grant visibility in contemporary Mexico. The first question Heli must answer, "¿Es usted el jefe de familia?" (Are you the head of the family?), conveys the implicitly patriarchal gaze of the survey, whose objects are invoked as private, domestic embodiments of the dominant masculine power that supposedly underpins collective national unity. Heli's momentary pause before answering in the affirmative offers a telling sign of both the hegemonic function of this category and the gaps separating him from its normative assumptions. His responses to the remainder of the questions underscore the contradictory logic of a system that enshrines the ideal of the male family provider while generating material conditions that preclude the lower-class majority from embodying this role in any meaningful sense. Beyond the inconsistency stemming from the fact that the employment incomes of both Heli and his father appear insufficient to raise the family above their current level of basic subsistence, the census interview calls attention to further disjunctions between economic realities in rural Mexico and "el jefe de familia" as a governing representational category of social identity. For example, the discrepancy between the number of bedrooms in the small home (two) and the number of people living together as a household unit (five) suggests how "familia" comes to signify a maldistribution of material resources for which the individual "jefe" may be held responsible, according to the neoliberal rationale of self-sufficiency informing the privatization of the national economy.

The paradoxes of a national patriarchal ideology that ostensibly grants agency and power to men within the private domestic sphere while simultaneously compelling them into deeper incorporation with neoliberal structures of exploitation are also apparent in the film's portrayal of the factory labor regimen to which Heli and his father are subjected. There is a notable incongruity in the census when the interviewer asks Heli if he is currently searching for additional employment after he has already stated that he works full time on the night shift at the assembly plant. Heli responds somewhat incredulously, "¿Otro trabajo? No" (Another job? No), but the question registers the implication that a more ambitious "jefe de familia" might be expected to pursue more advantageous opportunities. What the film shows, however, is that prospects for competitive advancement in the labor market in rural Mexico are highly constrained, not only by deficiencies in the public education system[17] but also by a lack of state investment in infrastructure. Heli and his father make daily journeys of what appear to be several kilometers along an unlit and unpaved road to and from the factory by bicycle or by foot, and there is no sign of any form of public transportation. Moreover, the broken-down car parked in the driveway of the family home conveys, with some irony, the vast discrepancy between the wages paid to Mexican auto industry workers and the consumer prices of the vehicles they produce. Within the factory setting, the constraints are even more apparent, as the laborers must not only perform repetitive tasks matching the pace and intensity of the mechanized manufacturing process but also submit themselves to a totalized system of discipline and surveillance. In a brief dialogue as they pass one another on the road, Heli mentions to his father that he plans to take a nap at work, and when his father warns him that he will be caught, Heli explains that he intends only to sleep during his lunch break. The scarcity of opportunities to recuperate energy is visually underscored by the sheer exhaustion evident in Heli's father's corporeal expression as he sinks into his chair upon arriving home from work, only to be promptly awakened by police violently breaking into the house in search of stolen drugs.

Different forms of control exerted on male bodies represented in *Heli* appear as a continuum linking factory labor to the mobilization of militarized law enforcement and the phenomenon of so-called narco violence. This is obviously not to suggest any simple equivalence between brutal torture and ordinary physical work, but rather to posit that mechanisms making lower-class rural men vulnerable to violence are closely related to those maintaining them in material precarity. Just as Beto's enforced state of fatigue resulting from his training routine marks him as weak in the eyes of his commanders and exposes him to more degradation, legitimating the imposition of still greater discipline, a similar cycle defines the experience of factory laborers who are coded as inadequate providers and compelled to accept detrimental working conditions that further diminish their economic agency. The corporeal correspondences of this viciously circular logic of control are evinced in shots connecting the robotic movements and calisthenic exercises the assembly workers are obliged to perform with the physical fitness drills, marching, and other coordinated activities of the police cadets. The image of Beto's thoroughly depleted body after his training session mirrors that of Heli's father after completing his shift at work. I have already discussed how the bodily suffering inflicted on Beto forms a bridge between discourses of public security and criminal spectacles of death, but the film also suggests how the brutalized body can be a means of regulating participation in the economic system of industrial labor. Not long after his horrific experience of being abducted and tortured, Heli receives a call to return to his position at the plant before his injuries have fully healed. His performance at work suffers as he can no longer keep pace with the physical demands of the job, and soon afterwards he is fired. From the perspective of the factory supervisors, a body that has been maltreated is not meaningfully distinct from one that is inherently deficient, which parallels the logic informing the police detectives' determination that Heli's murdered father can be considered a criminal. The sociocultural templates that configure prevailing perceptions of malformed masculinity are as instrumental in justifying state-organized violence as they are in rationalizing exploitative forms of control over the labor force.

Heli also illustrates how authoritative systems for surveilling and regulating women's bodies are integral to the structure of state-corporate power in neoliberal Mexico. In particular, medical and legal frameworks exercise patriarchal forms of governance over the sexual practices and reproductive health decisions of both Sabrina and Estela. The clearest example of this occurs after Estela escapes from her abductors and returns home. She is examined and treated by a local doctor, who explains that aborting her rape-induced pregnancy is not possible due to state laws in Guanajuato. The female body thus becomes a vehicle for advancing a specific political and economic agenda. A somewhat subtler manifestation of this power dynamic can be seen in an earlier sequence showing Sabrina receiving an internal postpartum pelvic exam during which the physician asks her to explain her reasons for not having resumed sexual relations during the several months since she gave birth, and she responds that she simply has not had the desire. In a contrasting sequence, Sabrina confides to a palmist that she wants to pursue a professional career as a nurse, following her mother's example. Sabrina's exchange with the obstetrician-gynecologist partly mirrors Heli's interview with the census taker in that both dialogues demonstrate how bodies are codified by patriarchal gender discourses. The normative assumption about Sabrina as a lower-class rural woman of child-bearing age, from the doctor's perspective, is that if there is no health issue preventing sexual relations with her spouse, she should naturally be reproducing without hesitation. Such assumptions create barriers to discussing family planning options and contraceptive methods within the setting of the medical office. Of course, other factors place constraints on Sabrina's agency, including the unpaid labor she is expected to provide to the private household, which remains a source of exploitable value fueling the neoliberal economy.

I understand the film's approach to narrativizing Heli's participation in perpetuating the rule of patriarchy in his relationship with Sabrina to be mostly coherent with the broader critique of how embodiments of masculinity are correlated with preexisting sociocultural categories and visual-discursive templates, but it also introduces certain inconsistencies. As my reading shows, Escalante generally avoids rendering realistic psychological portraits of the film's characters,[18] preferring instead to situate them within complex self-referential systems of signification that configure perceptions of their bodies to correspond with social categories and relations predetermined by the prevailing cultural politics of neoliberal Mexico. However, in representing Heli's response to violent trauma, the film uses elements of a more conventional emotional language to suggest an internal alteration outwardly expressed in terms of aggression, frustration, and despair. Several of his behaviors clearly correspond to cultural codes of malformed masculinity, as when he angrily lashes out at Sabrina and physically attacks her, but if this shift in his personality is taken to occur primarily as a consequence of his specific, individual, affective experience of anguish and grief, the effects of dominant gender codifications represented in the film may go unnoticed. In this case, his embodiment of violent machismo could be misconstrued as an inner defect, a latent tendency unleashed by trauma, but nonetheless a natural manifestation of his essentially flawed, overbearing masculinity and misogyny. Although such an interpretation runs contrary to other dimensions of the film where emphasis falls on external assemblages of meaning affixed to the bodies of social subjects, the evidence relating to the protagonist's posttraumatic conduct is arguably sufficient to support it, especially if one is persuaded that *Heli* primarily offers a realistic representation of an ordinary individual's experience as a victim of the drug war. Rather than treating this inconsistency as detrimental to the film's overall coherence, I am inclined to attribute it to Escalante's tolerance for ambiguity in his work. In order to be effective as a self-reflexive critique of processes of constructing and disseminating dominant sociocultural narratives, the film must incorporate elements of these familiar discourses, exposing their contradictions indirectly.

To account for Heli's aggravated response to violence without essentializing him in terms of gendered pathology, we may consider how the film frames his actions in relation to his contradictory alignment with the model of patriarchal citizenship articulated and enforced by the neoliberal state. The representational systems that mark lower-class rural men as inadequate family providers and as potential criminals establish that Heli does not have control over the perceptions that configure his social being or the meanings sutured to his body. Ideas of masculine superiority are deeply enmeshed with Mexico's dominant framework of neoliberal cultural politics, but not as realistic aspirational objectives available for lower-class rural men, who are generally precluded from approaching contemporary models of normative male subjecthood. Heli cannot reasonably align himself with patriarchal forms of masculine power, so his gender performances inevitably register as unreasonable misalignments—as evidence of malformation. His violent attacks on Sabrina may therefore be understood as paradoxical affirmations of powerlessness. This is not to justify or absolve such behavior or to deny the harm Heli causes to his wife, but rather to question prevailing assumptions of an imbalance of power in Mexico that absolutely favors male over female subjects across the social spectrum. *Heli* challenges the reductive idea that lower-class men may be disempowered economically and socially but still enjoy unquestioned gender privilege in the private domestic sphere. Heli undoubtedly abuses Sabrina, but in order to accurately describe this abuse as a manifestation of a system of patriarchy one must address its oppressive, negative effects on Heli rather than to presume his positive affiliation with its power.

The film facilitates such a description by using various strategies I have already analyzed to make evident the visual-discursive mechanisms acting on the bodies of lower-class men in rural Mexico, but in one sequence specifically related to Heli's conduct toward Sabrina in the aftermath of the kidnapping, torture, and murder, the visual language registers how the gender-based subjugation of Heli pervades the private domestic sphere. When Sabrina declines to have sexual intercourse with him, Heli loses his temper and violently tears her shirt as he leaves the bedroom. The next shot looks over his shoulder as he stares pensively at his own reflection in the bathroom mirror, but this gaze is interrupted by a sudden noise and powerful vibrations. The subsequent shot provides a first-person perspective from inside an oversized tactical pickup truck equipped with a heavy automatic weapon manned by a uniformed member of the militarized police force. As the vehicle pulls up to the house and Heli comes out to confront it, the camera looks down on him, positioning his head and shoulders at the very bottom of the frame (fig. 3.6). In the next shot, a forced perspective low-angle composition of Heli standing in front of the truck embellishes the size differential, significantly diminishing the appearance of the protagonist's physical stature (fig. 3.7). By introducing these shots into this part of the narrative, *Heli* visualizes the symbolic disparity and antagonism between the structures of state-organized oppression and lower-class rural males. Far from being elevated and empowered by systems of patriarchal authority, the main character experiences a profound lack of agency over his own subjective and corporeal embodiment of masculinity, which manifests as futile—though nonetheless injurious and condemnable—practices of domestic violence.

Figure 3.6. A high-angle shot minimizes the protagonist's stature from the implied perspective of members of the violent paramilitary police force (*Heli*).

Figure 3.7. A forced perspective technique similarly reduces the apparent size of the protagonist relative to the forces that threaten him (*Heli*).

The film's conclusion further develops the theme of futility by illustrating how the physical and symbolic wounds inflicted on lower-class men by gender-based mechanisms of oppression in neoliberal Mexico contribute to generalized, pervasive, cyclical patterns of violence and exclusion. Cultural discourses and imagery marking hierarchical distinctions between normative masculinity and its malformed variants feed a circular, self-referential system of representation in which certain classes of men are intelligible chiefly in terms of their perceived deviations from normative gender paradigms. The positive ideal of the powerful, rational, affectionate, expressive, and economically autonomous male providers continues to be articulated as a meaningful cultural category, but one that constitutively excludes most lower-class rural men. Whatever steps these men may take to appear "manly" paradoxically make them more vulnerable, exploitable, disposable, and killable. *Heli*'s final sequences demonstrate this by staging a vacant parody of the narrative formulas and performances of dominant masculinity in mainstream cinema's representations of justifiable, restorative, liberating violence. Heli wants to enact vengeance on those responsible for his sister's abduction and rape, so he asks for her help in seeking them out. Unable to speak, Estela draws up a rudimentary map from memory, which leads Heli to a small, isolated, dilapidated house, not entirely dissimilar from his own. As if by chance, a man arrives and enters the home while Heli observes from a distance before approaching the door, with the camera positioned behind him. The act of breaking open the door to kill the man inside echoes the way the police broke into Heli's home and murdered his father, though of course Heli does not use sophisticated weapons and armor to carry out his solitary attack. The man attempts to escape through an open window, but Heli gives chase, pushing him to the ground and kicking him repeatedly before strangling him to death. The camera remains inside the house so that the violence is visible only through the darkened frame of the window. In this way, Escalante highlights the selectivity of the cinematic perspective to bring attention to Heli's lack of narrative agency and the groundlessness of his actions. The possibility of a cathartic, conclusive, movielike, male-driven revenge story is denied, and what we see instead is a powerless individual carrying out a meaningless act of brutality against another powerless individual, as the representational framework registers the incompatibility between idealized performances of masculinity and lower-class subjects in rural Mexico.

The lovemaking scene between Heli and Sabrina that immediately follows this killing may appear to be at odds with the sense of futility that permeates much of the film, but if it serves to suggest a healing process and a potential return to normalcy, this can only underscore that what is normal for rural communities in neoliberal Mexico involves bearing the overwhelming burdens of structural violence and economic precarity held in place by a constrictive array of gender-based systems of cultural signification. The fairly traditional family portrait that Heli placed on the wall earlier on, which may have initially appeared as a galvanizing memory of a prior wholeness lamentably shattered by violence, ultimately serves to affirm the impossibility of approaching the conventional standards of domestic subjecthood established in dominant configurations of positive cultural imagery. The fiction of the stable nuclear family exerts power as a function of its irreconcilability with the social conditions inhabited by a majority of Mexicans, especially those in rural regions under sustained assault by a conjunction of neoliberal forces.

Using a variety of self-reflexive strategies, *Heli* illustrates how visual-discursive representational templates that organize authoritative sociocultural perceptions of divergent masculinities function as instrumental mechanisms of political and economic control in neoliberal Mexico. My approach identifies the film's critical insights into codes of malformed masculinity that not only serve to legitimate direct forms of oppression and exploitation but also contribute indirectly to perpetuating a generalized condition of powerlessness by forming a web of constraints and categorial exclusions around lower-class rural men. There exists a prevailing assumption that capitalism's utilization of male subjects' labor and physicality for profit and power is enhanced via their positive alignment with patriarchal values, but in the film's portrayal of rural Mexico, impoverished men such as Beto, Heli, and Heli's father are predefined in negative terms, condemned as criminals or defective family providers, or both. Their incorporation into the neoliberal state's economic and sociocultural structures therefore occurs not as an attempted approximation of some abstract notion of hegemonic masculinity, but rather as a perverse reaffirmation of their ineligibility to be fully recognized as men.

Chapter Four

Neoliberal Masculinities between Romance and Realism in *Te prometo anarquía*

I. Loving/Killing Each Other: Images of Mexican Men in Neoliberal Culture

In the opening of his book, *Queer Mexico* (2017), Paul Julian Smith observes a disconnect between the prevalence of an "apocalyptic vision of Mexico" and the many signs of a new openness toward expressions of sexual diversity in the country's media landscape, as well as in his own anecdotal experience of everyday life in certain quarters of the capital, officially declared as an "LGBTTTI-friendly" city (4–5).[1] Without denying the existing conditions of intensified violence, endemic corruption, and socioeconomic stratification that inform the catastrophic characterizations of Mexico's transition to neoliberalism, Smith points out how the obsessive public attention to these phenomena puzzlingly coexists with a divergent transformative trajectory in Mexican cultural politics and media representation. Amid widespread preoccupation with the supposedly imminent or already transpiring breakdown of state and society, Smith finds there has emerged in Mexico an increasingly coherent "queer cultural field" that manifests a tenuous but undeniable shift in public attitudes, perceptions, and sensibilities regarding same-sex desire and romantic affect (3). While Smith's impressive study of queer media representation across diverse genres and platforms does not engage in a full analysis of how these creative practices may or may not respond to the widely circulated sociocultural discourses and images of Mexico's variously defined apocalypse, I suggest that the concurrence of these trends may be further explored from the standpoint of Mexican masculinities in cinema.

One recent film that thematically situates itself at the intersection of Mexico's socially disintegrative experience of neoliberalism and its changing cultural politics of gender and sexuality is *Te prometo anarquía*, written and directed by Guatemalan-Mexican filmmaker Julio Hernández Cordón. Set in present-day Mexico City, the film centers on two young male skateboarders, Miguel (Diego Calva) and Johnny (Eduardo Martínez), who are entangled in a complicated sexual relationship as well as an illicit scheme to traffic human blood on the black market, an enterprise that ultimately implicates them in mass kidnapping and murder. The combination of a crime story with a same-sex romance narrative stands out as somewhat unusual, though it is not entirely exceptional in Mexican and international cinema of recent decades.[2] *Te prometo anarquía* is the fifth feature-length project by Hernández Cordón, and his first filmed in Mexico. The film received state financial support from FOPROCINE as well as international backing from the Berlinale World Cinema Fund. It attracted significant attention on the global festival circuit, garnering several awards, and although it did not have a substantial theatrical run in Mexico, some prominent critics in major national publications have praised the film.[3]

The relevance of *Te prometo anarquía* to this discussion derives from two conjoint distinctions in the film's form and content. The first lies in its portrayal of homosexuality with an approach that sidesteps the aesthetics and politics of particularity by positing romantic affect as a common ground on which to formulate ethical responses to sexual and gender diversity. In other words, the film never pedagogically confronts the spectator with a gay rights/liberation agenda, nor does it stress the sensory exploration of queer difference as a mode of defying entrenched heteronormativity. Instead, the filmmaker crafts a perspective designed to make Miguel, the principal protagonist, embody the universally identifiable emotional anguish of love and desire. The focalization of Miguel's experience elicits recognition and empathy from the audience in response to his feelings toward Johnny, the object of his affections. At the same time, the highly aestheticized framing of their ill-fated romance sets up a somewhat self-reflexive contrast with another distinctive element of the film.

This second distinction arises from the language of cinematic realism that Hernández Cordón employs to make quotidian life in Mexico City appear, if not fully apocalyptic, at least semidystopian.[4] This is achieved in sequences focused on the socioeconomic conditions inhabited by the heterogenous and segmented population of the sprawling megapolis. The depiction of the urban geography emphasizes spatial fragmentation through the proliferation of barriers, conduits, enclosures, and other physical features that reflect the dissolution of social bonds, particularly within and between collectivities of men represented in the film by a cast of nonprofessional actors. The camerawork often visually underscores how homosociality and affective attachments among men are subordinated to the ruthless economic logic of the market. Advanced capitalism's abstract life-sucking modalities of commodity production, exchange, and consumption are concretized through the trade in blood as a central plot device, and the narrative's culmination in abduction and brutality may be taken as a commentary that points to an unmediated accumulative-consumptive drive as a root cause of contemporary social degeneration. With its focus on material relations between men and the uncomfortable proximity of its fictional kidnapping scenario to topical events in Mexico, the film's realism conveys the not-so-subtle suggestion that neoliberal conditions and processes of subject-formation carry the potential to generate malformed masculinities associated with criminal violence.

In my interpretation of *Te prometo anarquía*, these two dimensions of the film—that is, (1) its affective engagement with same-sex desire using a recognizable cinematic language of romance, and (2) its realist representation of the detrimental consequences of advanced transnational capitalism for local social structures and masculine subjectivities—form a contrapuntal pattern. The protagonist's romantic sensibility initially offers the spectator a framework of identification and empathy aligned with liberal-progressive values and shared structures of feeling. The filmmaker partially destabilizes this alignment by illustrating the main character's simultaneous enmeshment in a coexisting and contradictory structure of morally corrupt acquisitive desires and consumption habits linked to violence and death. While this creative juxtaposition opens possibilities for a critical dialogue counterposing distinct ethico-aesthetic conceptions of gendered subjectivity, the director's strategy ultimately proves unsatisfactory. *Te prometo anarquía* not only moves to resolve its productive tension by positing the redemptive, humanizing potential of romantic affect as an antidote to negative models of masculinity defined by aggressive forms of accumulation and hyperconsumption, but also reserves this prospect of moral redemption exclusively for the privileged-class protagonist. In order to separate Miguel from the abject category of cold-blooded criminality, the film deploys familiar tropes of victimization and opaque masculine monstrosity organized by neoliberal capitalism's politics of fear. In this regard, the film rearticulates a distorted ontology of malformed lower-class Mexican maleness and reterritorializes the patriarchal symbolic order in a new configuration that justifies state violence and the exclusionary social practices of the privileged classes.

Reading *Te prometo anarquía* as an enactment of an antagonistic—yet paradoxically co-constitutive—relationship between Mexico's contemporary "apocalyptic" cultural discourses of masculine deficiency and the new "LGBT-friendly" cosmopolitan networks of affective relationality will require examining broader questions on both sides of the conjunction. To help address how the film reflects and participates in this convergence of representational tendencies, I engage with further contributions from Smith and other scholarship dealing with the relatively recent transformative expansion of sexual diversity in Mexican media production. Also relevant to my discussion is Ignacio Sánchez Prado's identification of a class-based pattern of realignment in postnational cinema's prevalent structures of affective relationality, which he correlates to material shifts within the film industry and wider processes of neoliberal politico-economic reorganization. A particularly illustrative link between Mexico's reconfigured cultural parameters of subject-formation and the socially degenerative effects of neoliberalism is provided by Sayak Valencia's theorization of "gore capitalism," a concept describing an array of economic practices that derive profits from violence and bloodshed, which Valencia explicitly associates with lower-class nonwhite masculinity. Within these coordinates, I make the case that *Te prometo anarquía*'s sexually progressive and ostensibly redemptive portrait of masculine subjectivity in Mexico's neoliberal context reproduces essentializing codes of gender malformation inherited from nationalist cultural politics.

II. Networks of Empathy in Queer Cinema

In keeping with my understanding of *Te prometo*'s dyadic composition, this part of my analysis addresses the portrayal of romance in the film, while the subsequent section turns toward its realist representation of material conditions framed as conducive to crime and social violence. The final part of the chapter offers reflections on the consequences of the contrast created by the film's dual dimensions and the filmmaker's approach to resolving the tension between them. Here, my initial questions consider how the film's treatment of homosexual relations, articulated with a somewhat conventional aesthetic and cultural grammar of romantic love, invites a dialogue with some recent critical approaches to mass market cinema.[5]

Hernández Cordón's previous full-length films, all of which were shot and produced in Guatemala, resist any such approximations to mainstream movies. After studying at the Centro de Capacitación Cinematográfica in Mexico City, he opted to return to Guatemala, where he had lived previously, to develop a do-it-yourself filmmaking practice using improvisatory strategies to achieve an original artistic vision, resulting in a succession of low-budget art house films characterized by unconventional narratives and experimental aesthetics. In works such as *Gasolina* (Gasoline) (2008), *Las marimbas del infierno* (Marimbas from Hell) (2010), *Hasta el sol tiene manchas* (Even the Sun Has Stains) (2012), and *Polvo* (Dust) (2012), he cultivated a distinctive creative ethos by embracing both the freedom and the challenge of working outside of established institutional models of cinema production (González de Canales 3). A more recent film, *Atrás hay relámpagos* (Lightning Falls Behind) (2017), made in Costa Rica, recuperates elements of his idiosyncratic free-form style of audiovisual storytelling. *Te prometo* is Hernández Cordón's first project to be filmed in Mexico, and its enhanced production values evince the substantial funding and technical resources provided by the state-sponsored cinema institute (Garba), but the film still manifests significant elements of the director's auteurist practice, particularly in his decision to use a cast of nonprofessionals, some of whom were selected on the basis on their social media profiles (Pickard). Furthermore, the fragmentary storyline and unrehearsed dialogue in many scenes instill a sense of spontaneity into the film's overall presentation. *Te prometo*'s long takes, distinctive shooting locations, and shadowy nocturnal exterior sequences also recall the aesthetics of realism found in some of Hernández Cordón's previous cinema.

At the same time, *Te prometo* occupies a unique space within the director's oeuvre given that its cinematographic composition and organizational structure emphasize romantic love and erotic desire, themes that do not figure prominently in any of his other works. While he has shown repeated interest in thematizing class relations, youth culture, and even violent crime, only *Te prometo* delves so fully into the amorous sentiments of one of its main characters. As I have already suggested, the film deliberately evades any direct engagement with identitarian discourses on plural sexualities, but its portrayal of the homosexual relationship between

Miguel and Johnny is one the film's distinguishing features and has been a focal point for reviewers and critics.[6] Even though the visual language is suffused with romantic affects, the plot does not take shape as a typical cinematic love story. The film shows only what appear to be the final stages of an intimate affair between two late-adolescent lovers, providing little information about how they initiated their relationship or how long it has lasted. From the few details conveyed through the narrative and dialogue, it can be pieced together that Johnny's mother, Brenda, works as a live-in domestic servant for Miguel's family, and the two young men appear to have spent part of their childhood or early adolescence together in the same home. How much about their sexual partnership is known to their parents remains unclear, but we learn that Miguel's mother apparently forced Johnny out of the house at some recent point, though for reasons that are never stated. In addition to registering compulsory silences surrounding the violation of class boundaries, these narrative elisions also illustrate the filmmaker's avoidance of subject matter connected to sexual identity in favor of foregrounding the affective currents generated by the romantic tension. Miguel evidently pursues Johnny with more fervor than the latter is willing to reciprocate, yet both partners fail to articulate or otherwise mutually establish the terms of their involvement with one another. At the outset of the film, Johnny has a newfound love interest in a young woman named Adri, provoking jealous rivalry in Miguel, though her presence does not prove to be the decisive factor in the terminal course of their relationship. As the main narrative thread follows the two male characters through a series of events leading up to the mass kidnapping and its aftermath, the film underscores the intensity of Miguel's emotional and erotic attachment to Johnny with prominent love sequences.

In Smith's brief commentary on *Te prometo anarquía* near the end of his book, he classifies it alongside Carlos Reygadas's and Amat Escalante's "art movies seasoned with sex and ultraviolence for foreign cinephiles," and he adds that the "fact that the sex (unlike in Reygadas and Escalante) is gay now seems indifferent" (*Queer Mexico* 138). Although I distance myself from Smith's rather dismissive and reductive take on the commonalities between this trio of auteur filmmakers, his remarks raise valid questions regarding how to map *Te prometo anarquía*'s representations of homoeroticism and social violence relative to current parameters of (trans)national reception. On one hand, Smith is undoubtedly correct about the film's intention to appeal to global festival audiences located mostly outside of Mexico, but on the other, the conception of its themes, content, creative strategies, and representational framework cannot be so easily disarticulated from the contemporary Mexican context and its internal reconfigurations of spectatorship, cultural politics, aesthetic taste, and sociality.[7] As I will argue in this chapter, the particular constellation of homosexual love and desire, neoliberal values, violent crime, and masculine subjecthood in *Te prometo anarquía* reflects some paradigmatic shifts as well as prevalent patterns of rearticulation that define Mexican postnational filmmaking practice more generally.

Along these lines, I consider the film in relation to the altered trajectories of romantic affect and intimacy that several scholars have identified in recent Mexican cinema. Current critical interest in affective dimensions of contemporary Mexican films can be viewed as part of a wider "affective turn" in cinema studies and other areas of sociocultural analysis that has resulted in a proliferation of new research focused on formulations of, and responses to, emotional and sensorial appeals in creative and political projects of various kinds.[8] Here I limit my discussion to a few relevant works of scholarship on transformations of national cinema that register correspondences between structures of feeling articulated in recent films and the political, economic, moral, and ideological reorganization of Mexico's social order under neoliberalism. This includes engagement with accounts of the increasingly visible representation of homosexual relations in Mexican film and other mass media, but with the qualification that *Te prometo anarquía* has not generally been presented or received as "queer cinema," despite its forthright depictions of homoerotic desire between men.[9]

The film's apparent indifference toward exploring any specific aspects of queer social identities or LGBTQ+ politics has been acknowledged and even underscored by Hernández Cordón himself. As he emphasizes in interviews, the normalization of the film's same-sex romantic relationship aims to transcend the particularism of classificatory labels: "Apart from the other issues it addresses, it seems to me to be a love story, even though it is a story of gay love, it is a story of love and love is universal" (Garba). The deployment of romantic love as a unifying theme that obviates the need to explicitly defy or deconstruct sociopolitical boundaries of gender and sexuality is not an unusual move in Mexico's contemporary field of cultural production. Smith describes similar discursive framing in a selection of somewhat more mainstream Mexican films dealing with sexual diversity, *Todo el mundo tiene a alguien menos yo* (Everybody's Got Somebody . . . Not Me) (2012, dir. Raúl Fuentes), *Cuatro lunas* (Four

Moons) (2014, dir. Sergio Tovar Velarde), and *Carmín tropical* (2014, dir. Rigoberto Perezcano),[10] which he sees as promoting "an unapologetically assimilationist politics" (85). For Smith, this approach does not necessarily have negative implications as it represents a viable integration strategy for LGBT-themed cinema and television productions seeking to enter a national media market still constrained in many areas by prevalent conservative tendencies. However, he also suggests that new films defined by an assumed social acceptance of homosexual affection and aspirations to commercial success (however modest) call for interpretative criteria distinct from those that might be applied to queer cinema with more challenging artistic ambitions or political motives. In his chapter on Mexican LGBT films that "no longer present themselves as resistant to a dominant cinematic and political regime," Smith offers three "prisms" to analyze their modes of appeal: cinephilia, fandom, and posthegemony (86). While in many other respects Hernández Cordón's auteurist filmmaking quite clearly stands apart from the lighter cinematic fare studied by Smith in his chapter, *Te prometo*'s mobilization of gay romance as a universal human factor finds common ground with this selection of (semi)mainstream movies. Smith's first two prisms may have some limited relevance to *Te prometo anarquía*, but here I engage with his description of a posthegemonic mode of "performance that effects a change in the world it claims to simply represent" (88), which closely parallels my understanding of the construction and deconstruction of romantic appeal in Hernández Cordón's film.

The concept of posthegemony has been given various definitions in recent political theory, but in a broad sense it refers to the diffuse exercise of sovereign power without the assumption of an underlying mass social consensus.[11] In Mexico, where the state has historically lacked popular legitimacy, the ruling order has been upheld not by citizens' rational consent to a governing ideology, nor by centralized totalitarian structures of coercion and control, but rather by selective enforcement of an inchoate and inequitable social contract through both official and unofficial actions (including violence), which unsettles the conventional political dynamics of hegemony and counterhegemonic opposition. Within these posthegemonic conditions, Smith explains, liberatory social transformations, such as increased acceptance of sexual diversity, occur not as outcomes of large-scale organized resistance movements but rather as dispersive alterations of "habit and affect" within "provisional collective grouping[s]" (88).[12] As opposed to political suasion, the cultural mobilization of passionate intensities becomes the primary means of effecting collective change by provoking shifts in habitual patterns of sociality and existing structures of feeling. Smith argues that his examples of mainstream LGBT cinema perform a desirable change by habitualizing the representation of romantic relations between same-sex partners and soliciting affective responses from the audience. Of course, he acknowledges the limits of such change in terms of the relatively narrow reach of these films, which circulate mainly among "a loose collective of cinephile viewers" (94). Among the broader field of (trans)national publics, these mostly affluent Mexican audiences who seek out uncontroversial cinema dealing with homosexual themes form only a small subset, one without any activist or oppositional inclinations, or, as Smith puts it, "an atomized multitude unable or unwilling to organize itself as a historical agent" (94). Nonetheless, for Smith, this "emerging, fragile collective of a queer-interested audience between the art house and multiplex" represents a key sociocultural network forming the basis of "a new kind of consensus for a modern Mexico eager to show off its recently acquired social liberalism, at least in the middle-class milieu" (106).[13]

Smith's interpretation of normalized queer romance in current Mexican cinema as a performative act of posthegemonic consensus-building aimed at mostly privileged metropolitan spectators corresponds quite closely to my understanding of *Te prometo anarquía*'s appeals to love and desire. As I will show later in this section, the film channels the flow of affect through the main protagonist, Miguel, inviting the audience to share in sensible associations enacted through his romantic experience, or, in Smith's terms, his performance of a desirable change. However, unlike the films examined by Smith, *Te prometo* deliberately interrupts or suspends the performative-affective connection by introducing elements of social realism preoccupied with certain destructive phenomena—that is, violent masculinities fomented by neoliberal socioeconomic conditions—that are driving Mexico's gradual descent into a lawless narco state. I argue that while Hernández Cordón purposefully structures his film around this counterpoint to expose underlying tensions in contemporary filmmaking practice, he ultimately reaffirms the capacity of affective intensities to reduce or reverse social deterioration by promoting new models of ethical relations, at least among the presumably affluent spectators who can empathize and identify with Miguel's feelings, redeeming him as a moral subject. Smith's brief reading of *Te prometo* implies that its representation of criminal violence is formulated to appease a different audience, that is, First World festivalgoers who demand bleak images of Third World ruin and chaos, whether to satisfy a morbid fascination or to symbolically confirm their own compassionate cosmopolitan values.[14] While I suggest that this characterization downplays the prominent romantic framework in the film and overstates the level of brutality it depicts, I also submit that Smith's position coincides more closely with mine as soon as one begins to question his firm separation between foreign and national audiences. In my view, the same affluent Mexican spectators described by Smith, who enjoy mainstream movies that reflect and reinforce their habitual and affective acceptance of sexual diversity, have implicit interests in consuming representations of social violence and criminality, provided that these are suitably codified as recognizable threats to the desirable change being performatively enacted. Their class-limited social consensus is arguably strengthened through shared antipathy toward the regressive or hostile forces symbolically depicted onscreen. Jumping ahead, I will argue that *Te prometo* complements its positive affective/ethical alignments to sexual difference with representations of threats to social progress crystallized as malformed masculinities.

Vinodh Venkatesh is another scholar whose work similarly addresses the recent surge in cinematic representations of gayness in terms of deployments of empathetic, emotional, and sensorial appeals, though with a scope that encompasses films produced in various parts of Latin America and the United States. In his book *New Maricón Cinema* (2016), Venkatesh's main arguments take shape around a posited distinction between Maricón and New Maricón cinemas, interconnected categories that chart an evolutionary shift away from older stereotyped depictions of homosexuality designed to voyeuristically distance the viewer from abject alterity, toward newer films that "transmit and relay affective intensities that align the viewer with sex and gender difference" (7). New Maricón films are distinguishable by this "affective schema" that generates "new structures of feeling vis-à-vis bodies and desires," through they do not constitute an absolute rupture since they often revisit dimensions of the earlier "scopic regime" associated with Maricón cinema (7). Venkatesh elaborates on these genre classifications throughout the text, adding more theoretical nuance than can be properly accounted for here. While he does not discuss *Te prometo*, I would suggest that many aspects of the film correspond to his basic description of how New Maricón cinema aims to generate pathos via sensual alignments, though more parallels occur with his identifications of recent cinematic trajectories that do not coincide fully with either of his main categories (10). These include descriptions of a "post-New" or "urban-New" subcategory, as exemplified by Argentine director Marco Berger's *Plan B* (2009), a film that (like *Te prometo*) "succeeds in 'naturalizing' same-sex desire, which emerges in the practice and texture of [the characters'] lives, situating itself thus at a point of escape from overt lesbigay politics" (151, 153–154). Also relevant, for my purposes, is Venkatesh's chapter on LGBT-themed commercial films "that do not adhere to the aesthetics or poetics of the New Maricón genre but that *were* made with an emancipatory and empathic politics in mind" (175). Here he offers an insightful analysis of the Mexican film *La otra familia* (The Other Family) (2011, dir. Gustavo Loza), which bears a very slight resemblance to *Te prometo* in the way it combines its main narrative focus on a same-sex couple (in this case situated within a family melodrama rather than a romance) with an intersecting plotline dealing with criminal violence in contemporary Mexico.

The similarities between these two films do not extend beyond this superficial connection at the level of content but engage with Venkatesh's understanding of how commercial LGBT films, such as *La otra familia*, align with neoliberal structures of feeling, which facilitates a discussion of *Te prometo*'s romantic affects in related terms. Like Smith, Venkatesh observes that mass market cinema tends to take an integrationist approach to issues of sexual diversity, "examining how subjects who identify with gayness negotiate their identity within a strongly conservative telos," while also aiming to "unravel the presuppositions of traditional normativity" (175–176). These narratives about "the normality of being 'gay' today in an urban setting" reflect a new "popular consensus on difference," which Venkatesh links, on one hand, to innovative aesthetic breakthroughs by New Maricón films and, on the other, to a broader "neoliberal turn" in commercial cinema (175, 176). Recent mainstream films that form part of this trend may reproduce some of the formulaic tropes and images of homosexuality found in Maricón cinema, but these are reframed in accordance with new cultural and ethical parameters associated with a "neoliberal agenda" that not only promotes an "awareness of gender difference" but also makes expressions of such awareness into a "sign of social and economic modernity and advancement" (176). Venkatesh adopts an ambivalent stance toward the gender politics that organize neoliberalism's cultural itineraries. Drawing upon the work of Sánchez Prado, who has provided a thorough account of the post-1988 transformation of Mexico's national cinema in terms of new structures of feeling closely identified with privileged-class perspectives and neoliberal ideology, Venkatesh recognizes how a film such as *La otra familia* mobilizes modern, globalized, and potentially Anglo-imperialist gender discourses in ways that reinforce classist and racist codes of social differentiation (176). Yet despite these discriminatory and hierarchical tendencies, he identifies significant ethical advancement manifested in the neoliberal turn's cultural "ostracizing of traditional machismo and homophobic sentiment" (176). In his final analysis of *La otra familia*, Venkatesh suggests that the film's combination of conventional conservatism with a neoliberal progay agenda offers a "stepping-stone . . . to true sociocultural emancipation" (191).

On this issue, Venkatesh coincides with Smith's position that appealing to the class-specific sensibilities of affluent audiences constitutes an appropriate and even necessary approach for filmmakers whose work aims to promote social equity by engendering empathy toward sexually diverse subjects. According to both scholars, it is to be expected that mainstream cinema will harmonize its modes of appeal with the aspirations of its target audience, and if in the context of the neoliberal turn more films put forward emotionally engaging articulations of sexual and gender pluralism, so much the better for progressive social values. In his dialogue with Sánchez Prado's historicization of the structures of affective relationality in recent cinema, Venkatesh suggests that certain revisions would help to account for the desirable effects of the emancipatory gender politics that are intertwined with other aspirational ideals of modern, global citizenship represented in commercial films. Whereas Sánchez Prado emphasizes how current Mexican cinema tends to consolidate existing class- and race-based social barriers, Venkatesh advocates for accentuating the inclusive, gay-positive side of the neoliberal cultural agenda, "even if it regiments and reiterates an overall regime of plural inequities" (177).

Smith's and Venkatesh's critical endorsements of the structures of feeling assembled in recent commercial films, at least those designed to foster empathetic alignments vis-à-vis sexually diverse constituencies, raise questions regarding the ethical trade-offs that filmmakers and audiences implicitly accept in order to create and maintain self-referential images of a sexually progressive cosmopolitanism in Mexico. The affective imaginaries that enable cinemagoers to recognize themselves and others as modern, global citizens circulate within a representational regime that has been shaped by neoliberal processes to conform with (rather than unsettle) the aspirational self-perceptions of Mexico's privileged classes, a point on which both scholars concur with Sánchez Prado. The commercial viability of Mexican mainstream cinema undoubtedly depends on filmmakers' proficiency at projecting a desirable reflection of the segments of society that comprise the bulk of the audience, facilitating what Smith calls "narcissistic identification" with onscreen characters (96). However, both Smith and Venkatesh also suggest that the motives of recent LGBT-themed movies transcend commerce because they promote an "emancipatory and empathic politics" (Venkatesh 175) or offer a "gift of love" to "queer-interested audiences" (Smith 106).

In my reading of Hernández Cordón's film, questions arise regarding the hidden costs within the emotional economy that organizes contemporary Mexican cinema. Can cinema's gifts of love and empathy be given and received across sexual orientations as freely as Smith and Venkatesh imply, or do they come with strings attached? If the neoliberal network of shared sentiment levies an unseen toll, who pays? Part of the way *Te prometo anarquía* attempts to address such questions, as I have already suggested, is through its contrapuntal arrangement of distinct cinematic languages, one romantic, designed to be affectively engaging, and the other realist, intended to be more reflective of material and socioeconomic conditions in Mexico City, particularly as experienced by masculine subjects belonging to diverse classes. As will become clear through my examples and analysis, the lines separating these two registers are sometimes blurred to achieve certain effects, but the counterpoint may still be discerned as a deliberate strategy. The filmmaker sets these two dimensions of *Te prometo* side by side partly in order to gesture toward aspects of social reality unrepresented in the genres of mainstream cinema most fully invested in manufacturing neoliberal structures of feeling, such as romantic comedies and light melodramas. This intention, and my arguments concerning its inadequate realization, will be discussed in more detail further on, but first I show how the strategy relies on an initial deployment of affective intensities, inviting the audience into the intimate space of the main protagonist's experience of desire.

The opening sequence of *Te prometo* sets up Miguel's emotional core and romantic outlook as appealing points of entry for the receptive spectator. The first shot shows Johnny emerging from the top hatch of a tanker trailer out of the red glow of its interior into a dark and seemingly empty alleyway. We see him only as a shadowy figure who remains at a distance and with his back mostly turned toward the camera. In the next shot, we briefly see Johnny from a closer perspective, but he covers his face with his hand in order to consume an inhalant, which we subsequently learn is glue. After Johnny calls out to Miguel, the camera moves to position the latter's face near the center of the frame, situating Johnny just outside its edge, barely visible. The effect of the cinematographic composition, in conjunction with the dialogue, is to bring Miguel's sentimental perspective into the foreground for the audience. From the disjointed conversation, we gather that Miguel has been jealously brooding over Johnny's burgeoning interest in Adri, whom Miguel considers an interloper. There are also vague hints in their remarks suggesting Johnny's reluctance to be fully open about his involvement with Miguel. The film's refusal to provide a full diegetic exposition of the relationship between the two young men has several consequences. As already discussed, sidestepping issues related to the characters' public identities signals a disengagement from certain didactic formulas associated with LGBT politics in mass media. At the same time, commencing this romantic scenario in media res with allusions to an array of unexplained facets of the relationship may arouse curiosity in certain viewers, drawing them into the intimate lives of the characters. More importantly, the dearth of narrative content moves the emphasis to the visual and sensual elements of the scene. The cinematic language and corporeal performance convey Miguel's sense of betrayal and his yearning for reconciliation, as the shot remains close enough to show the sullen expression on his face while he sits down and then stares up longingly at Johnny (fig. 4.1). The inscription of Miguel's subjectivity through such recognizably coded romantic behaviors recurs at several points throughout the rest of the film, but already in the first sequence he is established as

Figure 4.1. Miguel (Diego Calva) gazes up longingly at his lover, Johnny (Eduardo Eliseo Martínez), in the opening sequence of *Te prometo anarquía* (2015, dir. Julio Hernández Cordón).

the main beacon of affect, emitting palpable emotional wavelengths for the audience to home in on.

The next sequence includes a love scene between Johnny and Miguel inside the tanker trailer, which serves as Johnny's makeshift home. Once again, the visual arrangement of the subjects within the frame emphasizes the centrality of Miguel's erotic gaze and affective desire. In one carefully composed shot with a static camera situated above the performers, we see Johnny reposed with his head and shoulders cradled by Adri, who lies asleep, and his bare legs wrapped around Miguel, who faces Johnny from the opposite side of the improvised bed. While Johnny occupies himself with a portable videogame console, Miguel watches him and teases him before playfully initiating sexual contact. Johnny at first resists Miguel's entreaty, pointing to Adri's obvious presence, but Miguel continues his sexual advances. As Miguel stands up, undresses, and places himself in a hammock hanging in an adjacent section of the tanker's interior, the camera keeps his eyes near the center of the frame, capturing his line of sight as he observes Johnny rising to join him. Johnny caresses and kisses Miguel tenderly, but he is positioned with his back to the audience and his upper body remains out of frame during most of the shot. The camera remains fixed at a medium distance as we see them begin to have intercourse in the hammock, but Miguel's expression of sensual pleasure is visually prominent while Johnny continues facing away from the spectator (fig. 4.2).

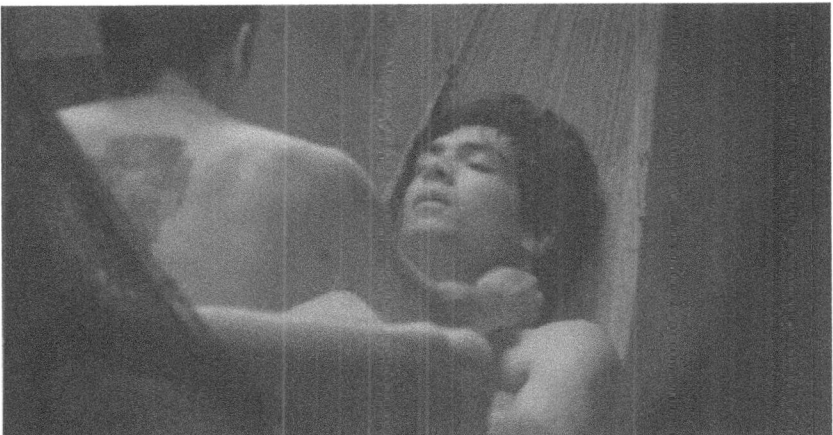

Figure 4.2. This shot of Miguel (right) and Johnny (left) having intercourse centers Miguel's expression of desire and pleasure, while Johnny faces away from the camera (*Te prometo anarquía*).

The film registers even more clearly that its affective focalization is tied to Miguel in a later sequence that begins by showing an intimate moment shared between Johnny and Adri. Preceding sequences and elements of dialogue establish that Miguel is growing anxious about being out of contact with Johnny for some interval, perhaps a day or two (the passage of time is not clearly marked). A medium-long shot shows Johnny and Adri alone together in the jai alai courts that double as a skatepark. They are both undressed, and their playful interaction soon turns into a sexual embrace, but they are positioned at a significant distance from the camera, preventing the image from generating any erotic intensity. The next shot cuts to Miguel standing just outside the court, and it suddenly becomes clear that we have been watching the scene unfold from his perspective. Even before any dialogue begins, the sound helps to transmit Miguel's jealous anxiety as we hear Johnny's telephone ringing unanswered throughout the first part of the sequence. By linking this sound to a dial tone heard in the previous sequence, the film's editing discloses how Miguel is confirming his suspicions that his calls are being ignored because Johnny is amorously occupied with Adri. The camera closely tracks Miguel's movements as he aggressively confronts both his lover and his romantic rival, his temper flaring as they trade accusations. The film's narrative mostly bypasses the issue of whether Miguel's feelings of betrayal are justifiable within the terms of the relationship. Even if his conduct appears rather immature, this may in fact help to establish that Miguel is experiencing—likely for the first time in his young life—the anguish of unrequited love, and to bring these feelings to the film's surface for the audience.

It should be added that *Te prometo* does contain shots and sequences conveying Johnny's perspective, but these are distinctly *not* constructed in a romantic or affective register. For example, in a montage set to a soundtrack of melancholy indie-rock music, we first see Miguel getting out of the bed in the tanker and driving himself home well before dawn, leaving Johnny by himself. The rest of the sequence shows what may be taken as a typical morning for Johnny, as he rises early, practices skateboarding, and makes his way to the jai alai courts, where he showers before beginning his workday as a janitor. Throughout most of these shots, Johnny is framed from medium and long distances, showing him in the context of the urban environment without the camera getting close enough to transmit any distinct expression of feeling or emotion (fig. 4.3). The tenor of the music complements the general mood of the film, but it does not obviously correspond to any specific sentiments embodied by

Johnny himself.[15] The banality of his routine activities partly pertains to the film's realist dimension, to be described more fully in the next section, but the images in this sequence also provide a contrast with the visual language used in comparable shots focused on Miguel. For instance, the same montage includes an over-the-shoulder shot of Miguel's perspective as he drives himself home. The camera aligns with his gaze as he playfully pretends to bite the streetlights he passes, a highly stylized visual device that relays the sense of bliss he likely feels after reconciling with his lover. Earlier in the film, when Miguel is alone in his own bedroom after making love to Johnny in the tanker the previous night, we see him framed in a very tight close-up shot with an expression that similarly suggests a kind of postcoital serenity.

While Hernández Cordón's camerawork and editing choices clearly draw the spectator toward identification with Miguel's affective sentiments and romantic gaze, the contrastive portrayal of Johnny simultaneously introduces possibilities for more critical consideration of the main protagonist's perspective. Other elements of the film similarly contribute to exposing Miguel's point of view to scrutiny. For instance, the distinctive red-tinged interior lighting of the tanker trailer aligns with the erotic connotations that it holds for Miguel as the site of his sexual encounters with Johnny, but it also imbues these scenes with aesthetic artifice, especially in contrast with the duller palette of colors that defines the film's many exterior

Figure 4.3. A long shot of Johnny contextualizes him in the urban environment, avoiding any suggestion of his emotional interiority (*Te prometo anarquía*).

shots of Mexico City. This disparity suggests how the tanker sequences are colored by Miguel's emotional presence and eroticizing perspective. Twice in the film we see Miguel and Johnny being intimate together inside the tanker, both times following quarrels arising from Miguel's fits of jealousy. On each occasion, the red glow may be understood to reflect the impassioned sensibility that pervades Miguel's perception of Johnny. Of course, it may be taken for granted that the interior light remains red while Johnny is alone or with Adri, but from the audience's perspective the film's composition associates this altered color scheme with Miguel's erotically charged gaze.

The intended effect of these visual prompts, I am suggesting, is not to fully undo the alignment with Miguel, but to indirectly mark the perimeter of his romantic outlook. Presenting Johnny alone in a quotidian context and making the affective framework that centers Miguel's desire artificially explicit are two correlated techniques that facilitate at least a partial questioning of the structures of feeling assembled through the film's romance. Although this strategy never arrives at a fully self-reflexive mode of cinema, it combines coherently with the film's thematic and aesthetic engagement with economic precarity, social fragmentation, and violent crime. The realist depiction of some bleaker aspects of Mexico City offers a more direct contrast with the affect-driven intimate scenes, but through the approach I have described, the film already alerts the spectator to the horizons of the romantic mode of perception associated with the main protagonist. In this way, the film's juxtaposition of its two main cinematic grammars, romance and realism, does not simply generate a clash of irreconcilable formal/aesthetic disparities, but rather a contrapuntal pattern of representational oppositions. In other words, the romantic language defines itself in dialogic contradistinction to the language of social realism.

It is in this aesthetic practice of counterpoint that I locate the film's attempts to intervene critically in Mexican cinema's tendency to foster what Sánchez Prado describes as an "increasing separation between the cultural languages of different social classes and social geographies" (*Screening* 63). The patterns of divergence and compartmentalization that, according to Sánchez Prado, have redefined how cultural representations are produced and consumed in Mexico are deeply intertwined with processes of structural transformation associated with the neoliberal political and economic agenda implemented from the 1980s onwards. In his analysis, the rise of the romantic comedy as a major commercial genre of Mexican cinema in the 1990s and 2000s serves as a paradigmatic illustration of the effects of privatization on systems of film production and exhibition. Market deregulation and drastic reductions in state subsidies were among the factors that brought the national film industry to the brink of collapse in the 1980s, but a revised aesthetic language combining elements of U.S. indie filmmaking, TV sitcoms, and Hollywood romantic comedy eventually succeeded in attracting new audiences to the cinema by offering an updated "structure of feeling . . . based on the aspirations of the middle and upper classes to achieve the promise of individual success brought forward by neoliberalism" ("Regimes" 5). Drawing on the concept of "emotional capitalism," developed by sociologist Eva Illouz to describe the close correlation of economics and intimacy in capitalist modernity, Sánchez Prado accounts for romantic comedy's successful integration into Mexico's new cultural economy by highlighting its capacity to articulate discourses of love and desire assembled and packaged to be fully compatible with idealized neoliberal models of consumption and professional ambition (*Screening* 88–89). In order to circulate effectively as "cultural commodities that engage affect through the market" (88), these films abandon the allegorical frameworks of traditional romantic cinema and television in Mexico designed to codify common identities within an imagined national community. Instead, they adopt a distinct filmic language intended to "reflect the experiences of a middle class whose social and cultural identities are framed by discourses of consumption, such as advertising" (71). In the new romantic narratives, contemporary meanings of love and intimacy are explored and defined in private, individualized, and market-oriented registers by characters who inhabit sociocultural spaces insulated from the political tensions, economic instability, and collective insecurity affecting the wider social formation. To sustain affective identification with class-specific audiences, romantic comedies of this period cultivated an exclusive association between the aspirational ideals of modern love and positions of social privilege, creating a "representational economy of Mexico where the lower classes have no significant role" ("Regimes" 7).

For Sánchez Prado, the self-enclosed, elitist worlds represented in these films are not merely a symptom of filmmakers' reluctance to jeopardize the entertainment value of their cinema with more realistic treatments of class diversity and social conflict. Rather, the "self-referential space" of romantic comedies mirrors actual socio-spatial transformations of Mexico's urban geography, especially in Mexico City and other urban centers where the construction of exclusive residential developments, luxury shopping malls, and high-priced multiplex cinemas manifests the willingness of the privileged classes "to isolate themselves from the rest of the social spectrum" (*Screening* 91). From this perspective, it is not entirely accurate to suggest that these films lack realism, or that they ignore socio-material relations, since they actually do represent—albeit one-sidedly and uncritically—new economic realities in which racialized and impoverished constituencies are considered inadequate to, and therefore legitimately excludible from, neoliberal Mexico's growth, remodernization, and progress. To better explain the general invisibility of lower-class Mexicans in commercial romantic cinema, Sánchez Prado emphasizes that, within the emotional economy defined by neoliberalism, "unequal access to the structures of representation and consumption of feelings create[s] distinct regimes of affect that replicate rather than question existing ideological, racial, and class separations" ("Regimes" 2). As a genre thoroughly woven up with privileged-class affinities, lifestyles, and consumer habits, romantic comedy articulates the prevailing cultural language of love as a monologue that not only fails to address social difference but disavows inequality by reproducing discourses that hide or naturalize it. While Sánchez Prado attaches particular significance to affect-driven narrative cinema that uses humor and romance to codify the class-specific cultural sensibilities of affluent Mexicans adjusting to the neoliberal order, he also suggests that the patterns of social partitioning reflected in romantic comedy's themes, content, and visual language have influenced corresponding transformations in other kinds of film, including those made with political and auteurist intent (*Screening* 104).

As a cultural medium that grants its audiences commoditized access to a network of modern sentiments, Mexican cinema simultaneously fosters moral compromise with the ruthless socioeconomic order of transnational capitalism. I contend that at least part of Hernández Cordón's intention in *Te prometo anarquía* lies in critically exposing the concealed underside of neoliberal cinema's prevailing emotional economy, not merely by staging a love story that cuts across class lines to incorporate lower-class characters and spaces, but by implicating solipsistic structures of feeling in the deteriorating social condition of Mexico outside its islands of prosperity. The director attempts to open a space between distinct cinematic languages that can begin to show how the contemporary cultural meanings of love, intimacy, sexuality, and desire in Mexico under neoliberalism are indissolubly bound up with the racialized class system, economic precarity, power differentials, and social violence. With strategies designed to highlight the dissonance and interplay between the romantic sensibilities of the privileged-class protagonist, Miguel, and the insecurity pervading the social environment he traverses, *Te prometo* begins to elucidate the narrow and selective conduits cinema offers for the circulation of pathos as well as the obstacles impeding other potential routes it might take.

III. Material Relations and Masculine Malformation under Neoliberalism

The realist language in *Te prometo*, which I interpret as a critical counterpoint to the grammar of intimacy and romance, deals with the dystopic conditions of neoliberal capitalism in Mexico City that contextualize Miguel and Johnny's doomed scheme to traffic blood on the black market. This dimension of the film presents itself as an approximation of real-life phenomena of social violence and organized crime in Mexico, especially in the depiction of a mass abduction. At first, however, the protagonists' involvement in the blood trade merely skirts the boundaries of illegitimacy. Collaborating with a corrupt paramedic named Gabriel, their main activity is simply to recruit donors from among their friends and acquaintances who will accept cash payments for their plasma without asking any questions. Johnny and Miguel earn a procurement fee from Gabriel for each donor they enlist, and they readily sell their own blood as well. Gabriel's larger than usual request for fifty donors signals an opportunity for deeper integration into the shadow economy and serves as a central plot device, providing the rationale for a string of sequences showing various locations around the city where the boys seek out additional sources of blood. It is here that the directorial focus turns toward aspects of the material reality of contemporary Mexico City, mapping out an urban geography defined by heterogenous, fragmented patterns of informal economic activity and consumption-based sociality that have become hallmarks of Mexico's neoliberal era.[16]

Initially, what is most relevant about these sequences is the tension they generate vis-à-vis the affective intensities emanating from the film's romantic and intimate dimensions. As outlined in the previous section, Miguel's passionate desire for Johnny contrasts dialogically with elements of the film that illustrate the characters' mutual enmeshment in webs of uneven economic power relations, systemic social injustice, and overt forms of exploitation. The realism not only functions to supply a critical perspective on Mexico's processes of neoliberal transformation, but also serves Hernández Cordón's intention to open fissures in the prevailing structure of feelings assembled by mainstream Mexican cinema. The neoliberal cultural regime of affect thus comes to be seen in light of co-constitutive experiences of social fragmentation under advanced capitalism. In an early sequence, one of several filmed on location inside Mexico City's metro system, Miguel is headed to the jai alai courts to meet Johnny and organize blood donors when he runs into a younger friend known as Techno, who sells pirated music to train passengers. Lugging his backpack full of CDs through crowded carriages and calling out for customers, Techno's occupation typifies those of countless other impoverished youths who eke out a meagre livelihood in the city's informal economy, subjects who normally form only part of the background or are simply invisible in romantic comedies and other mainstream affect-driven genre films. Hernández Cordón introduces Techno into the narrative structure of *Te prometo* not simply as a referent to quotidian reality, but as a way of gesturing to the limits of pathos in the prevailing cultural imaginary. When Techno suddenly collapses from exhaustion, the camera barely registers his small, unconscious body crumpled on the floor of the train (fig. 4.4). Other passengers hardly take notice, and even when Miguel attends to him and drags him unceremoniously onto the platform at the next station, his attitude conveys as much annoyance as concern, as he

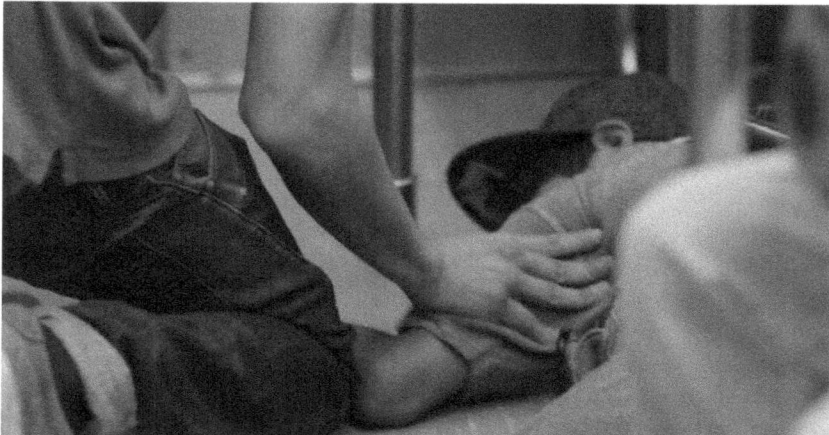

Figure 4.4. An obscured shot of Techno (Diego Escamilla Corona) shows him collapsed on the floor of a subway train carriage while Miguel prepares to drag him onto the platform (*Te prometo anarquía*).

complains out loud, "Pinche Techno, ¿porqué no comes bien, cabrón?" (Damn it, Techno, why don't you eat well, asshole?). In contradistinction to the emotional intensity that organizes the perspective in the preceding erotic scene and close-up shots of Miguel alone in his bedroom, the realist language in this sequence transmits a pervasive sense of social apathy and collective callousness.

This lack of empathy acquires additional layers of meaning soon afterward when the dialogue reveals that Techno's chronic fatigue is attributable not simply to hunger but to anemia caused by overfrequent blood donations done without Miguel's knowledge. When Miguel learns about these surplus extractions during an informal business meeting with Gabriel, he seems more alarmed at losing out on the procurement fee than by his young friend's self-imperiling behavior. This conversation between Miguel and Gabriel provides the film's most substantial description of the commercial logistics of the blood trade, though even here the dialogue omits a full explanation of the market for this illicit plasma supply. More revealing are the terms they use to articulate the profit-making imperatives of their enterprise, which suggest how material motives thoroughly displace ethics in interpersonal relations. Gabriel explains that Johnny tested positive for hepatitis C, insinuating that Miguel may also be infected, which presents a problem because the blood must be uncontaminated in order to be effectively commoditized. In other words, the issue is not the boys' well-being or the risks of unprotected sex, but rather the threat that infectious disease poses to the profitability of their venture. As Gabriel rebukes Miguel for not exercising proper discipline in his business practices, their language reflects the dehumanizing logic that structures their economic outlook. The euphemism they use to refer to withdrawing blood, 'ordeñarse' (to get milked), makes the donors into the equivalent of "vacas" (cows). The fact that Miguel uses the milking metaphor to refer even to his own blood withdrawals does not diminish the objectifying tone in his assertion, "Son vacas, Gabriel, allí está" (They're cows, Gabriel, that's it), or in his eager acceptance of the assignment to gather fifty donors at once for a threefold escalation in the payout. Later, when Miguel and Johnny survey the full assembly of *vacas* they have amassed from various sources, the dialogue again underscores their detachment from the human dimensions of their "product" as they abstractly tally the sum of cash they are about to receive.

Complementing the characters' direct expressions of this ruthlessly reductionist reasoning, the director's cinematographic techniques also convey how the neoliberal order impinges on intersubjectivity and social relations. One illustrative sequence deals with members of Miguel and Johnny's own peer group made up of adolescent male skateboarders, who may represent a range of social classes but mostly appear to share a stratum of relative privilege. Unlike some other *vacas* in the narrative, these youths do not seem to be selling their blood out of necessity or coercion; rather, they treat the scheme as a convenient means to supplement or enhance their participation in the globalized consumption practices that define skateboarding subculture. This becomes especially apparent in a sequence that takes place at a small skate shop, where Miguel and a group of skateboarders gather after a session of getting "milked." In a long, slow-motion tracking shot that follows them through the corridors of a large urban marketplace on their way to the shop, the camera shows them moving together on their boards as a cohesive unit. Inside the store, they engage in playful roughhousing, shoving, slapping, and climbing on top of one another in ways that approach the homoerotic. However, the visual language seems designed to complicate the impression of strong, intimate bonds of male desire and friendship by showing how their relations are thoroughly mediated by commerce and consumption. Not only are the boys surrounded by prominent displays of the branded skateboarding merchandise through which they configure their shared consumer identities, but as the camera slowly pans across the room, emphasis falls on the distribution of the cash payments for the blood donations. The director intensifies the evocative conjunction of homosocial attachment and market-based exchange by filming the handover of money while the boys (and the audience) listen to the young store clerk recite a sentimental poem extolling the love that unites his generation despite the dreadful conditions of their existence.

Just as male friendship appears inextricably entwined with materialist motives and desires, so too does romance. Indeed, Johnny and Miguel's relationship is suffused with signs of economic contingency, and although it is never fully spelled out in the narrative, their shared involvement in the blood business appears to be a major factor sustaining their romantic partnership. While it would not be accurate to suggest that the film reduces their love affair to a transactional exchange, allusions to the economic wages of intimacy are woven into nearly every interaction between Miguel and Johnny. Sometimes clear references are directly expressed in the dialogue, as when Miguel makes a point of mentioning that he paid for all of Johnny's clothing. At other times, the material factors mediating their affective bond are articulated visually, such as in the montage of realist imagery contrasting Miguel's comfortable and secure domestic circumstances with Johnny's quasi-homelessness. Miguel's emotional expressions of fealty to Johnny coexist with relational dynamics verging on those between benefactor and dependent. From this perspective, the insulated, individualistic, consumer-oriented discourses of love and desire that organize Mexican romantic comedies become implicated in the darker side of emotional capitalism, unveiling how the social distribution of pathos entails a financial calculus.

The counterpoint between Miguel's intense romantic sensibilities and the cold economic logic governing his network of interpersonal relations constitutes a primary aspect of the film's critique of neoliberal cultural politics in Mexico. As Sánchez Prado argues, contemporary Mexican films articulating mostly privileged-class experiences of intimacy do not typically address current material issues affecting constituencies across a wider range of social locations, as these tend to "occupy altogether separate paradigms in the new cinema" ("Regimes" 12). In another essay, Sánchez Prado describes how recent mainstream Mexican cinema has begun to introduce more socially diverse themes and content as a way to "break its allegiance to the values of its middle-class spectators" ("Humorous" 216), but the films he describes, whether configured by commercial or auteurist aesthetics, offer a very limited scope of criticism.[17] *Te prometo* clearly aims for a critical perspective beyond the horizon of what would be possible within the aesthetic and thematic conventions of romantic comedy or related commercial genres, but it nonetheless positions itself to be read against the grain of existing structures of feeling codified by these films. More than using social realism to expose the exclusionary regime of affect and self-interested social blindness underpinning Mexican cinema's commoditized cultural discourses of love, Hernández Cordón's contrapuntal mode of critique in *Te prometo* attempts to raise questions about the detrimental consequences of neoliberalism's transformed parameters of citizenship, subjectivity, desire, and ethics. The connections drawn by the representations of the characters' market-based reasoning, consumer habits, masculine identities, and approximation to dystopic practices of social violence may be understood as critical reflections on contemporary cultural conditions shaped by the dominant material and ideological forces of neoliberal Mexico. However, while the film successfully locates convergences within the cultural network of feelings where well-defined trajectories of romance and pathos intersect with cruelty and exploitation, *Te prometo* finally moves into alignment with the prevailing parameters of modern, liberal, progressive subjecthood. I argue that this occurs via the film's incongruous preoccupation with redeeming Miguel in the eyes of the audience, categorically separating him from culturally overdetermined signifiers of malformed Mexican masculinity.

The gender malformations I am describing in this context are strongly associated with lower-class, racialized masculine subjects represented as culpable for Mexico's social epidemic of routine violence, mass killings/disappearances, drug trafficking, and other kinds of organized crime. *Te prometo*'s blood trade plotline leads to the protagonists' pivotal encounter with a menacing group of armed men who embody signs of violent Mexican masculinity made recognizable through ceaseless reiteration in mass media. Driving an oversized vehicle with ostentatious colored lighting on the wheels, these men arrive at the assembly point where the fifty *vacas* gathered together by Miguel and Johnny are waiting to give blood and receive their promised payment. The leader of the armed men, David, takes Miguel aside to inform him of the terms of their transaction, brandishing money and weapons while uttering vague threats of trouble with "los de arriba" (the higher-ups) in order to make it clear that there is no room for negotiation. David's intimidation tactics compel the blood donors to agree to be transported en masse to a separate location, which was not part of the prior arrangements. Forced to accept their powerlessness in the situation, all fifty *vacas* comply with David's commands, giving up their cell phones and loading themselves into the back of a freight truck, adding another dimension to the livestock metaphor. After rushing to fetch beverages for the group from a nearby corner store, Miguel and Johnny return to find that the truck has disappeared along with its human cargo, and they come to the immediate and devastating realization that they have unknowingly facilitated a mass abduction.

The sudden, unexplained appearance of the kidnappers and the undetermined fate of their victims form part of a narrative strategy to generate suspense, as the audience does not have the benefit of full knowledge of the depicted events and must instead approach them through the constraints of the protagonists' subjective standpoints. Furthermore, Hernández Cordón's decision to withhold contextual details of the kidnapping scenario and to make its outcome inconclusive allows the film to allude to the full gamut of terrifying possibilities without having to reproduce any scenes of spectacular violence. In this sense, the film assumes its audience will be familiar with the profusion of sensationalized media representations of "apocalyptic" brutality in Mexico and relies on this existing cultural imaginary to evoke habitual reactions, for example, fear, antipathy, revulsion, and compassion for the victims. While these factors are relevant to my reading, I suggest the most significant effect produced by the absence of a backstory and full continuation of this central narrative thread is to lay critical emphasis on the ethical subjecthood of the two male protagonists. Because the immediate motives of the crime are kept hidden, along with the precise rationale tying it to the blood trade, the only causal factors for the viewer to consider are the choices made by Miguel and Johnny, positioned against the social backdrop of neoliberal Mexico City.

This approach allows the film to articulate a social critique at two interrelated levels, one general and the other more specific. First, the broader set of issues being addressed has to do with late capitalism as a system of sociocultural practices that commoditizes everything and displaces all ethical restraints on profitability. Neoliberal Mexico's new economic imperatives entail profit-seeking through the privatization and marketization of every facet of life, so the blood trade comes to represent a concretization of the fundamental precept that life itself is a natural resource like any other to be extracted for material gain. Miguel and Johnny's involvement in this semi-illicit business venture logically coheres with the perverse norms of a socioeconomic order that generates unconstrained hyperconsumption, calculated scarcity, commercialized intersubjectivity, and objectified corporeality. That the two protagonists occupy distinct spheres in the class system carries certain implications for the film's framing of their decisions and conduct (still to be discussed), but their apparently mutual entanglement in the tendrils of the corrupt economy conveys a general indictment of neoliberalism's pervasive tendency to degrade interpersonal relations, collective values, and processes of ethical subject formation across the social spectrum.

This macro-level critique contains within it a more particular examination focused on masculinity's role in propelling the degenerative cycle set off by Mexico's neoliberal transition. In its bleak panorama of the unforgiving conditions of advanced capitalism, the film demonstrates specific critical concern with the options available to Mexican men and the factors apparently inducing them toward socially destructive trajectories. Compelled by an array of ideological and material forces and desires, men in the film are shown to be particularly susceptible to entrapment within the dichotomy of either becoming monstrous or being reduced to hapless victims. The narrative situates Miguel and Johnny at this tense intersection, showing how their active complicity with the cruel logic of exploitation pulls them, perhaps unwittingly, toward the monstrous side of the divide. The confrontation with David and the kidnappers underscores the protagonists' growing proximity to the malformed masculinities embodied by the criminals. Following the abduction, their impulsive decision to seek a futile vengeance by inflicting deadly violence on Gabriel, who falsely denies knowledge of the crime, offers a further indication of the film's preoccupation with the presumptive tendency of male subjects to be enticed by monstrous masculine agency.

Te prometo's critical articulation of a late capitalist dystopia in Mexico defined by brutal forms of masculine self-realization and ruthless practices of material acquisition shares numerous coordinates with Sayak Valencia's sociocultural theorization of "gore capitalism." Developing this concept in her eponymously titled book, Valencia offers an account of neoliberalism's close historical, political, and practical integration with diverse manifestations of violence and bloodshed typically associated with black market criminality, practices that modern economic analysis disregards by consigning them to the "realm of the irrational" (24). For her, rethinking the experience of advanced capitalism from the perspective of recent Mexican history (more specifically from the Tijuana border zone) means that one "cannot ignore the relationships between legal and illegal economies and the rampant use of violence as a mode of *necro-empowerment* and wealth accumulation" (25).[18] Valencia works to build a theoretical discourse with the critical capacity to interpret and explain the correlation between the globalized expansion of market-based rationality into state-administered systems of justice, governance, social policy, and so forth (that is, neoliberalism) and the intensification of violence as routine praxis in territories of the so-called Third World. The concept of "gore," appropriated from cinema, signifies for Valencia the materialization of a "grotesque and parodic element of the spilling of blood and guts, which as it is so absurd and unjustified, would appear to be unreal, gimmicky and artificial" (31). The routinization of such extremes in contemporary reality crystallizes neoliberalism's underlying "*episteme of violence*, its logics and practices," especially to the extent gore functions as a "tool used against bodies by the global economy" (31). Valencia's formulation "gore capitalism" refers to a deep structural correspondence between neoliberal economic principles and "ultraviolent forms of capital accumulation, practices we categorize as gore" (20). She is careful to add that these phenomena are not geographically confined within the borders of the Third World, but tend to be concentrated where multiple, overlapping factors reproduce ongoing conditions of socioeconomic insecurity, encompassing all manner of devastated communities including those situated in very close proximity to centers of global finance and commerce (70).

In these general dimensions, Valencia's interpretative description of neoliberalism as a political economy fueled by gore converges quite closely with *Te prometo*'s realist depiction of contemporary material conditions in Mexico City. Although the film does not rely on gruesome images of butchery that have become all too familiar in the news media and in certain popular cinema and television productions claiming to represent Mexico's spurious drug war, its narrative content dealing with the blood business and mass kidnapping, along with certain visual strategies I have already described, approach vectors of neoliberal cultural and economic transition coinciding with those delineated by Valencia's notion of gore capitalism. By opting to organize the film's storyline around the black market trade in blood products, Hernández Cordón not only avoids a plethora of cinematic clichés surrounding the narcotics industry[19] but also encounters a somewhat original entry point to the thematic of the hypercommercialized body, conveying its radical and inherently violent transformation into a commodity—a source of profit and object for consumption. In Valencia's work, this process constitutes a paradigmatic reconfiguration currently unfolding within the global regime of capitalism, which she defines in terms of a "transition from biopower to necropower" (222). Whereas influential political theories of modernity have focused on the body as a locus of subjugated subjectivity forming a nexus between individual rights/freedoms (habeas corpus) and the penetrative corporeal operations of state power (biopolitics), Valencia argues that the hyperconsumerist demands of contemporary capitalist societies exercise another modality of governance by rendering "the body as an increasingly valuable asset as it is reinterpreted as merchandise" (207). "Necropower" refers to the violent and macabre strategies implemented by agents of gore capitalism to push this ruling logic to its limits, particularly in the establishment of a "gore marketplace" offering an array of products and services that fully capitalize on perverse appetites for consumable bodies: "the sale of illegal drugs, violent activities, the sale of human organs, murder, trafficking of woman and children, et cetera" (225).

At the outset of *Te prometo*, Miguel and Johnny may be only fringe participants in this market, but the narrative illustrates their swift and seamless integration into more advanced economic practices of gore, positioning them on the cusp of being fully engulfed by the dystopian capitalist regime, at least until the film's final act when Miguel is redeemed. Still, throughout much of the film's fragmentary storyline, Hernández Cordón invites viewers to contemplate the male protagonists' distinctive motives, choices, and constraints in relation to Mexico's contemporary social reality, which appears to be crumbling around them. Like the film, Valencia's work takes up questions of how and why individuals are compelled to adopt gore strategies in response to the precarious conditions of neoliberalism. While her theorization encompasses a range of internal and external factors that contribute to the production of "gore subjectivity" (195), the central elements of her analysis are oriented around the axis of masculinity. The most significant objects in her study are the legions of men excluded from the mainstream side of the global economic system, condemned to poverty, redundancy, and powerlessness, who nonetheless desire forms of self-affirmation that "comply with the orders and directives of the heteropatriarchal and misogynist capitalism of the West, as it is only through this inherited discourse that they are able to feel legitimated and empowered" (108). Due to their frustrated, peripheralized position in the legal economic sphere, they turn to the illegal gore marketplace to find opportunities to embody "the masculinist figure of *the self-made man*" (40; original emphasis). In doing so, they re-create themselves as "endriagos," a term Valencia borrows from medieval Spanish literature to identify these debased, monstrous counterparts to the dominant neoliberal male: "the endriago subject—that is, *the entrepreneurs of gore capitalism*—can be understood as a new creature, an amalgam of *economic entrepreneur, political entrepreneur* and *violence specialist*" (64; original emphasis).

Just as *Te prometo*'s overall portrayal of the adverse consequences of the neoliberal project in Mexico resonates strongly with Valencia's account of gore capitalism, the film likewise shares certain aspects of her approach to masculinity as the sociocultural ground on which violent endriago subjectivities most readily take root. At the same time, however, there are some apparent differences, particularly related to the privileged-class position occupied by Miguel, which seemingly controverts the basic premise of Valencia's arguments concerning how advanced capitalism's globalized conditions of extreme socio-material inequality foster the spread of resentment and hopelessness, crucial precursors in the formulation of gore masculinities (107–109). Of course, there is nothing exceptional about bourgeois citizen-subjects who participate in illicit economic activity, either as consumers or (in)direct beneficiaries. Indeed, throughout her analysis Valencia identifies structural elements constituting a "web of almost imperceptible connections between the legal and illegal economies" (61). In the film, Miguel marshals his family's legitimate business resources to enhance his gains on the blood market when he coercively recruits a large group of *vacas* from the staff at the concert venue owned by his mother. His conduct corresponds with Valencia's understanding of how the logic of accumulative exploitation extends organically from conventional capitalism into the field of criminality, and of how subjects located on both sides of the spectrum equally embrace the same entrepreneurial ideal of masculinity. This dimension of Miguel's character is further emphasized when he engages—with some trepidation—in transactional deal-making with David as a fellow businessman and accepts—albeit under duress—a large cash payment from him for the work of assembling the *vacas* about to be abducted.

As much as Valencia stresses the definition of gore capitalism as a profound and radical convergence between the praxis of bloodshed and Western modernity's prevailing forms of economic rationality, consumer culture, gender identity, and so forth, her conceptualization maintains a decisive separation at the level of embodied masculine subjectivities, of which only certain subgroups come to be constituted as abjectly vicious endriagos. The difference is articulated primarily along racialized class lines,[20] with the caveat that the "poor no longer belong to a single social class" (134). Middle-class and elite males may participate actively as consumers, investors, facilitators, trainers, and so forth in the gore economy, but Valencia does not consider them to be endriagos because they already have access to conventional avenues of social status and gender legitimacy without relying on practices of necropower. By contrast, she understands the use of direct violence by the poor as "a response to the fear of demasculinization that haunts many men as a consequence of rising workplace precarity and their own subsequent inability to legitimately take on the role of male provider" (134). While emphasizing that the entire globalized economic system of neoliberalism is epistemically underpinned by the logic of exploitative violence and ideologies of male supremacy, Valencia associates only a specific subclass of men with the instrumentalization of gore "for personal self-affirmation and simultaneously as a means of subsistence" (135). Her analysis explicitly endeavors *not* to engage in deterministic socioeconomic reasoning that would *other* these men as "irreversible phenomena" (121), but at the same time, she invokes material poverty and precarity, accompanied by requisite feelings of frustration and alienation, as necessary elements—interfaced with an array of cultural and discursive factors, from *narcocorridos* to violent videogames—in the production of savage masculine subjectivities. What this implies, in my understanding of Valencia's thought, is that social privilege, along with a basic level of cultural-aesthetic-ethical discernment, provides a screen of immunity against the personalized, embodied effects of becoming-gore. A middle- or upper-class man (or woman) purposefully involved in unmediated gore practices can only ever be an individual exception, a mere curiosity, some kind of psychopath, or a perverse thrill seeker. Meanwhile, racialized subaltern men may be theorized as endriagos, an ontological category of singularly threatening, bestial beings who commit violent crimes for a shared set of reasons related to their maladjusted masculine gender identities.

On the surface, *Te prometo*'s portrayal of Miguel's trajectory from the outer orbit of the gore economy nearer to its occluded center of gravity, where he discovers himself to be capable of committing cold-blooded murder, might seem to offer a partial counternarrative to the myths of malformed, lower-class Mexican masculinity rearticulated in Valencia's work. Despite his privileged social position, Miguel not only absorbs himself in (semi-)illegal activity but readily accepts the prospect of deeper involvement in the criminal underworld. During a dialogue with Johnny, in which Miguel relays what he has learned from Gabriel about the workings of the blood trade controlled by narco gangs, both characters share an attitude of apathy and resignation:

> MIGUEL: ¿Qué piensas de venderle sangre a los narcos? (What do you think of selling blood to narcos?)
>
> JOHNNY: Me vale pito. (I don't give a shit.)
>
> . . . .
>
> MIGUEL: Medio pinche México es narco, ¿no? (Half of fucking Mexico are narcos, right?)
>
> JOHNNY: Como si no supiéramos. (As if we didn't know.)

Their common perspective on the dystopian capitalist context suggests how such amoral responses are not dependent on a disadvantaged social location. Ostensibly at least, the potential for masculine malformation is not represented as the exclusive property of lower-class bodies. Just as it attempts to contravene the class-restricted cultural codes of affective relationality in Mexican cinema, which typically enable privileged-class audiences to view themselves and their practices of intimacy in isolation from wider social problems, the film also appears to contest the prevailing representational regime's tendency to naturalize stereotypes of criminalized lower-class males. Beyond Miguel's own conduct, several other elements of the film could support this interpretation, such as the narrative positioning of impoverished male workers and street vendors primarily as victims of social violence rather than as potential perpetrators.

When considered in more depth, however, *Te prometo* fails to consistently hold up a critical mirror to the dominant gaze of Mexico's privileged classes, and instead returns to myths of malformed masculinity, not unlike those reiterated by Valencia, which reaffirm class- and race-based essentializations. As I have already suggested, my reading finds that despite efforts to construct a coherent critique of the paradigms of subjectivity validated by neoliberal cultural politics, the film ultimately legitimates the virtuous self-perceptions of the privileged classes and the redemptive social narratives of the neoliberal order. This is most evident in the restoration of Miguel to ethical masculine subjecthood in the film's final sequences, which I discuss in the concluding section of this chapter, but there are also additional factors that contribute to my interpretation. Specifically, signs pointing to Miguel and Johnny's distinct motivations and emotional dispositions found throughout the film help to naturalize the focus on Miguel's affect-driven reintegration into the prevailing sociocultural consensus in the finale.

Johnny's exclusion from an equivalent process is already prefigured in the film's comparatively uncomplicated construction of his relationship to crime and violence. The loosely assembled fragments of the narrative make the specific motives of both protagonists relatively opaque to the audience, but while Miguel embodies a complex and paradoxical conjunction of gore capitalist ethos and romantic sensibility reflected in the contrapuntal cinematic language, the film's portrayal of Johnny tends to frame him in more straightforwardly materialist terms. In other words, while Miguel's participation in the blood trade generates intrigue (enhanced by his somewhat playful vampire-like aesthetic), Johnny's role in the scheme can be ascribed to economic necessity. This differentiation does not cast Johnny as a hardened pragmatist in the criminal economy, but it does entail downplaying his emotional and moral interiority. This becomes most apparent in a series of sequences following the abduction. Miguel and Johnny angrily confront Gabriel outside Mexico's City's Churubusco Studios, where he apparently works as a part-time actor, but he deflects their accusations and explains that he must go into the studio to make phone calls to find out what happened. In one of the film's most visually remarkable shots, the camera captures the two protagonists from behind, creating a shared perspective as they stealthily follow Gabriel into the studio, stalking him like prey.[21] The shot fades to a blank screen just as they begin their brutal attack, though the sound conveys the violence and the sequence closes with a brief image of Gabriel lying dead in a pool of his own blood. Even if the murder is carried out in terms of a diluted notion of justified vengeance, the composition seems designed to convey the dystopian culmination of the characters' transformation into predatory killers. However, the film also emphasizes that this shift does not occur uniformly, as Miguel's reaction to the events diverges significantly from that of Johnny. The next sequence contains a long shot of the two boys on a pedestrian bridge where we see Miguel in the midst of an emotional breakdown, while Johnny consoles him and appears relatively dispassionate by comparison (fig. 4.5).

This divergence continues into the film's denouement, which reemphasizes Miguel's romantic sensibility and leaves Johnny conspicuously absent from the reconnected circuit of empathy. Following the killing

Figure 4.5. A long shot of the protagonists on a pedestrian overpass shows Miguel evidently undergoing a crisis while Johnny consoles him (*Te prometo anarquía*).

of Gabriel, the two protagonists spend the night in a hotel room, where Johnny introduces Miguel to the practice of inhaling glue, ostensibly to help him forget about his problems temporarily. As the solvents take effect, Johnny initiates physical play that transitions into seduction. Just as in an earlier erotic scene, the camera lingers on Miguel's face to highlight his sensual experience, but here the rationale for this framing acquires a distinct significance within the diegesis. Miguel's genuine passion creates a greater contrast with Johnny's materialist mindset because the audience has prior knowledge of the imminent betrayal. Just before the sex scene, Johnny is seen having a private telephone conversation with his mother, in which he convinces her to abandon her job as a domestic and leave the city with him. Later, while Miguel lies asleep under the effects of the neurotoxic chemicals he inhaled, Johnny takes all the money received from the kidnappers and leaves the hotel on his own. Although there is potential pathos in Johnny's desire to liberate his mother from servitude, this dissipates soon after they take refuge with a relative in a remote rural location. Appearing restless and bored, Johnny complains to his mother about not having a suitable spot to practice skateboarding, and when he suggests that he might call Miguel to pick him up, his mother strikes him in anger. With that, Johnny grabs the remaining money, leaving only a few notes for his mother, and begins skating along the highway alone.

The film's final narrative inscriptions of Johnny's character make it relatively clear that his experience has not fundamentally altered his social/ethical parameters of masculine selfhood. Even if his actions may be partly construed as resistant to Mexico's exploitative system of class relations, the film denies the possibility of Johnny being transformed by his encounter with the radical vicissitudes of gore capitalism. While his fate at the end of the story is inconclusive, Johnny has arguably become even more vulnerable to violence because of the events that transpired before his escape, and so his apparent desire to return to his former circumstances implies a regressive, self-imposed subjugation and a blind resignation to the limited options offered to male subjects by the prevailing order. This coheres with Valencia's definition of marginalized endriagos in terms of their "obedience to hegemonic, capitalist, and heteropatriarchal masculinity," which renders them "unable to question the assumptions of the system as it is imposed on them in the name of power, economics, and masculinity" (256). One might argue that avoiding a direct representation of any predetermined dystopian outcomes serves at least to defer Johnny's reinsertion into the victim/victimizer dichotomy, creating space for undetermined future alternatives. Indeed, this could be inferred from a dialogue between Miguel and his mother after she learns about the abduction. As she drives to the airport, she explains to her son that he must flee to safety with a friend of the family in Texas, and when Miguel asks what will happen to Johnny, she replies, as though speaking for the filmmaker, "No sé" (I don't know).

Perhaps it would be easier to accept this as an invitation to contemplate Johnny's unknown transformative trajectory were the film not so explicitly invested in foregrounding a redemptive transformation for Miguel. Both characters seemed to be caught in the same neoliberal web of material and discursive forces governing their embodiments of male subjecthood, and while Johnny appears to remain trapped at the conclusion, the film explicitly highlights Miguel's capacity to begin extricating himself. In Valencia's terms, he discovers his latent potential to "deconstruct and reinvent masculinity . . . outside the limits set by heteropatriarchy and violence as a tool for male self-affirmation" (274). What is most incongruous about the film's approach to illustrating this change is that Miguel's path to redemption leads back into the affective sphere of romance, where the dominant cultural imaginary and cinematic language suppress recognition of the harsh realities of neoliberalism. In his exile, Miguel works as a menial laborer in a botanical garden and engages in glue-sniffing, approximating the earlier portrayal of Johnny, but he avoids succumbing to total debasement by strengthening his romantic imagination—something Johnny was unable to do. Still protected by privileged-class connections, and now insulated from the worst excesses of gore capitalism, Miguel creatively transforms his surroundings into a utopian space, a *locus amoenus* inspired by idealized daydreams of lost love. By the film's logic, this does not imply a retreat from reality but rather a maturation of his sentimental outlook. After his close call with monstrosity, Miguel reenters empathetic alignment with modern structures of feeling by embracing love as a universal, liberatory, ethical, and aesthetic ideal. The requisite omission of Johnny from this process implicitly reinstalls myths of malformed lower-class masculinity.

IV. Reasserting Masculine Hierarchies

My arguments concerning Hernández Cordón's attempts to question pervasive structures of affect in Mexican cinema lead to a twofold conclusion positing that the universalized and naturalized treatment of same-sex desire contributes to *Te prometo*'s critical intervention while also becoming a source of the film's major contradictions. On the first side, *Te prometo* provides a timely response to the restricted modes of diversification that have been observed in established genre films and in Mexican cinema production at large. The increasing incorporation of sexual difference into a broader range of films addressed to affluent audiences across orientations, as described by Venkatesh and Smith, has generated little or no critique of the consequences of neoliberalism for lower-class and racialized constituencies. Indeed, mainstream films articulating narratives of LGBTQ equality, acceptance, and integration have, in some cases, been among the most conformist in constructing new affective arrangements and cultural identities in terms that unquestioningly endorse the neoliberal state's uneven distributions of economic, political, and social power. From this perspective, *Te prometo* may be seen as issuing a provocative challenge to current gay-themed cinema in Mexico, questioning the conditions of access to the normative, privileged sphere of emotional affinities. The film sheds critical light on the adaptive capacity of neoliberal cultural politics to incorporate new and diverse objects of compassion while maintaining the same narrow, closed criteria of subjecthood and citizenship. By the same token, seemingly expanded horizons in other kinds of Mexican films, such as the recent crop of romantic comedies Sánchez Prado approvingly describes as "more directly engaged with Mexico's social inequalities" (204), are similarly called into question by *Te prometo*'s contrapuntal grammar. The strategies Hernández Cordón develops in his film illustrate how ostensibly inclusive cultural discourses of intimacy and romance may continue to deny, distort, and erase the correspondence between systemic social inequity and neoliberalism's prevailing cultural codes of subjective desire. Without sustained critical reflection on this correlation, Mexican cinema's more diverse array of romantic narratives simply reaffirm existing codifications of bourgeois sensibility by making empathy and love appear as forces capable of overcoming material, social, and ideological barriers—a logic consistent with the erasure of meaningful histories of intersected class-, race-, and gender-based oppressions.

While my analysis concedes that *Te prometo* is partly successful in exposing the inherent tensions of emotional capitalism normally suppressed and disavowed in Mexican cinema of the neoliberal era, the converse side of my twofold interpretation argues that Hernández Cordón ultimately reburies this tension in order to provide the audience a narrative resolution imbued with redemptive pathos. As I have already suggested, unsettling the audience's initial alignment with Miguel's romantic, homoerotic perspective constitutes a central element of the film's critical strategy, as this is what enables the language of counterpoint to create a relational dialogue between the prevalent sentimental register of Mexican cinema and the realist evocations of the country's ongoing crisis of social violence. However, after following the main characters through their complicit self-involvement in a nightmarish ordeal, which they survive but their relationship does not, the film's closing trajectory takes a disappointing turn.

The final act reestablishes the spectator's implied affective identification with Miguel by allowing him to transcend the ethical quandaries arising from the socio-material dimensions of his desire for Johnny, and to redeem himself through pure emotional experience. Paradoxically, part of what facilitates this drive toward redemptive closure are elements of the same modern regime of liberal, sexually progressive but class-restricted emotional affinities that, as I have argued, were thrown into question by the film's contrapuntal language. The closing sequences reconnect the viewer to a shared circuit of feelings via a highly aestheticized romantic reverie in which Miguel, now alone and relocated to Texas, imagines an affectionate reunion with Johnny. Miguel's impossible fantasy, which revels in a universal ideal of love removed from the context of neoliberal Mexico's stratified and fragmented social structure, amounts to what might be called, using Smith's terms, a performative change. Leaving the audience with this desirable imaginary alternative is a deliberate choice by Hernández Cordón to de-emphasize the social realism that was contrastively in play throughout much of the film, and in this sense the move is more self-conscious than the changes performed by the mainstream representations of sexual diversity in the Mexican films described by Smith, but it nonetheless partakes in the same affect-driven liberal consensus, which is gay-positive but strictly class-bounded. Achieving this effect requires excluding Johnny's lower-class male subjectivity from the sphere of empathy, even as his image is instrumentally deployed in the service of Miguel's moral redemption. Social differentiations rooted in Mexico's racialized class system are removed from critical consideration as Miguel appears naturally and unquestionably capable of embodying emancipatory, humanizing expressions of love, while Johnny is at best neglected as an unknowable alterity, and at worst condemned as a malformed, disposable object.

Afterword

By some measures, Mexican cinema has arguably never been more viable as a sphere of cultural production than it is today, two decades into the new millennium.[1] The annual statistical reports published by IMCINE (Instituto Mexicano de Cinematografía) attest to the continuing overall expansion of the domestic market for Mexican films, especially mainstream comedies and light melodramas but also arthouse and independent cinema. Established auteur directors produce strikingly original projects on a regular basis, often to widespread acclaim. And although the pipeline for emergent filmmakers remains relatively narrow, a steady stream of new Mexican talent exhibits impressive work at international festivals year after year. Yet, in spite of healthy outward appearances, there are significant underlying weaknesses in the contemporary field of Mexican cinema, including its persistent inability to break with its inherited repertoire of cultural myths correlating to the transhistorical category of malformed masculinity. To be sure, there exist prominent examples of films offering substantive challenges to prevailing rearticulations of fictive essentialisms that have historically defined subordinate maleness in cinema.[2] But these remain the exceptions in a domain of cultural representation reliant as ever on formulaic images of racialized, lower-class Mexican men designed to signify regressive, dangerous, defective models of subjectivity. As I have argued throughout this book, various iterations of these representational formulas have pervaded Mexican cinema since at least the mid-twentieth century.

The persistence of cinematic signifying practices that symbolically conflate brown male bodies with submasculinity, racial inferiority, intellectual deficiency, improvidence, criminality, cultural backwardness, and an array of other markers of social abjection reflects long-standing categorial binaries that are structurally reproduced in every dimension of Mexico's hegemonic racialized and class-defined regime of gender politics. In this sense, the problem of malformed masculinity far exceeds the cultural and historical scope of Mexican cinema, as this classification is ultimately founded upon the logic of the modern/colonial distinction between the human and the subhuman, the origins of which trace to sixteenth-century imperialism, early formations of global capitalism, and the cognitive consolidation of a Eurocentric worldview.[3] As long as the overarching order of cultural politics in Mexico continues to be organized by this dominant rationale, representational possibilities in all fields will be constrained by existing parameters of humanness. The goal of contesting these constraints partly informed transnational currents of radical political filmmaking in the 1960s, '70s, and '80s, which are sometimes gathered under the umbrella term Third Cinema, but these films typically lacked intersectional perspectives that could target racialized gender formations for critique. They also had only limited influence in Mexico and generally failed to extend their appeal beyond audiences who already identified with leftist revolutionary and Third World nationalist ideologies. In the sphere of contemporary commercial and arthouse filmmaking, the potential to challenge the logic of coloniality is inherently restricted, since the film industry as a whole remains closely aligned with the cultural agendas of the neoliberal state. This makes it all the more significant that at least some filmmakers working in Mexico today have managed to articulate considerable critiques of racial and class-based categories of gender discrimination without fully alienating the mostly affluent spectators who comprise their main audiences.

While it would be wrongheaded to study mainstream or independent filmmaking in present-day Mexico with the expectation of encountering radical efforts to unsettle deep structures of modern Western knowledge and power that have remained embedded in dominant cultural imaginaries for centuries, one can certainly take these structural dimensions of oppression into consideration when analyzing observable processes of transformation at the level of aesthetic practice. Indeed, not doing so risks rendering invisible cinema's reproductions of the colonial logic of modern power, allowing legitimations of exploitation to pass unnoticed and fictive categories of difference to be reintegrated into normative patterns of representation. For this reason, my discussions have focused on how recent films respond—or fail to respond—to rearticulated myths of Mexican masculinity that carry forward racializing assemblages from the past and reconfigure them in terms of the current neoliberal order. The prevailing language of cinema in Mexico has undoubtedly been altered over the past several decades, and many recent films share a preoccupation with representing "new" masculinities no longer defined by traditional macho expressions of virility and homosocial affinity. These transformations have facilitated the circulation of a range of distinct sociocultural possibilities for masculine self-realization by turning away from compulsory heterosexuality, homophobia, misogyny, and other antiquated dimensions of conventional machismo. It must be acknowledged, however, that these progressive trajectories of representational change tend to be aligned with the cultural, political, and socioeconomic itineraries of the neoliberal state. The highly successful commercial film *Hazlo como hombre* (Do It Like a Man) (2017, dir. Nicolás López) illustrates this alignment quite clearly, as it shows how the same generic formulas that made the romantic comedy into the paradigmatic expression of neoliberal culture in Mexico are fully compatible with mainstream narratives of gay liberation and masculine self-reformation. Much like *Y tu mamá también*, López's film reterritorializes traditional macho archetypes in order to portray middle- and upper-class metropolitan men engaged in redemptive processes of self-discovery and self-improvement, overcoming detrimental cultural legacies of gender oppression and toxic masculinity, thereby bringing themselves up to date with modern liberal-progressive standards of manhood. The self-enclosed worlds of social privilege represented in these kinds of films may avoid making any specific assertions about lower-class, racialized masculinity, but the cultural logic they endorse is altogether consistent with the reproduction of predominant stereotypes of malformed men frustrated by their own inability to fulfill the promises of self-realization offered by neoliberal capitalism. The success of *Hazlo como hombre* can therefore be understood in terms of the same structural mechanisms driving the proliferation of cultural imagery that attributes the rise of social violence to criminal gangs made up of savage men originating from impoverished rural parts of the country.

This critique certainly does not amount to suggesting that more "positive" representations of lower-class men would help to resolve the problem. Taking such an approach from within the currently prevailing climate of cinema production is far more likely to lead to outcomes akin to *Como caído del cielo* (2019, dir. José Bojórquez), Netflix's disastrous attempt to resurrect the ghost of Pedro Infante. What is instructive about this film, however, is that it openly and explicitly exhibits certain paradigmatic patterns of rearticulating mythic Mexican masculinity that more often unfold at the subtextual level. In brief, the film's plotline begins with the immortal spirit of Infante (Omar Chaparro), who is trapped in limbo due to his serial womanizing and other notorious macho behaviors. Granted a final opportunity to atone for the masculine sins that defined him as an onscreen persona as much as in reality, Infante returns to life in present-day Mexico by inhabiting the body of Pedro Guadalupe (also played by Chaparro). Whereas films like *Y tu mamá también* and *Hazlo como hombre* tacitly encourage viewers to infer that the male protagonists' initial shortcomings are somehow inherited from outmoded Golden Age icons of machismo and mexicanidad, in *Como caído del cielo* the legacy of Pedro Infante is fully enunciated as the cultural patrimony of contemporary masculine subjects such as Pedro Guadalupe, who not only earns a living by performing as an Infante impersonator but also follows in his idol's footsteps by pursuing extramarital relations. The challenge that Infante must complete to attain absolution involves occupying Pedro Guadalupe's body and his domestic circumstances in order to undergo a moral transformation by proving to his wife, Raquel (Ana Claudia Talancón), that he is capable of romantic commitment and sexual fidelity. In other words, the narrative structure uses the same blueprint of masculine self-reformation that organizes so many other recent Mexican films, but makes a much more overt claim in attributing contemporary men's gender defects to their supposedly natural affinity with obsolete models of traditional machismo.

As I have already suggested, the more important distinction is that, unlike the vast majority of recent Mexican romantic comedies set in affluent metropolitan neighborhoods, *Como caído del cielo* offers a portrait of what are supposed to be working-class characters living in the provincial border city of Tijuana. Part of the premise of the narrative is that the couple find themselves deeply in debt because Pedro Guadalupe lay in a coma on life support in a private hospital for three months (before the arrival of Infante's spirit triggers his miraculous recovery). Raquel works as a police officer on traffic patrol and her insurance does not cover the accumulated medical bills. In addition to the financial stress, their marriage is already fractured because of Pedro's disloyal past. Putting aside the film's total disinterest in representing the actual living conditions of impoverished working families in places like Tijuana, what is most puzzling—and yet simultaneously revealing—about the depiction of Pedro and Raquel as an illustration of lower-class gender relations is that the resolution to their conflict lies with a corrective process of masculine self-improvement involving Pedro's adoption of transnational, cosmopolitan values reflected in neoliberal cultural politics. It is clearly not sufficient to transpose positive aspects of Infante's mythic machismo—for example, his strong work ethic, physical toughness, charm, and musicality—from the nationalist past to the neoliberal present. Instead, to achieve the desirable change in his gender identity, Pedro must learn to enact a model of masculinity that brings him into alignment with the demands and expectations of globalized culture. This chiefly involves didactic dialogues with Jenny Infante, Pedro Infante's granddaughter, a young, independent, transnational Mexican woman studying for a law degree in nearby San Diego, who openly questions the nationalist cultural legacy of Golden Age films starring her ancestor. With only the slightest touch of irony, the film shows Pedro absorbed in critical lessons on patriarchy at an academic seminar delivered by a European feminist intellectual. Equipped with this knowledge of progressive gender politics, Pedro is better prepared to turn away from his conventional macho posturing and embrace "new" masculinity. Curiously, however, the film's convoluted climax reintroduces further allusions to the past when Pedro must endure a brutal boxing match reminiscent of the classic melodrama *Pepe el Toro*. In a final twist, the narrative undercuts conventional male heroism by refusing to culminate with Pedro's athletic triumph. Instead, he winds up being kidnapped by criminals and then rescued by Raquel and her motorcycling squad of women police officers.

Obviously, this light romantic comedy, which trafficks in confused forms of nostalgia, does not pretend to issue a serious or coherent call for lower-class men to abandon their supposed fixation on old-fashioned Mexican machismo and begin studying the precepts of white, Western feminism. Yet I find it quite illustrative that the iconic figure of Pedro Infante is invoked as both the ultimate source of Mexican men's failed masculinity and as the instigating basis for a necessary transformation articulated in terms that correspond with current cinema's dominant logic of representation. Within this paradigm, one of the few feasible ways to create a positive image of lower-class Mexican masculinity is to present it as a project involving an evolutionary transition that naturally begins from archaic machismo and inevitably culminates with a reformed model of male gender identity legitimated by association with globalized circuits of cultural capital. The image retains its Mexican specificity chiefly as a problematic point of origin that must be effectively disavowed to ensure a properly redemptive self-realization of the neoliberal masculine ideal. As should be clear by the arguments I have elaborated throughout my book, I find this conjunctive pattern of evolution and disavowal to be thoroughly distortive as it places the racially dichotomizing function of mestizo nationalism's gender ideology under complete erasure. Choosing from the plethora of confirmatory examples of this in *Como caído del cielo*, I would mention only how the film reinscribes the duality of mestizaje by allowing Infante's enabling whiteness to be seamlessly overlain by that of Chaparro, meanwhile projecting disabling brownness and malformation onto the portrayal of two inarticulate, cartoonish thugs whose clumsy attempts to subdue Pedro serve only to generate some minor narrative tension. That the filmmakers evidently expect their audience to accept this predetermined arrangement of racialized bodies and gender identities as natural underscores their decision to elide the history of social hierarchies consolidated by mestizo nationalism and reproduced by the neoliberal state. Criticism that ignores this decision implicitly condones its repercussions.

I have been arguing that these kinds of elisions and distortions arise from an underlying transhistorical system of classification that seeks to separate human subjects from those classified as less than human on the basis of invented categories of distinction, particularly racialized gender difference. The logic of coloniality that organizes this system can manifest itself in cinematic representations regardless of the particular aesthetic language filmmakers may employ. Hence, my position is distinct from that taken by recent critics who argue that distortive images of Mexico's underclasses are being proliferated mostly by a recent stylistic trend toward realism in cinema. In a discussion exploring the problematic contours of this movement, Emmelhainz, Sánchez Prado, and Zavala call out the "constante y repetitivo agotamiento del paradigma del cine real, que se conforma con la exhibición de las vidas de los mexicanos de clases bajas como centro de su política" (continuous and repetitive exhaustion of the paradigm of realist cinema, which is content to exhibit the lives of lower-class Mexicans as the center of its politics) ("Nunca estuvo ahí"). Their analysis focuses on the recent film *Ya no estoy aquí* (I'm Not Here Anymore) (2019, dir. Fernando Farías), but also addresses a broader selection of recent realist cinema dealing with poverty, migration, crime, and violence produced in Mexico and other parts of Latin America, including *La jaula de oro* (The Golden Dream) (2013, dir. Diego Quemada-Diez) and *Chicuarotes* (2019, dir. Gael García Bernal). They regard these films as casting an objectifying, *othering* gaze on the subaltern from a self-referential standpoint intended to confirm the progressive social values, aesthetic sensibilities, and cultural whiteness of progressive middle- and upper-class audiences, who are ultimately most interested in concealing the political and economic processes that create and sustain massive wealth disparities and violent forms of state oppression. Realism promotes this kind of representational relationship because it preserves the privilege of understanding for the viewer, reducing the onscreen characters to mostly silent, unthinking figures who are compelled to act by their circumstances and not by their own sense of agency: "nunca se reconocen como sujetos políticos o participantes conscientes dentro su propia realidad" (they never recognize themselves as political subjects or conscious participants in their own reality).

To describe this subalternizing gaze primarily as the consequence of a relatively recent turn toward cinematic realism is to decontextualize both of these phenomena, bypassing not only correlated processes equally governed by the neoliberal politics of representation but also downplaying historical connections to earlier stages of Mexican filmmaking practice, which laid the foundations for the contemporary imagery of dehumanization. It is certainly true that we are now faced with a more diverse and productive cinema industry in Mexico that appears increasingly to thrive on denigrating depictions of the poor and the marginalized, but in my view, film studies can do more to explain present configurations of film production in relation to the prevailing politico-economic structures by critically situating them together in broad networks of power with deep historical roots. Representational patterns that assign subhuman status to certain categories of Mexicans are as old as Mexican cinema itself, and in fact even much older than that. I would suggest that a film such as *Ya no estoy aquí* could be productively approached in terms of how it uses new aesthetic strategies to rearticulate existing categorial exclusions and hierarchies. By engaging with the underlying logic that enables recent films to activate—and contest—the long-standing cultural mythology of malformed masculinity, I have attempted to demonstrate what this kind of approach entails.

In closing, I would emphasize that the critique of gendered cultural politics proposed by *Mexico Unmanned* does not posit that the symbolic violence generated by rearticulated myths of malformed masculinity is necessarily more sinister than that of conventional stereotypes of women and sexual minorities structured in misogyny and homophobia, but it does suggest that the former has been largely invisible and too readily justified in contemporary cinema and criticism. The lack of critical engagement with the overdetermined meanings of masculinity attached to racialized male bodies illustrates the extent to which their malformation has been naturalized and dehistoricized, to the point where it can be unquestioningly accepted even by astute readers of Mexican film. My aim in writing this book has not been to displace discussions oriented by feminism and queer politics in Mexican film studies, but rather to open relational dialogues at the intersection of multiple oppressions. Creative and critical projects with emancipatory goals must avoid jockeying for privileged status in the neoliberal order of cultural politics and rather learn to recognize their mutual enmeshment in a larger network of power. This book has sought to contribute to this goal by challenging the cultural logic that gives coherence to oppressive categorial conceptions of masculinity in Mexico.

Notes

Preface

1. The quotation comes from Julia Tuñón's extensive interviews with Fernández, published in *En su propio espejo*. The fuller quote is as follows: "Yo soñaba en un cine, todavía sigo soñando en un cine distinto, ¿no?, pero mexicano puro. Yo ahorita tengo un afán enorme de mexicanizar a los mexicanos, nos estamos apochando" (I dreamed and keep dreaming of a distinct cinema, but pure Mexican. Now I have a great desire to Mexicanize the Mexicans, we're becoming *pochos*) (72).

2. The critical account of Golden Age cinema's popular reception I am outlining here is well known in Mexican cultural studies. In broad terms, this view regards the establishment of a domestic film industry capable of reaching a mass spectatorship as a cornerstone of the postrevolutionary state's efforts to construct an imagined community, a shared national identity that would serve to legitimate the ruling political order. Cultural critic Carlos Monsiváis, a leading proponent of this perspective, has put forward highly influential arguments about the role of filmmaking as a didactic ideological mediator between the modern nation-state and the masses, including the claim that "No se acudió al cine a soñar: se fue a aprender. A través de los estilos de los artistas o de los géneros de moda, el público se fue reconociendo y transformando, se apaciguó y se resignó y se encumbró secretamente" ([Mexican audiences] did not go to the cinema to dream, but to learn. Through the performers' styles or fashionable genres, the public recognized and transformed itself, becoming secretly pacified, resigned, and self-satisfied) ("Notas" 446). Monsiváis repeatedly refers to the enduring appeal of Pedro Infante's performances of machismo as evidence of mass identification with myths of Mexicanness ("Notas" 446, 454). These ideas informed the work of media theorists such as Nestor García Canclini (see *Hybrid Cultures*) and Jesús Martín Barbero (see *Communication, Culture, and Hegemony*), who analyzed popular culture in Mexico and Latin America as a contested intermediary space between hegemonic conceptions of national (or transnational) modernity and heterogenous

local traditions. The cultural studies paradigm of reading Mexican national cinema as a medium encoded with dominant discourses prescribing normative modes of subject-formation and social identity remains widely accepted, even as more recent film researchers (such as those mentioned in this preface) have developed a range of new strategies for interrogating the spectator-screen relationship beyond the interpellative effects of state-sponsored mass media apparatuses. For an overview of these issues, see Tierney *Emilio Fernández* (17–45), as well as Noble (70–94).

3. Gender-based theories of reception have been particularly influential in the development of critical challenges to the supposedly determinative function of the masculinist gaze in Golden Age cinema. In addition to the mentioned works by de la Mora, Noble, Tierney, and Dever, also see Ana M. López "Celluloid Tears" and "Tears and Desire," and Joanne Hershfield *Mexican Cinema/Mexican Woman, 1940–50*. Existing criticism has offered insightful analyses of how national cinema's prevailing models of masculinity shifted in relation to sociohistorical transformations in spectatorship (e.g., Noble), but there has not been any study that seriously questions the presumptive alliance between ordinary Mexican men and the patriarchal nation-state.

4. I discuss some of Ramos's and Paz's specific contributions to the essentialist conceptualization of Mexican masculinity in the introduction.

5. Federico Navarrete, drawing upon the work of philosopher Bolívar Echeverría, explains that "whiteness" as a sign of cultural or civilizational superiority (*blanquitud*) is not equivalent to "white skin" or other physical features (*blancura*) in the racist configuration of Mexico's assimilative projects of westernization (10). Similarly, I am suggesting that the racializing inferiority of "brownness" may be signified independently of skin color and physiognomy in visual mediums such as cinema.

6. Of course, Mexican national cinema of the 1930s, '40s, and '50s also contains many examples of principal protagonists who meet this description of malformed masculinity. The comedy films of Cantinflas (Mario Moreno) typically center on variants of the "pelado" figure, a recognizable stereotype of the racialized urban subproletariat embodying socially undesirable gender traits. With his characteristic style of linguistic prevarication, Cantinflas lightly mocks aspects of Mexican society while avoiding any truly subversive satire. By reproducing the stereotype of the inveterate idler who breeds chaos and confusion, these films tend to confirm rather than challenge predetermined conceptions of the lower-class mestizo's natural inferiority. Something similar could be said of Tin Tan (Germán Valdés) and his portrayals of the criminalized "pachuco" figure. Comedies starring Cantinflas and Tin Tan have rarely, if ever, been studied in terms of how their representations of lower-class males might map onto the larger symbolic matrix of Mexican masculinities, but I would argue that they provide fairly stable and coherent expressions of several modalities of gender malformation outlined here and developed more extensively in later chapters.

7. In *The Cage of Melancholy*, Bartra is more directly concerned with critiquing intellectual discourses that construct authoritative definitions of the national character, but his analysis is also attentive to film and other forms of popular culture that promulgate these myths of nationhood on a massive scale. Partly coinciding with Monsiváis and others who regard Golden Age cinema as an ideological means of consolidating Mexican identity, Bartra writes that "the mass media recycle the popular stereotypes fabricated by the hegemonic culture so that, in their turn, they exercise an influence on the lower classes' way of life" (127). An important distinction, however, is that Monsiváis describes film spectators of the 1930s through the 1950s experiencing genuine forms of recognition that generated "an alliance between the film industry and the audiences of the faithful, between films and communities that saw themselves represented there" ("Mexican Cinema" 142), whereas Bartra emphasizes that "the popular components of the national culture are mere fragments (often very distorted ones) of what is in reality the everyday life of the social class whence they are taken" (127).

Introduction

1. See María Lugones "Heterosexualism and the Colonial/Modern Gender System."

2. Another author who examines the deterioration of Mexican filmmaking during the same approximate period is Jorge Ayala Blanco in *La condición del cine mexicano*, though, unlike Ramírez Berg, he offers little attention to gender.

3. See Sayak Valencia *Gore Capitalism* and Sergio González Rodríguez *Huesos en el desierto* and *The Femicide Machine*.

4. In defining the analytic category of malformed masculinity, I am certainly aware of the influential schema developed by theorist Raewyn (R. W.) Connell, which attempts to identify the major relational patterns of masculine practice constructed by Western modernity (76–81). Connell's well-known framework of hegemonic, subordinate, complicit, and marginalized masculinities is a frequent starting point for critical reflections on male gendering arrangements in Latin American literary, cinema, and cultural studies (e.g., Vinodh Venkatesh *The Body as Capital*, and the anthologies *Lo masculino en evidencia*, edited by José Toro-Alfonso, and *Modern Argentine Masculinities*, edited by Carolina Rocha). Without disputing the overall merit of Connell's ongoing scholarly project to establish transcultural parameters for the analysis of men and masculinities situated within global capitalism, I find her contributions to have limited applicability to my approach in this book. To explain Mexican cinema's role in upholding the logical dichotomy between positive and negative masculinities in terms of malformation, I ground my analysis in an understanding of the specific historical systems of sociocultural classification that shaped Mexico's postrevolutionary gender order. This includes

consideration of the particular effects of the state's assimilative modernizing project of mestizaje, which conceals racializing modalities of social differentiation within gendered affirmations of shared cultural identity. Furthermore, I suggest that the rationale separating citizen-subjects with fully formed modern gender identities from those whose deficient maleness (or femaleness) marks them as intrinsically malformed—a rationale that continues to organize the cultural politics of neoliberal Mexico—expresses what Lugones calls the "coloniality of gender" ("Toward" 743). Connell's original accounts of the interdependency of race- and class-based oppressions in the development of globalized patterns of masculine practice grant some limited attention to the history of Western imperialism (185–203), but in my view she overlooks the continuing consequences of the racialized human/subhuman divide that remains strongly embedded in modern/ colonial gender politics. In more recent writings, Connell herself recognizes the need for an epistemological shift in gender theory that would decenter European knowledge paradigms in dialogue with perspectives formulated from "the global South" ("Rethinking Gender" 534). However, Connell's brief and underinformed engagement with Lugones—which includes deriding her as a "schematic" thinker while grudgingly acknowledging the correctness of her position—indicates to me that she has not yet fully digested the meaning of coloniality as it has been theorized in relation to racialized gender hierarchies ("Rethinking Gender" 532).

5. See discussions of national cinema's prostitution melodramas in Hershfield and de la Mora. In literary studies, see Debra Castillo *Easy Women* and Alicia Gaspar de Alba *[Un]framing the "Bad Woman."*

6. On the modern colonial gender system, see Lugones "Heterosexualism and the Colonial/Modern Gender System" and "Toward a Decolonial Feminism." Studies of the coloniality of gender in Mexican contexts include Sylvia Marcos *Taken from the Lips* and Rosalva Aída Hernández Castillo "Feminismos Poscoloniales: Reflexiones desde el sur del Río Bravo."

7. The transition to postnational filmmaking in Mexico described by Sánchez Prado and others begins in earnest in the late 1980s though it does not find full expression until at least a decade later, with the romantic (tragi-)comedy *Sexo, pudor y lágrimas* (1999, dir. Antonio Serrano) serving as a particularly notable landmark. A more comprehensive study of masculinity in Mexican cinema would need to consider films produced before and during this transition to thoroughly investigate how myths of national identity were maintained. However, there is a general consensus in current Mexican film scholarship (cited throughout this book) that no lasting departures from the nationalist ideological agenda occurred in cinema until those that accompanied the neoliberal restructuring of the film industry and the corresponding apparatus of cultural politics. While there are many gaps in the existing research on cinema from the end of the Golden Age to the 1980s, I have found no strong reasons to doubt that most representations of masculinity throughout these decades typically maintained the same core cultural

logic regardless of thematic, stylistic, or genre variations. This claim is supported in particular by Ramírez Berg's *Cinema of Solitude*, which pays close attention to gendered imagery not only in well-known films by "prestige" directors, such as Felipe Cazals, Luis Alcoriza, and Arturo Ripstein, but also in popular genres neglected by scholarship, such as sex comedies and boxing films produced during the decades preceding the neoliberal era. He finds that representations of Mexican masculinity throughout this period remained stubbornly consistent with the patriarchal ethos formulated in the 1930s and '40s (100, 136).

8. This line is taken from the speech by López Obrador (better known as AMLO) outlining his government's "Plan Nacional de Desarrollo 2019–2024," which was delivered in March 2019, only a few months after his inauguration as president. More than a year later, in July 2020 and in the midst of a global pandemic, AMLO made his first official trip abroad, traveling to Washington, D.C., to celebrate the official commencement of the new North American free trade agreement with President Donald Trump (Lubold and Montes). For a brief critical discussion of the continuity of neoliberalism in Mexico under AMLO, see Rafael Rojas "La cuarta invención del liberalismo oficial." Also see Rafael Lemus "AMLO en el laberinto neoliberal." Other valuable resources chiefly concerned with the economic dimensions of neoliberalism in Mexico include María Eugenia Romero Sotelo *Los orígenes del neoliberalismo en México* and James Cypher and Raúl Delgado Wise *Mexico's Economic Dilemma*. Mexican author Fernando Escalante Gonzalbo's *Historia mínima del neoliberalismo* offers a critical historical overview but contains little discussion of the Mexican context. Just coming to press as corrections to this book are being completed, Lemus's *Breve historia de nuestro neoliberalismo* promises to offer an up-to-date critical analysis of cultural and politics in neoliberal Mexico that includes the initial stages of AMLO's presidency.

9. On Mexican literature in the neoliberal era, see Sánchez Prado *Strategic Occidentalism* and Miguel López-Lozano *Utopian Dreams, Apocalyptic Nightmares*. On popular music, see the anthology *Decentering the Nation*, edited by Jesús A. Ramos-Kittrell. On transformations in the sphere of visual art and other forms of "high culture," see Emmelhainz *La tiranía del sentido común*.

10. The phrase "structure of feeling" was coined by British cultural theorist Raymond Williams in 1954 to refer to dominant frameworks of thought and sensibility that may exist only as shared trajectories rather than as complete ideological, aesthetic, or epistemic paradigms (Buchanan 454–455). The term has become widely used in recent theorizations of affect. See, for example, the anthology *Structures of Feeling*, edited by Devika Sharma and Frederik Tygstrup. For a discussion of neoliberal affect with some relevance to Latin American contexts, see Dierdra Reber *Coming to Our Senses*.

11. In addition to the works discussed here, also see Pilar Calveiro *Resistir al neoliberalismo* and Gareth Williams *The Mexican Exception*.

12. All translations from Spanish in the text are mine.

13. For an excellent set of reflections on pluriversality as a conceptual underpinning for ongoing practices of resistance and reexistence by indigenous and Afro-descendent communities throughout Latin America in the face of neoliberal devastation, see Arturo Escobar *Pluriversal Politics*.

14. Emmelhainz uses the concept of calculated sovereignty as developed by anthropologist Aihwa Ong in *Neoliberalism as Exception*.

15. Valencia takes the term *endriago* from the medieval romance *Amadís de Gaula* (Amadis of Gaul). She explains that in its original context, the endriago is "a monster, a cross between a man, a hydra and a dragon. It is noted for its large stature, agility and beastliness; it is one of the enemies that Amadis of Gaul is forced to confront" (132). I address specific problems with Valencia's conceptualization of the *endriago* as the paradigmatic masculine agent of gore capitalism in chapter 4.

16. There exists a significant body of research that seeks to approach the phenomenon of drug-related crime in Mexico through the lens of masculinity. See, for example, the multidisciplinary anthology *Masculinidad, crimen organizado, y violencia*, edited by Luis Gerardo Ayala Real and Luis Fernando Rodríguez Lanuza. While some of these studies offer sound analysis, others are grounded in distortive categories and concepts consistent with official discourses that erase the role of the neoliberal state in sustaining oppressive social conditions marked by extreme violence. This is particularly true when researchers engaging in ethnographic fieldwork and other empirical methods use the depoliticized concept of "narcocultura" to classify the social and cultural practices of impoverished young men in rural Mexico, taking them out of context and identifying them with the nihilistic glorification of death while ignoring systemic patterns of violence arising from the aggressive expansion of transnational capitalism. For example, see the work of Guillermo Núñez Noriega and Claudia Esthela Espinoza Cid published in the volume mentioned above (19–42) and elsewhere, for example, "El narcotráfico como dispositivo de poder sexo-genérico: Crimen organizado, masculinidad y teoría queer." Scholarship in cultural studies also participates in fetishizing the phenomenon of so-called narcocultura in ways that perpetuate myths of masculine malformation. See, for example, *Narcocultura de norte a sur*, a volume of essays edited by Ainhoa Mejías Vásquez.

17. For a detailed discussion of the processes that have contributed to the internationalization of Mexican star directors, see the chapters on Mexico in Tierney *New Transnationalisms in Contemporary Latin American Cinemas* (33–121). Also see chapter 4 of Sánchez Prado *Screening Neoliberalism*.

18. Women's experiences of exclusion from nonacting creative roles in the history of Mexican filmmaking have been well documented, as have some of the major contributions by female directors, writers, and editors to the tradition of national cinema. In particular, see Dever's discussions of Matilde Landeta and Marcela Fernández Violante in *Celluloid Nationalism and Other Melodramas*. Of

course, acknowledging the structural impediments to women's participation as filmmakers goes only part of the way toward addressing the range of prohibitive barriers that have made the field most accessible to members of Mexico's socially privileged minority. Still, considering this book's interest in the sphere of contemporary independent Mexican cinema, it should be mentioned that there exists today a growing cohort of young female film directors, many of them nonwhite, whose work merits wider critical engagement, for example, Daniela Alatorre, Natalia Almada, Lila Aviles, Tatiana Huezo, Luna Marán, Ale_andra Marquez, Yulene Olaizola, María Sojob, and Dinazar Urbina, to name only a handful.

19. Also see the anthology *Modern Masculinities in Mexico*, edited by Víctor M. Macías-González and Anne Rubenstein.

20. See Doris Sommer *Foundational Fictions*.

21. Gayle Rubin's influential essay, "The Traffic in Women," is referenced by Irwin (112), de la Mora (93), and Domínguez-Ruvalcaba (83) in each of their accounts of the homosocial dimensions of Mexican masculinity. Eve Kosofsky Sedgwick's *Between Men* is another important source cited in their discussions of this issue (Irwin xxvii; de la Mora 92–93).

22. Connell's work, especially *Masculinities*, is referenced directly by Irwin (231n15) and Domínguez-Ruvalcaba (100), as well as indirectly by de la Mora (30) by way of Deniz Kandiyoti. Gutmann's well-known ethnographic study, *The Meanings of Macho*, is also mentioned by all three authors.

23. These ideas from Butler's *Bodies That Matter* are cited by Irwin (xxi) and Domínguez-Ruvalcaba (85).

24. Also see the discussions of Ramos and Paz in Irwin (xxii–xxvii, 187–196), Domínguez-Ruvalcaba (97–111), and de la Mora (16, 108, 120–128).

25. Bartra's *The Cage of Melancholy* remains one of the most original and compelling critiques of Mexico's nationalist myths of cultural identity, focusing on the expression of mestizaje in terms of stalled metamorphosis. Also see the work of Claudio Lomnitz in *Exits from the Labyrinth* and *Deep Mexico, Silent Mexico*. More recent studies dealing with mestizaje as national ideology include Joshua Lund *The Mestizo State*, Pedro Ángel Palou *El fracaso del mestizo*, and David S. Dalton *Mestizo Modernity*. In some cases, the question of machismo is broached in these authors' discussions, though it is generally not understood as a fundamental component of the state's racializing ideology.

26. One must not discount the prominence of feminine symbols in the construction of mestizo nationalism, the most obvious being the Virgin of Guadalupe. However, even though the Virgin was unsurpassable as the most recognized and widely accepted figure of Mexican unity and shared tradition, the imaginary ideal of the modern mestizo citizen-subject described by nationalist intellectuals was almost invariably male. This is unsurprising for several reasons, including the fact that the intellectuals in question were exclusively male, and that suffrage was not granted to women until 1953. Even by 1950, Paz could barely bring himself to

conceptualize a place for female subjectivity in his opus on the Mexican national character, infamously defining woman as the "Enigma" (89).

27. One could compile a lengthy list of the major ideologues who contributed to formulating these agendas, but the most prominent nationalist thinkers I have in mind here are Andrés Molina Enríquez, Manuel Gamio, and José Vasconcelos.

28. Quijano's theorizing provided significant stimulus for the researchers associated with the modernity/(de)decoloniality group. See Walter Mignolo and Catherine Walsh *On Decolonialtiy*.

29. I am aware of existing accounts of audience responses to Golden Age films, but these are generally gathered from a retrospective standpoint, making them unreliable as indications of the original spectators' reactions. My position is that there is no way to know with certainty what lower-class men and women thought of these films when they were first shown.

Chapter 1

1. In addition to the research cited below dealing with *Y tu mamá también* in relation to Mexican national cinema, also see Vek Lewis "When 'Macho' Bodies Fail: Spectacles of Corporeality and the Limits of the Homosocial/sexual in Mexican Cinema." Discussions of Cuarón's engagement with global filmmaking currents include Hester Baer and Ryan Long "Transnational Cinema and the Mexican State in Alfonso Cuarón's *Y tu mamá también*" and Alberto Ribas "'El pinche acentito ese': Deseo transatlántico y exotismo satírico en el cine mexicano del cambio de milenio."

2. The idea is so frequently repeated that it hardly registers as a conscious claim for many authors. Among the most prominent proponents of this view is Carlos Monsiváis. See *Pedro Infante: Las leyes del querer* and "¡Quien fuera Pedro Infante!"

3. María Novaro's *Sin dejar huella* (2000) and Juan Carlos de Llaca's *Por la libre* (2000) are two examples of Mexican road movies that preceded *Y tu mamá también*. Another instance of the genre, released several years after Cuarón's film, is Gerardo Tort's *Viaje redondo* (2009).

4. It is worth noting that *El gavilán pollero* involves a road trip of sorts, in which the two protagonists, José and Luis, make their way (mostly on horseback) from the countryside into Mexico City, where they sojourn for a short time. However, their trip does not result in any major transformation. After a dramatic split, instigated by Antonia, they both leave the city only to be reunited in a rural setting where they ultimately reseal their friendship by dumping Antonia into a shallow creek.

5. This reading is frequently suggested or implied in critical responses to the film, for example, Caitlin Benson-Allot "Sex versus the Small Screen."

6. Vasconcelos is often characterized as an antipositivist thinker because he expressed doubts about some of the reigning scientific paradigms of his day, particularly rejecting theories of racial miscegenation, though he did not fully reject all positivist models of knowledge-making. For him, the truth, as such, exists only as transcendental, metaphysical ideal, and he argues against relying solely on modern science and pure reason to achieve it. For a discussion of Vasconcelos's antipositivist views on science and objective truth, see Dalton (31–58).

7. As the first film released by Cha Cha Chá, the production company cofounded by Alfonso Cuarón, Alejandro González Iñárritu, and Guillermo del Toro in partnership with Universal Pictures, *Rudo y Cursi*'s commercial success helped to consolidate transformations in the Mexican film industry that had been taking place since the 1990s (Tierney *New Transnationalisms* 41).

8. By contrast, these traditional sporting ideals are clearly articulated in many conventional soccer movies, including those mentioned in Sánchez Prado's analysis (*Screening* 194), such as the *Goal!* trilogy (2005, dir. Danny Cannon; 2007, dir. Jaume Collet-Serra; 2009, dir. Andrew Monahan), and *Bend It Like Beckham* (2002, dir. Gurinder Chadha). Historian J. A. Mangan discusses how the modern ethical code of sport derives from the imperial ideology of nineteenth-century Britain. Athletic games were understood as a civilizing mechanism that would inculcate colonial subjects with British virtues such as "promptitude . . . honor, cooperation and unselfishness" (41).

9. A relevant example that comes to mind in this context is the mutually supportive collaboration between some of the most celebrated men in the Mexican cinema industry with the backing of a major Hollywood studio.

Chapter 2

1. Lahr-Vivaz follows Julianne Burton-Carvajal's conceptualization of melodrama as a "metagenre . . . that subsumes and hybridizes with other generic categories" (191).

2. See, for example, Cypher and Delgado Wise (8).

3. A rather less subtle example of a similar defamiliarization technique is used in one of the film's final shots, which shows a group of men ringing an oversized church bell. On the audio track, we hear the ambient rainfall, but the tolling of the bell is absent, even as the images depict actions that we expect to produce the corresponding sound.

4. See, for example, Alison Griffiths *Wondrous Difference*.

5. For further discussion of this scene, see Ordóñez "Carlos Reygadas's *Batalla en el cielo*" (86–87).

6. Here, Eisenman cites Jean Jacques Rousseau's *Discourse on Inequality*, which establishes a comparison between horses and men in terms of their desire

for liberty: "An unbroken horse erects his mane, paws the ground and starts back impetuously at the sight of the bridle; while one which is properly trained suffers patiently even whip and spur: so savage man will not bend his neck to the yoke to which civilized man submits without a murmur, but prefers the most turbulent state of liberty to the most peaceful slavery" (Rousseau qtd. in Eisenman 147).

7. Berger explains that one of the most predominant categories of subject matter for oil paintings produced between 1500 and 1900 includes "objects that can be bought and owned" (85). Canvases often represented items possessed by the artist or, more often, his patron: livestock and other animals, land, buildings, women, jewelry, and so forth (85). For Berger, these tendencies in art are part of the inauguration of a new way of seeing the world, which was governed by attitudes concerning private property and the free exchange of goods.

8. Another European oil painting that appears in this sequence, Vermeer's *Girl with a Red Hat* (1665–67), may be similarly understood to reflect intersecting histories of modern gender categories, commodity fetishism, and colonial power relations. It is beyond the scope of this chapter to fully explore such an interpretation, but suggestive connections between Vermeer's paintings and imperial formations of global capitalism are offered by historian Timothy Brook in *Vermeer's Hat*.

9. I acknowledge that Reygadas himself denies any significant connection between himself and Juan, but I take this to mean that he does not want the film to be understood as a straightforward self-portrait. My argument does not rest on the notion of a biographical correspondence between Juan and Reygadas. Rather, I am suggesting that the director's decision to include his own children, dogs, and house in the fictive representation of Juan's life supports the idea that filmic perspectives are inextricably entangled with social positionalities and unequal configurations of power.

Chapter 3

1. One obvious incongruity in Hind's critique—though hardly unique to her—is that the definitive division between *capital* and *provincia* already implies centering Mexico City while lumping diverse regions and cultures together into the same category by virtue of their supposed contrast with a metropolitan standard—itself a very problematic homogenization.

2. Of course, the crime-related anxieties of privileged-class Mexicans are also reflected in films with urban settings. See Sánchez Prado "*Amores Perros*: Exotic Violence and Neoliberal Fear." While Sánchez Prado pays little attention to race and gender in this analysis of Alejandro González Iñárritu's debut film, what he describes as the class-based fears organizing the director's depiction of crime and violence in Mexico City has some correlation with my understanding

of how malformed masculinities reappear as logically necessary elements for neoliberal cultural politics.

3. These include the films *Un dulce olor a muerte* (A Sweet Scent of Death) (1998, dir. Gabriel Retes), *Sin dejar huella* (Leaving No Trace) (2000, dir. María Novaro), and *El crimen del padre Amaro* (The Crime of Padre Amaro) (2000, dir. Carlos Carrera).

4. The four films Sánchez Prado discusses in this brief text are *El infierno* (Hell) (2010, dir. Luis Estrada), *Salvando al soldado Pérez* (Saving Private Pérez) (2011, dir. Beto Gómez), *Miss Bala* (2011, dir. Gerardo Naranjo), and *Heli*.

5. Sánchez Prado's argument also underscores how these recent films displace the popular mythology of the narco as a heroic bandit celebrated in Mexican B movies such as *La banda del carro rojo* (The Red Car Gang) (1978, dir. Rubén Galindo).

6. There are, of course, significant differences between the critical positions of these two authors. For example, in terms of what *Heli* can achieve as a politico-ethical discourse on Third World violence directed mainly at global elite audiences, Llamas-Rodríguez is much more confident about the film's possibilities of "forcing an orientation" (35), whereas Podalsky remains circumspect regarding these kinds of claims (251). As I explain in detail below, what these authors (and others) share is an understanding of the filmmaker's primary intention to transmit sensory perceptions of violent Mexican realities.

7. See, for example, Sophia A. McClennen "From the Aesthetics of Hunger to the Cosmetics of Hunger in Brazilian Cinema: Meirelles' *City of God*."

8. See Valencia (99–111).

9. See Iddo Dickmann *The Little Crystalline Seed* and Marcus Snow *Into the Abyss: A Study of the Mise en Abyme*.

10. Zavala writes, "El supuesto debilitamiento del Estado con el advenimiento del neoliberalismo se registra principalmente a un nivel discursivo que invisibiliza las estrategias de control disciplinario por medio de las cuales el Estado se ha relacionado con el crimen organizado a partir de la segunda mitad del siglo XX. . . . Pero el narcotráfico no es un factor causal del discurso securitario sino un objeto de ese discurso. En otras palabras, lo que comúnmente llamamos 'narco' es la invención de una política estatal que responde a intereses geopolíticos específicos" (The supposed weakening of the State with the advent of neoliberalism is registered principally at a discursive level that hides the strategies of disciplinary control through which the State has related to organized crime from the middle of the twentieth century. . . . Yet drug trafficking is not the causal factor of the securitarian discourse but rather its object. In other words, what we commonly call the 'narco' is the invention of a state policy that responds to specific geopolitical interests) (62).

11. Valencia's influential theorizations on this theme may appear to be relevant to *Heli*, but as I show in my discussion of *Te prometo anarquía* in chapter

4, I find her work to be rather problematic, especially when it takes up questions of masculinity.

12. See Zavala (30), and Paley *Guerra neoliberal* (33).

13. To observe the circulation of misleading or incomplete narratives about drug-related violence in the Mexican media is not to impugn the news industry as a whole. Many dedicated journalists and reporters routinely put their own lives at risk to gather and distribute information on organized crime and its ties to state and corporate entities. Oswaldo Zavala begins his book *Los cárteles no existen* with a brief discussion of his own work as a news reporter with *El diario de Juárez* in northern Mexico, and he cites the influential mentorship of Ignacio Alvarado and Julián Cardona (8).

14. In the same interview with Solórzano, Escalante makes reference to prevalent narrativizations of crime and violence in U.S. television programs in relation to his earlier film, *Los bastardos* (2008):

[Solórzano]: ¿Crees que la televisión ha jugado un papel en el clima actual de rechazo hacia los inmigrantes mexicanos? (Do you think that television has played a role in the current climate of rejection toward Mexican immigrants?)

[Escalante]: Así es como llegó a la presidencia Donald Trump, ¿no? A través de explotar el miedo. También tienes ahí programas como *Cops*—que es el que sale en la película—, que trata de arrestos solo a negros y mexicanos. (Isn't that how Donald Trump became president? By exploiting fear. You also have programs there like *Cops*—which appears in the film—that deal only with arrests of blacks and Mexicans.) (Solórzano "Retratos" 31).

15. See Valencia (237–244).

16. See Sánchez Prado *Screening Neoliberalism* (62–64), and my discussion of this text in chapter 4.

17. Heli states to the census taker that he has completed *secundaria* (junior high school) but not *preparatoria* (high school). In 2012, the Mexican government implemented a policy to make *preparatoria* compulsory and free for all students in the national public education system. However, few rural communities in Mexico have the capacity to provide this level of schooling locally and sending children to attend classes in a different town or city would be an extra expense most rural families could not afford.

18. Podalsky makes a similar point in "The Aesthetics of Detachment," though for reasons that are distinct from mine.

Chapter 4

1. A variation on the common acronym for categories of sexual and gender diversity, LGBTTTI denotes Lesbian, Gay, Bisexual, Transsexual, Transgender, Transvestite, Intersex (Espinosa). For more information on the declaration, see

"Declaratoria CDMX, Ciudad Amigable LGBTTTI" on the government of Mexico City's official website for the Consejo para prevenir y eliminar discriminación de la Ciudad de México (Council to Prevent and Eliminate Discrimination from Mexico City, COPRED).

2. *Te prometo anarquía* is fairly unique in the particulars of its narrative content, but its combination of homoeroticism with elements of film noir, along with an aesthetics of realism focused on marginalized youths, elicits comparisons to films by Gus Van Sant, especially *Mala Noche* (1985) and *My Own Private Idaho* (1991), but also aspects of *Elephant* (2003) and *Paranoid Park* (2007). A relevant early forerunner in Mexican cinema is Jaime Humberto Hermosillo's violent yet lighthearted crime story, *Matinée* (1977). Other thematically related films include *Plata quemada* (Burnt Money) (2000, dir. Marcelo Piñeyro) and *La virgen de los sicarios* (Our Lady of the Assassins) (2000, dir. Barbet Schroeder).

3. Carlos Bonfil commends the film in his review in *La Jornada*, and Fernanda Solórzano, writing in *Letras Libres*, calls it the best Mexican film of 2015 ("Las ciudades invisibles"). According to the *Anuario estadístico de cine mexicano 2016* published by IMCINE, *Te prometo anarquía* was shown on thirty screens to slightly more than fourteen thousand viewers (95). The 2017 edition of the same publication shows that the film was among the most viewed on FilminLatino, an online video streaming service in Mexico (225). The film's many festival prizes include the Horizons Award at the San Sebastián International Film Festival and the FIPRESCI Prize at the Rio de Janeiro International Film Festival. An early version of film also received the Primera Mirada award for completion funds at the Panama International Film Festival. In Mexico, the film won the Guerrero Award for best feature-length picture at the Morelia International Film Festival. It was also nominated for an Ariel award for best direction.

4. In his more recent film, *Cómprame un revolver* (Buy Me a Gun) (2018), Hernández Cordón shifts toward a more fully dystopic view of Mexico, imagining a near-future scenario in which the country is overrun by brutal narco gangs who target women and children for violent exploitation.

5. For reasons that become clear in this discussion, the term "mass market cinema" must be contextualized by some understanding of the current contours of film production and exhibition in Mexico. The phrase is somewhat of a misnomer in the sense that mainstream commercial films are not marketed to a mass audience, but rather to a relatively narrow, economically privileged sector of society that has the means to pay for tickets that are priced out of all proportion to the incomes of the majority of Mexicans.

6. See, for example, Solórzano "Las ciudades invisibles" and Laplante "Love under Siege."

7. To be clear, Smith recognizes the sphere of transnational festival cinema as an important sector of Mexican film production, and he even posits it as one of "two futures" available for Mexican queer filmmaking (139). Although Smith

favors the alternate sphere of more commercially oriented media productions with mainstream domestic appeal as offering "the greatest potential for achieving a 'social contribution' to a modern Mexico that can still be dangerously conservative" (139), he still gives thoughtful appraisals of queer films with challenging formal approaches that seek legitimation on the global festival circuit. For example, see his chapter on the films of Julián Hernández, as well as in his insightful interview with the filmmaker, in *Queer Mexico*.

8. Examples of recent work within this critical framework in Latin American studies include the essays anthologized in *El lenguaje de las emociones*, edited by Sánchez Prado and Mabel Moraña, as well as Podalsky *The Politics of Affect and Emotion in Contemporary Latin American Cinema*.

9. Although the director dissociates his work from the global queer/LGBT cinema movement (Pickard), *Te prometo* was recognized with a jury award at the Queer Porto international film festival. Of course, the director's objections do not preclude the possibility of approaching the film through a queer studies hermeneutic. As David William Foster explains in *Queer Issues in Contemporary Latin American Cinema*, "any cultural text—hence, any film—can be read from a queer perspective," by which he refers to a critical practice of subverting heteronormative politics that may underpin a given articulation of culture (ix). In another sense, he takes queer cinema studies to mean addressing how films "promote principles of an anti-heterosexist stance," particularly in terms of challenging homophobia as an "instrument of heteronormativity" (x). My analysis of *Te prometo*'s indirect approach to thematizing queerness takes into account Foster's broad definition of what comprises a threat to homophobia: "These phenomena are beliefs, behavior, or specific acts in themselves, or they are reflexes of them, signs that are read as indicative of a belief, behavior, or specific act such that the signs themselves do not constitute a challenge to heteronormativity in any direct sense but are taken to point to something that is" (x–xi).

10. Smith uses a rather loose definition of "mainstream" in this context. Obviously, it does not imply levels of distribution, exhibition, and popular appeal proximate to those of Hollywood films (Smith 92–93). Indeed, *Todo el mundo tiene a alguien menos yo* is a film that registers as thoroughly *un*-mainstream in its complete absence from regular commercial circulation on DVD or any existing streaming service (as of 2020).

11. For a brief overview of intellectual debates on this topic, see Beasley-Murray (xi–xv).

12. Here, Smith draws upon Beasley-Murray's work in *Posthegemony*.

13. Smith explains that the film *Carmín tropical* constitutes somewhat of an "outlier" since it depicts regional expressions of sexual diversity in Oaxaca, but he also remarks that its representation of *provincia* is rather sanitized (105–106). For Smith, the avoidance of "social realism" is suggestive of a refusal to conform to First-World audience expectations of poverty and misery, supporting his idea that the film is designed to appeal primarily to middle-class Mexican spectators (105).

While I do not wholly disagree, I would add that there is likely equal interest among both domestic and international metropolitan audiences in consuming idyllic, sensual, exoticizing, touristic images of Oaxacan beaches, towns, and other settings of the kind seen in *Carmín tropical*. This transnational appeal is perhaps even more apparent due to the film's close conformity to the widely established commercial genre conventions of a noir thriller/murder mystery.

14. Smith's comments on the film's appeal to "foreign cinephiles" quoted above may be contextualized by his broader claims about how audiences outside Mexico "prefer to believe that the more explicit the evidence of poverty and violence is in a Mexican film, the truer that film is to the experience of that country" (105). Other critics have made similar criticisms of *Te prometo*. For example, see Andrea Penman-Lomeli, "Consumption of Culture as Politics."

15. This, despite that the lyrics of the song contain lines sung in English, repeating his name, for example, "Johnny doesn't like the sun." In a sense, the music conveys a feeling *about* Johnny, but not *belonging* to him.

16. See Néstor García Canclini *Consumers and Citizens* (18–19).

17. For example, he describes the romantic comedy *Cásase quien pueda* (2014) as "a veiled critique of the audience's preference of the rich" because of the "unflattering rendering of the protagonist's superficiality and upper-class behavior" (211).

18. The term "necroempowerment" derives from Achilles Mbembe's conceptualization of "necropolitics," itself a critical reworking of Foucauldian "biopolitics." Throughout her book, Valencia often engages with these and other contemporary political and philosophical discourses on violence and power. All italicizations in my quotations from Valecia's text occur in the original.

19. In an interview (Vargas), Hernández Cordón explains that he originally conceived the film as a drug trafficking story but decided to change it after reading media coverage of a clandestine market for human blood.

20. Valencia specifies that the endriagos are "mostly non-white and non-First World subjects" (125), and she also ties the category to "the campesino (peasant) classes" (105).

21. The shot is somewhat reminiscent of horror film genre conventions, in which killers/monsters stalk their victims. The on-location shooting at Churubusco Studios and the fade to a green screen at the end of the sequence add to the metafilmic dimension of these images. However, I do not think these few reflexive gestures add up to a fully self-aware mode of representation in the film, especially at the intersection of class, masculinity, and violence.

Afterword

1. The first version of this afterword was written in early March 2020, just before the devastation of the global COVID-19 pandemic began to unfold. At the

time of completing the final changes to the text, in May 2021, signs of the fragility and unevenness of recovery are everywhere apparent, and it feels too soon to make any conclusive claims about the lasting effects of the past year's events. My remarks in the afterword's opening paragraph, which have not been substantially revised, originally aimed to suggest that more critical attention to the prevailing set of representational codes related to malformed masculine identities might serve to temper the positive outlook for Mexican cinema that seemed to be predominant at that moment. According to IMCINE's statistical yearbook for 2019, the total annual audience for Mexican cinema reached its largest size ever with 35.2 million tickets sold (9). Domestic production also rose to the record-breaking level of 216 feature-length films, 101 of which were screened in theaters (9). A majority of these Mexican films were funded solely with private investment (9). Now, in the enduring aftermath of catastrophe, while movie theaters across Mexico are still actively limiting attendance, the outlook for the national film industry cannot be the same as it was. The first reliable quantification of the pandemic's impact appears in the statistical report compiled by CANACINE (Cámara Nacional de la Industria Cinematográfica), which shows a 94 percent reduction in attendance for the period of March to December 2020, as compared with same period in the previous year. The IMCINE yearbook for 2020, which would be the most comprehensive source of quantitative data, is not yet available to be consulted. The ideas expressed throughout the rest of the afterword remain valid, even if filmmaking in Mexico currently faces a most uncertain future.

    2. In addition to the works of cinema discussed in the preceding chapters, filmmakers such as Fernando Eimbcke and Julián Hernández have also contributed to contesting symbolic frameworks surrounding masculine identities in Mexico.

    3. See Lugones "Heterosexualism" and "The Coloniality of Gender." For an illuminating set of responses to Lugones's thought, see *Speaking Face to Face*, edited by Pedro DiPietro, Jennifer McWeeny, and Shireen Roshanravan.

Works Cited

Acevedo-Muñoz, Ernesto. "Sex, Class, and Mexico in Alfonso Cuarón's *Y tu mamá también*." *Film & History*, vol. 34, no. 1, 2004, pp. 39–48.
Albarrán-Torres, César. "Spectacles of Death: Body Horror, Affect and Visual Culture in the Mexican Narco Wars." *Senses of Cinema*, no. 84, Sept. 2017.
Ayala Blanco, Jorge. *La condición del cine mexicano*. Editorial Posada, 1986.
Ayala Real, Luis Gerardo, and Luis Fernando Rodríguez Lanuza, editors. *Masculinidad, crimen organizado y violencia*. Colofón, 2016.
Baer, Hester, and Ryan Long. "Transnational Cinema and the Mexican State in Alfonso Cuarón's *Y tu mamá también*." *South Central Review*, vol. 21, no. 3, 2004, pp. 150–168.
Bartra, Roger. *The Cage of Melancholy: Identity and Metamorphosis in the Mexican Character*. Translated by Christopher J. Hall, Rutgers University Press, 1992.
Beasley-Murray, Jon. *Posthegemony: Political Theory and Latin America*. University of Minnesota Press, 2010.
Benson-Allott, Caitlin. "Sex versus the Small Screen: Home Video Censorship and Alfonso Cuarón's *Y tu mamá tambien*." *Jump Cut*, vol. 51, 2009.
Berger, John. *Ways of Seeing*. Penguin, 1973.
Bonfil, Carlos. "Foro de la Cineteca." *La Jornada*, 15 July 2016. www.jornada.com.mx/2016/07/15/opinion/a09o1esp.
Bordun, Troy. *Genre Trouble and Extreme Cinema: Film Theory at the Fringes of Contemporary Art Cinema*. Palgrave Macmillan, 2017.
Brook, Timothy. *Vermeer's Hat: The Seventeenth Century and the Dawn of the Global World*. Bloomsbury, 2007.
Buchanan, Ian. *A Dictionary of Critical Theory*. Oxford University Press, 2018.
Burton-Carvajal, Julianne. "Mexican Melodramas of Patriarchy: Specificity of a Transcultural Form." *Framing Latin American Cinema: Contemporary Critical Perspectives*, edited by Anne Marie Stock, University of Minnesota Press, 1997, pp. 186–234.
Butler, Judith. *Bodies That Matter: On the Discursive Limits of "Sex."* Routledge, 1993.

Calveiro, Pilar. *Resistir al neoliberalismo: Comunidades y autonomías*. Siglo XXI, 2019.
CANACINE. "Resultados Definitivos 2020." canacine.org.mx/wp-content/uploads/2021/02/Resultados-definitivos-2020.pdf.
Castillo, Debra A. *Easy Women: Sex and Gender in Modern Mexican Fiction*. University of Minnesota Press, 1998.
Connell, Raewyn. "Rethinking Gender from the South." *Feminist Studies*, vol. 40, no. 3, 2014, pp. 518–539
Connell, R. W. *Masculinities*. University of California Press, 2005.
COPRED. "Declaratoria CDMX Ciudad Amigable LGBTTTI." *Consejo para Prevenir y Eliminar la Discriminación de la CDMX*, 2015, copred.cdmx.gob.mx/acciones-estrategicas/declaratoria-cdmx-ciudad-amigable-lgbttti.
Couret, Nilo. "Enduring Art Cinema." *The Routledge Companion to Latin American Cinema*, edited by Marvin D'Lugo et al., Routledge, 2018, pp. 233–248.
Cypher, James M., and Raúl Delgado Wise. *Mexico's Economic Dilemma: The Developmental Failure of Neoliberalism*. Rowman & Littlefield, 2011.
Dalton, David S. *Mestizo Modernity: Race, Technology, and the Body in Post-Revolutionary Mexico*. University Press of Florida, 2018.
Dargis, Manohla. "Ducking Rain and Competition at Cannes." *New York Times*, 16 May 2013. www.nytimes.com/2013/05/17/movies/at-cannes-film-festival-ducking-rain-and-competition.html.
de la Mora, Sergio. *Cinemachismo: Masculinities and Sexuality in Mexican Film*. University of Texas Press, 2006.
de Luca, Tiago. "Natural Views: Animals, Contingency and Death in Carlos Reygadas's Japón and Lisandro Alsonso's Los Muertos." *Slow Cinema*, edited by Tiago de Luca and Nuno Barradas Jorge, Edinburgh University Press, 2015, pp. 219–230.
———. *Realism of the Senses in World Cinema: The Experience of Physical Reality*. I.B. Tauris, 2014.
Dever, Susan. *Celluloid Nationalism and Other Melodramas: From Post-Revolutionary Mexico to Fin de Siglo Mexamérica*. SUNY Press, 2003.
Dickmann, Iddo. *The Little Crystalline Seed: The Ontological Significance of Mise en Abyme in Post-Heideggerian Thought*. SUNY Press, 2019.
DiPietro, Pedro, Jennifer McWeeny, and Shireen Roshanravan, editors. *Speaking Face to Face: The Visionary Philosophy of María Lugones*. SUNY Press, 2019.
Domínguez-Ruvalcaba, Héctor. *Modernity and the Nation in Mexican Representations of Masculinity: From Sensuality to Bloodshed*. Palgrave Macmillan, 2007.
Eisenman, Stephen. *Cry of Nature: Art and the Making of Animal Rights*. Reaktion Books, 2013.
Emmelhainz, Irmgard. *La tiranía del sentido común: La reconversión neoliberal de México*. Paradiso Editores, 2016.

Emmelhainz, Irmgard, Ignacio M. Sánchez Prado, and Oswaldo Zavala. "Nunca estuvo ahí." *Revista Común*, 4 Sept. 2020, www.revistacomun.com/blog/nunca-estuvo-ahi.

Escalante Gonzalbo, Fernando. *Historia mínima del neoliberalismo*. El Colegio de Mexico, 2015.

Escobar, Arturo. *Pluriversal Politics: The Real and the Possible*. Translated by David Frye, Duke University Press, 2020.

Espinosa, Ana. "¿Qué significa LGBTTTI?" *El Universal*, 22 June 2018, www.eluniversal.com.mx/articulo/mundo/2017/06/24/que-significa-lgbttti.

EZLN (Ejército zapatista de liberación nacional). *EZLN: Documentos y comunicados*. Era, 1994.

———. "The People the Color of the Earth." *The Zapatista Reader*, edited by Tom Hayden, Thunder's Mouth Press/Nation Books, 2002, pp. 106–114.

Foster, David William. *Queer Issues in Contemporary Latin American Cinema*. University of Texas Press, 2003.

Gago, Verónica. *Neoliberalism from Below: Popular Pragmatics and Baroque Economies*. Translated by Liz Mason-Deese, Duke University Press, 2017.

Garba, Jaime. "Te Prometo Anarquía by Julio Hernández Cordón at the 13th FICM." *Festival Internacional del Cine en Morelia*, 29 Oct. 2015, moreliafilmfest.com/en/te-prometo-anarquia-de-julio-hernandez-cordon-en-el-13ficm/.

García Canclini, Néstor. *Consumers and Citizens: Globalization and Multicultural Conflicts*. Translated by George Yúdice, University of Minnesota Press, 2003.

———. *Hybrid Cultures: Strategies for Entering and Leaving Modernity*. Translated by Christopher L. Chiappari, University of Minnesota Press, 1995.

Gaspar de Alba, Alicia. *[Un]Framing the "Bad Woman": Sor Juana, Malinche, Coyolxauhqui, and Other Rebels with a Cause*. University of Texas Press, 2014.

González de Canales, Julia. "Marginalidad cinematográfica: Centroamérica y la obra de Julio Hernández Cordón." *Istmo*, no. 32, 2016, istmo.denison.edu/n32/articulos/15.html.

González Rodríguez, Sergio. *The Femicide Machine*. Semiotext(e), 2012.

———. *Huesos en el desierto*. Anagrama, 2002.

Griffiths, Alison. *Wondrous Difference: Cinema, Anthropology, and Turn-of-the-Century Visual Culture*. Columbia University Press, 2002

Gutmann, Matthew C. *The Meanings of Macho: Being a Man in Mexico City*. University of California Press, 1996.

Hale, Mike. "Film: 'Silent Light.'" *New York Times*, 19 Sept. 2008. www.nytimes.com/2008/09/21/movies/21weekfilm.html.

Harvey, David. *A Brief History of Neoliberalism*. Oxford University Press, 2005.

Hernández Castillo, Rosalva Aída. "Feminismos Poscoloniales: Reflexiones desde el sur del Río Bravo." *Descolonizando el feminismo: Teorías y prácticas desde* los márgenes, edited by Rosalva Aída Hernández Castillo and Liliana Suárez-Navaz, Ediciones Cátedra, 2011.

Hershfield, Joanne. *Mexican Cinema / Mexican Woman, 1940–1950*. University of Arizona Press, 1996.

Hind, Emily. "Provincia in Recent Mexican Cinema, 1989–2004." *Discourse*, vol. 26, no. 1, 2004, pp. 26–45.

IMCINE. *Anuario estadístico de cine mexicano 2016*. anuariocinemx.imcine.gob.mx/Assets/anuarios/2016.pdf.

———. *Anuario estadístico de cine mexicano 2017*. anuariocinemx.imcine.gob.mx/Assets/anuarios/2017.pdf.

———. *Anuario estadístico de cine mexicano 2019*. anuariocinemx.imcine.gob.mx/Assets/anuarios/2019.pdf.

Irwin, Robert McKee. *Mexican Masculinities*. University of Minnesota Press, 2003.

Lahr-Vivaz, Elena. *Mexican Melodrama: Film and Nation from the Golden Age to the New Wave*. University of Arizona Press, 2016.

Laplante, Jaie. "Love under Siege: Julio Hernandez Cordon's *I Promise You Anarchy* (*Te Prometo Anarquia*)." *Miami Film Festival*, 10 Aug. 2015, miamifilmfestival.com/2015/08/love-siege/.

Lemus, Rafael. "AMLO en el laberinto neoliberal." *New York Times*, 8 July 2019. www.nytimes.com/es/2019/07/08/espanol/opinion/lopez-obrador-neoliberalismo.html.

———. *Breve historia de nuestro neoliberalismo: Poder y cultura en México*. Debate, 2021.

Lewis, Vek. "When 'Macho' Bodies Fail: Spectacles of Corporeality and the Limits of the Homosocial/Sexual in Mexican Cinema." *Mysterious Skin: Male Bodies in Contemporary Cinema*, edited by Santiago Fouz-Hernández, I.B. Tauris, 2009, pp. 177–192.

Lim, Dennis. "All the Dreaminess of Reality: 'Post Tenebras Lux' by Carlos Reygadas at Film Forum." *New York Times*, 26 Apr. 2013. www.nytimes.com/2013/04/28/movies/post-tenebras-lux-by-carlos-reygadas-at-film-forum.html.

Llamas-Rodríguez, Juan. "Toward a Cinema of Slow Violence." *Film Quarterly*, vol. 71, no. 3, 2018, pp. 27–36.

Lomnitz, Claudio. *Deep Mexico, Silent Mexico: An Anthropology of Nationalism*. University of Minnesota Press, 2001.

———. *Exits from the Labyrinth: Culture and Ideology in the Mexican National Space*. University of California Press, 1992.

López, Ana M. "Celluloid Tears: Melodrama in the 'Old' Mexican Cinema." *Iris: A Journal of Theory on Image and Sound*, vol. 13, 1991, pp. 29–51.

———. "Tears and Desire: Women and Melodrama in the 'Old' Mexican Cinema." *Multiple Voices in Feminist Film and Criticism*, edited by Diane Cardon et al., University of Minnesota Press, 1994, pp. 254–270.

López-Lozano, Miguel. *Utopian Dreams, Apocalyptic Nightmares: Globalization in Recent Mexican and Chicano Narrative*. Purdue University Press, 2008.

López Obrador, Andrés Manuel. "Clausura del Foro Nacional para la elaboración del Plan Nacional de Desarrollo." *Sitio Oficial de Andrés Manuel López Obrador*, 17 Mar. 2019, lopezobrador.org.mx/2019/03/17/version-estenografica-clausura-del-foro-nacional-para-la-elaboracion-del-plan-nacional-de-desarrollo/.

Lubold, Gordon, and Juan Montes. "Trump, López Obrador Tout Cooperation." *Wall Street Journal*, 9 July 2020. https://www.wsj.com/articles/trump-lopez-obrador-tout-cooperation-11594250797.

Lugones, María. "The Coloniality of Gender." *The Palgrave Handbook of Gender and Development*, edited by Wendy Harcourt. Palgrave Macmillan, 2016, pp. 13–33.

———. "Heterosexualism and the Colonial/Modern Gender System." *Hypatia*, vol. 22, no. 1, 2007, pp. 186–209.

———. "Toward a Decolonial Feminism." *Hypatia*, vol. 25, no. 4, 2010, pp. 743–759.

Lund, Joshua. *The Mestizo State: Reading Race in Modern Mexico*. University of Minnesota Press, 2012.

Macías-González, Víctor M., and Anne Rubenstein, editors. *Masculinity and Sexuality in Modern Mexico*. University of New Mexico Press, 2012.

MacLaird, Misha. *Aesthetics and Politics in the Mexican Film Industry*. Palgrave Macmillan, 2013.

Mangan, J. A. *The Games Ethic and Imperialism: Aspects of the Diffusion of an Ideal*. Frank Cass, 1986.

Marcos, Sylvia. *Taken from the Lips: Gender and Eros in Mesoamerican Religions*. Brill, 2006.

Martín Barbero, Jesús. *Communication, Culture, and Hegemony: From the Media to Mediations*. Translated by Elizabeth Fox and Robert A. White, SAGE Publications, 1993.

McClanahan, Erik. "Brotherly Love: A Conversation with 'Rudo y Cursi' Director Carlos Cuarón." *Twin Cities Daily Planet*, 2 June 2009, www.tcdailyplanet.net/brotherly-love-conversation-carlos-cuaron/.

McClennen, Sophia A. "From the Aesthetics of Hunger to the Cosmetics of Hunger in Brazilian Cinema: Meirelles' *City of God*." *symplokē*, vol. 19, nos. 1–2, 2011, pp. 95–106.

Mejías Vásquez, Ainhoa, editor. *Narcocultura de norte a sur: Una mirada cultural al fenómeno del narco*. Universidad Nacional Autónoma de México, 2017.

Mignolo, Walter D., and Catherine E. Walsh. *On Decoloniality: Concepts, Analytics, and Praxis*. Duke University Press, 2018.

Monsiváis, Carlos. "Mexican Cinema: Of Myths and Demystifications." *Mediating Two Worlds: Cinematic Encounters in the Americas*, edited by John King et al., British Film Institute, 1993, pp. 139–146.

———. "Notas sobre la cultura mexicana en el siglo XX." *Historia general de México*, edited by Daniel Cosío Villegas, vol. 4, Colegio de México, 1977, pp. 303–476.

———. *Pedro Infante: Las leyes del querer*. Aguilar, 2008.

———. "¡Quien fuera Pedro Infante!" *Revista Encuentro*, Apr. 1986, pp. 1–16.

Navarrete, Federico. "La blanquitud y la blancura, cumbre del racismo mexicano." *Revista de la Universidad de México*, no. 864, Sept. 2020, pp. 7–12.

Noble, Andrea. *Mexican National Cinema*. Routledge, 2005.

Núñez Noriega, Guillermo, and Claudia Esthela Espinoza Cid. "El narcotráfico como dispositivo de poder sexo-genérico: Crimen organizado, masculinidad y teoría queer." *Estudios de Género de El Colegio de México*, vol. 3, no. 5, 2017, pp. 90–128.

Ong, Aihwa. *Neoliberalism as Exception: Mutations in Citizenship and Sovereignty*. Duke University Press, 2006.

Ordóñez, Samanta. "Carlos Reygadas's *Batalla en el Cielo* (*Battle in Heaven*) (2005): Disarticulating the Brown Male Body from Myths of Mexican Masculinity." *Studies in Spanish & Latin American Cinemas*, vol. 14, no. 1, Mar. 2017, pp. 77–94.

Paley, Dawn. "Countering Gore Capitalism." *Social Text Online*, 8 Nov. 2019, socialtextjournal.org/periscope_article/countering-gore-capitalism/.

———. *Guerra neoliberal: Desaparición y búsqueda en el norte de México*. Libertad bajo palabra, 2020.

Paley, Dawn, and Simon Granovsky-Larsen. "Introduction: Organized Violence and the Expansion of Capital." *Organized Violence: Capitalist Warfare in Latin America*, edited by Dawn Paley and Simon Granovsky-Larsen, University of Regina Press, 2019, pp. 1–20.

Palou, Pedro Ángel. *El fracaso del mestizo*. Ariel, 2014.

Paz, Octavio. *El Laberinto de la soledad*. 1950. Penguin, 1997.

Penman-Lomeli, Andrea. "Consumption of Culture as Politics." *Full Stop Quarterly,"* no. 5, 2017, www.full-stop.net/2017/08/29/features/essays/andrea-penman-lomeli/consumption-of-culture-as-politics/.

Pickard, Christopher. "IFF Panama: Julio Hernández Cordón's 'Te Prometo Anarquía.'" *Variety*, 14 Apr. 2015, variety.com/2015/film/markets-festivals/iff-panama-julio-hernandez-cordons-te-prometo-anarquia-1201472286/.

Podalsky, Laura. "The Aesthetics of Detachment." *Arizona Journal of Hispanic Cultural Studies*, vol. 20, 2016, pp. 237–254.

———. *The Politics of Affect and Emotion in Contemporary Latin American Cinema: Argentina, Brazil, Cuba, and Mexico*. Palgrave Macmillan, 2011.

Quijano, Aníbal. "Coloniality of Power, Eurocentrism, and Latin America." *Nepantla: Views from South*, translated by Michael Ennis, vol. 1, no. 3, 2000, pp. 533–580.

Ramírez Berg, Charles. *Cinema of Solitude: A Critical Study of Mexican Film, 1967–1983*. University of Texas Press, 1992.

Ramos, Samuel. *El perfil del hombre y la cultura en México*. Planeta Mexicana, 1951.
Ramos-Kittrell, Jesús A., editor. *Decentering the Nation: Music, Mexicanidad, and Globalization*. Lexington Books, 2019.
Reber, Dierdra. *Coming to Our Senses. Affect and an Order of Things for Global Culture*. Columbia University Press, 2016.
Ribas, Alberto. "'El pinche acentito ese': Deseo transatlántico y exotismo satírico en el cine mexicano del cambio de milenio: *Amores Perros, Y tu mamá también, Sin dejar huella*." *Hispanic Research Journal*, vol. 10, no. 5, 2009, pp. 457–481.
Rocha, Carolina, editor. *Modern Argentine Masculinities*. Intellect, 2013.
Roig-Franzia, Manuel. "Videos of Violent Police Training Appear as Mexico Awaits U.S. Aid." *Washington Post*, 2 July 2008, www.washingtonpost.com/wp-dyn/content/article/2008/07/01/AR2008070102624.html.
Rojas, Rafael. "La cuarta invención del liberalismo oficial." *Letras Libres*, no. 261, Sept. 2020, pp. 10–13
Romero Sotelo, María Eugenia. *Los orígenes del neoliberalismo en México: La escuela austriaca*. Fondo de cultura económica, 2016.
Rubin, Gayle S. "The Traffic in Women: Notes on the 'Political Economy' of Sex." *Toward an Anthropology of Women*, edited by Rayna Reiter, Monthly Review Press, 1975, pp. 157–210.
Sánchez Prado, Ignacio M. "*Amores Perros*: Exotic Violence and Neoliberal Fear." *Journal of Latin American Cultural Studies*, vol. 15, no. 1, 2006, pp. 39–57.
———. "El narco como arte y mercancía." *Confabulario*, 14 Sept. 2014, confabulario.eluniversal.com.mx/el-narco-como-arte-y-mercancia/.
———. "Humorous Affects: Romantic Comedies in Contemporary Mexico." *Humor in Latin American Cinema*, edited by Juan Poblete and Juana Suárez, Palgrave Macmillan, 2016, pp. 203–222.
———. "Regimes of Affect: Love and Class in Mexican Neoliberal Cinema." *Journal of Popular Romance Studies*, vol. 4, no. 1, 2014.
———. *Screening Neoliberalism: Transforming Mexican Cinema, 1988–2012*. Vanderbilt University Press, 2014.
———. *Strategic Occidentalism: On Mexican Fiction, the Neoliberal Book Market, and the Question of World Literature*. Northwestern University Press, 2018.
Sánchez Prado, Ignacio M., and Mabel Moraña, editors. *El lenguaje de las emociones: Afecto y cultura en América Latina*. Iberoamericana, 2012.
Schaefer, Claudia. "Parodying Paradise: When Mexican Buddy Films Turn *Rudo y Cursi*." *Quarterly Review of Film and Video*, vol. 30, no. 1, 2013, pp. 50–61.
Sedgwick, Eve Kosofsky. *Between Men: English Literature and Male Homosocial Desire*. Columbia University Press, 1985.
Seidler, Victor J. *Rediscovering Masculinity: Reason, Language and Sexuality*. Routledge, 1989.
Sharma, Devika, and Frederik Tygstrup. *Structures of Feeling: Affectivity and the Study of Culture*. Walter de Gruyter, 2015.

Smith, Paul Julian. *Queer Mexico: Cinema and Television since 2000*. Wayne State University Press, 2017.

Snow, Marcus. *Into the Abyss: A Study of the Mise en Abyme*. London Metropolitan University, 2016.

Solórzano, Fernanda. "*Heli* de Amat Escalante." *Letras Libres*, no. 176, Aug. 2013, pp. 90–91.

———. "Las ciudades invisibles de Hernández Cordón." *Letras Libres*, no. 213, Sept. 2016, pp. 66–67.

———. "Retratos de un país en llamas: Entrevista a Amat Escalante." *Letras Libres*, no. 223, July 2017, pp. 28–33.

Sommer, Doris. *Foundational Fictions: The National Romances of Latin America*. University of California Press, 1991.

Tierney, Dolores. *Emilio Fernández: Pictures in the Margins*. Manchester University Press, 2007.

———. *New Transnationalisms in Contemporary Latin American Cinemas*. Edinburgh University Press, 2018.

Toro Alfonso, José, editor. *Lo masculino en evidencia: Investigaciones sobre la masculinidad*. Publicaciones Puertorriqueñas, 2012.

Tuckman, Jo. "Amat Escalante: 'Batman Had More Killings Than *Heli*.'" *Guardian*, 15 May 2014. www.theguardian.com/film/2014/may/15/amat-escalante-heli-cannes-mexico-violence.

Tuñón, Julia. *En su propio espejo: (Entrevista con Emilio "El Indio" Fernández)*. Universidad Autónoma Metropolitana, 1988.

Valencia, Sayak. *Gore Capitalism*. Translated by John Pluecker, Semiotext(e), 2018.

Vargas, Andrew S. "Julio Hernández Cordón on Using Facebook to Cast the Skateboarding Stars of His Movie." *Remezcla*, 4 Dec. 2015, remezcla.com/features/film/julio-hernandez-cordon-on-how-his-script-about-drug-dealing-skaters-turned-into-a-movie-on-blood-traffickers/.

Vasconcelos, José. *The Cosmic Race: A Bilingual Edition*. Translated by Didier T. Jaén, Johns Hopkins University Press, 1997.

Venkatesh, Vinodh. *The Body as Capital: Masculinities in Contemporary Latin American Fiction*. University of Arizona Press, 2015.

———. *New Maricón Cinema: Outing Latin American Film*. University of Texas Press, 2016.

Williams, Gareth. *The Mexican Exception: Sovereignty, Police, and Democracy*. Palgrave Macmillan, 2011.

Wood, David. "Latin America at the (Sports) Movies: Winning, Losing and Playing in *Rudo y Cursi* and *En Tres y Dos*." *Bulletin of Spanish Studies*, vol. 90, no. 8, 2013, pp. 1357–1375.

Zavala, Oswaldo. *Los cárteles no existen: Narcotráfico y cultura en México*. Malpaso, 2018.

Zea, Leopoldo. "Vasconcelos y la utopía de la raza cósmica." *Cuadernos Americanos: Nueva Época*, vol. 37, 1993, pp. 23–36.

Index

Acevedo-Muñoz, Ernesto, 38
affect: and homosociality, 20, 40, 46, 147; and masculine subjecthood, 133–34, 138; and mestizaje, 56; and neoliberalism, 11, 16, 148, 163–64, 166, 182, 195n10; in recent cinema, 145, 148, 151–56, 163–64, 166, 177, 182; in *Te prometo anarquía*, 34, 146–50, 156–63, 177, 180–82; theories of, 195n10, 204n8; and violence, 111, 116. *See also* empathy; emotion; feeling, structures of; pathos; sentiment
African/Afrodescendent peoples, 1, 31, 196n13
Aguilar, Luis, 45
Alatorre, Daniela, 197n18
Albarrán-Torres, César, 115, 117, 122–23
Alcoriza, Luis, 195n7
Almada, Natalia, 197n18
Alonso, Lisandro, 116
Amores perros (González Iñárritu), 200n2
arthouse cinema, 114–15, 149, 153. *See also* auteurism; festivals, film; independent cinema
A toda máquina (Rodríguez), 45, 49, 52

Atrás hay relámpagos (Hernández Cordón), 149
audiences: and affect, 116, 146, 153, 156; class composition of, 10–11, 60, 108, 110, 153–54, 163, 169, 188–89, 203n5, 205n17; of current cinema, 7, 25, 43, 60, 68–71, 109, 151–54, 177, 184, 188–89, 203n3, 204n13, 206n1; of Golden Age cinema, xv, 25, 30, 51, 81, 191n2, 192n3, 193n7, 198n29; and identification, xv–xvii, 6, 11, 51, 77, 81, 147, 153, 155, 157, 161, 163, 182, 191n2, 192n2; and queer themes, 153, 156–57, 181; responses to violence, 116–17, 122–23, 127, 153–54, 201n6, 205n14; transnational, 71, 110–11, 117, 127, 150, 153, 204n13, 205n14
auteurism, 17, 73, 76–77, 105, 149–50, 152, 164, 169. *See also* arthouse cinema; festivals, film
Aviles, Lila, 197n18
Ayala Blanco, Jorge, 193

Bartra, Roger, xviii–xix, 23–24, 33, 50–51, 96–97, 193n7, 197n25
Batalla en el cielo (Reygadas), 33–34, 75–78, 82–94, 105, 111, 199n5

Beasley-Murray, Jon, 204nn11–12
Bend It Like Beckham (Chadha), 199n8
Berger, John, 91
Berger, Marco, 155. See also *Plan B*
blackness, 28
body, 32–33, 41, 75, 82, 85, 111, 114, 116, 122, 128–30, 133, 137–39, 173. See also corporeality
Bojórquez, José, 185. See also *Como caído del cielo*
Bordun, Troy, 73–75
Bourdieu, Pierre, 22
brownness, 48, 192n5; in *Batalla en el cielo*, 78–79, 82, 90–91, 94; and malformed masculinity, 6, 28, 34, 81–82, 94, 112, 183, 188; in *Post tenebras lux*, 94. See also indio; mestizaje; mestizo; racialization
buddy film, 40–42, 44–46, 49–55, 59–60, 65. See also *specific titles*
Burton-Carvajal, Julianne, 199n1
Butler, Judith, 22, 197n23

Calderón, Felipe, 107
CANACINE (Cámara Nacional de la Industria Cinematográfica), 206n1
Cannon, Danny, 199n8. See also *Goal!*
Canoa (Cazals), 108
Cantinflas (Mario Moreno), 192n6
capitalism: and coloniality, 12, 29–30, 184; and culture, xix, 26, 29, 48, 91–92, 112, 164–66, 200n8; and dystopia, 13, 35, 146–47, 165, 169, 172–74, 176; emotional (Illouz), 163, 169, 181; gore (Valencia), 12–14, 148, 172–80, 196n15; logic of, 147, 171; and masculinity, 5, 29, 33, 41, 47, 61–62, 69, 92, 112, 143, 147–48, 171, 174–75, 179, 185, 193n4, 196n16; and racialization, xvii, 2, 29; and the state, 1, 7–9, 14, 21–24, 29–30, 47–48, 69, 112. See also modernization; neoliberalism
Carmín tropical (Perezcano), 152, 204n13
Carrera, Carlos, 201n3. See also *El crimen del padre Amaro*
cartels. See drugs; narcos
Castillo, Debra, 194n5
Cazals, Felipe, 108, 195n7. See also *Canoa*
Cha Cha Chá Films, 199n7
Chadha, Gurinder, 199n8. See also *Bend It Like Beckham*
Chaparro, Omar, 186, 188
charro, 2, 45, 56
Chiapas, 12
Chicuarotes (García Bernal), 188
Chihuahua, xiv
Cidade de Deus (Meirelles and Lund, K.), 111
cine de oro. See Golden Age cinema
citizenship, 1, 10–11, 29–32, 44, 48, 80–81, 135, 139, 156, 169, 181
Ciudad Juárez, 5
class difference: in *Batalla en cielo*, 34, 83, 91; and cinema audiences, 11, 110, 156, 162–64, 169; and gender, 2, 21, 26, 28–30, 34; and malformed masculinity, xviii, 17, 33–34, 48, 79–80, 141; in *Post tenebras lux*, 34, 74, 76, 95, 100; and racialization, 2, 21, 26–30, 48, 50–51; in *Rudo y Cursi*, 33, 42–44, 69, 71; in *Te prometo anarquía*, 148–50, 157, 164, 168, 171, 179, 182; in *Y tu mamá también*, 33, 37–39, 41, 58, 60–62, 71
colonialism, 1, 24, 29–32, 184, 194n4, 199n8, 200n8. See also coloniality
coloniality, xviii, 184, 188; of gender (Lugones), 31, 184, 193n1,

194n4, 194n6, 206n3; of power (Quijano), 29, 30, 198n28. *See also* colonialism; racialization
comedia ranchera, 44–46, 49, 54, 108. See also *Los tres García*
Como caído del cielo (Bojórquez), 185–88
Cómprame un revolver (Hernández Cordón), 203n4
Connell, Raewyn (R. W.), 22, 193n4, 197n22
contract: gendered, 40, 45, 50–51; homosocial, 45–46; patriarchal, 5, 32, 38, 48, 50, 67; social, 152; in *Y tu mamá también*, 53, 55, 58–59, 61–62. *See also* pacts, thematization of
corporeality, 22, 28, 50, 78–83, 90, 130–32, 136–37, 140, 158, 171, 173. *See also* body
cosmopolitanism, xix, 5, 148, 154, 156, 186
Costa Rica, 149
Couret, Nilo, 117
COVID-19, 205n1
criminality: discourses and images of, 5, 12–13, 16, 26, 107, 109, 112, 133, 183, 196n16, 200n2, 202n14; in *Heli*, 34, 113–24, 133–39, 143; and homosexuality, 20, 146, 203n2; and malformed masculinity, xviii, 32, 34, 80–83, 90, 107, 137, 147, 185, 192n6; Paley on, 14–16; in *Te prometo anarquía*, 147–51, 153–55, 162, 165, 170–77; Valencia on, 14, 172, 175–76; Zavala on, 15–16, 113, 201n10. *See also* drugs; violence
criollo, 21, 29–30, 79
Cuáron, Alfonso, 17–18, 33, 37–44, 51, 55–62, 68, 71, 198n1, 198n3, 199n7, 199n9. See also *Sólo con tu pareja*; *Y tu mamá también*

Cuáron, Carlos, 17–18, 33, 37, 39, 42–44, 51, 62–65, 68, 70, 199n9. See also *Rudo y Cursi*
Cuatro lunas (Tovar Velarde), 151–52

Dalton, David, 197n25
Dargis, Manohla, 115
dehumanization, 16, 128, 133, 167, 189. *See also* humanness; racialization
de la Madrid Hurtado, Miguel, 9
de la Mora, Sergio, xvi–xvii, 18–26, 45–49, 76, 79–81, 87, 96, 192n3, 194n5, 197nn21–21, 197n24
de Llaca, Juan Carlos, 198n3. See also *Por la libre*
del Río, Dolores, 87
del Toro, Guillermo, 199n7, 199n9
de Luca, Tiago, 73–75, 93, 102–104, 114–15
Dever, Susan, xvi–xvii, 192n3, 196n18
Díaz, Porfirio, 21. *See also* Porfiriato
Domínguez-Ruvalcaba, Héctor, 18–26, 31–32, 45–49
drugs: in *Heli*, 34, 111–25, 131–36, 139; in *Rudo y Cursi*, 43, 67; trade, 5, 14–15, 109–10, 170, 205n19; use of, 56, 92; and violence, 110–14, 173, 202n13, 196n16; war on, 14–16, 107, 110–14, 173, 201n10. *See also* criminality; narcos

Echeverría, Bolívar, 192n5
effeminacy, xvi, xviii, 5, 20–21, 25, 32, 79
Eimbcke, Fernando, 116, 206n2
Eisenman, Stephen, 90–91
Ejército Zapatista de Liberación Nacional, 12
El crimen del padre Amaro (Carrera), 201n3
Elephant (Van Sant), 203n2

El gavilán pollero (González, R. A.), 46, 49, 52–54, 198n4
El infierno (Estrada), 121, 201n4
El lugar sin límites (Ripstein), 108
El Tigre de Santa Julia (Gamboa), 109
Emmelhainz, Irmgard, 12–13, 188, 195n9, 196n14
emotion: and attachment/connection, 16, 116, 134, 150–51, 154–59, 162, 177; and capitalism, 157, 163–64, 169, 181; and detachment/disconnection, 115, 160, 167, 177; expression of, xiv, 21, 79, 146, 169, 178, 182; and masculinity, 21, 79, 138. *See also* affect; empathy; feeling, structures of; melodrama; pathos; romance; sentiment
empathy, 11, 35, 78, 122, 146–47, 148–65, 167, 178, 180–82. *See also* affect; emotion; feeling, structures of; pathos; sentiment
Escalante, Amat, 7–18, 34, 105, 110–43, 150, 202n14. *See also Heli*; *Los bastardos*
Estrada, Luis, 109, 201n4. *See also El infierno*; *La ley de Herodes*
Eurocentrism, 29–30, 184
EZLN (Ejército Zapatista de Liberación Nacional), 12

family: provider role, 4, 66, 79, 83, 94, 135–36, 139, 143; structure, 42, 48, 75, 134, 142; values, 42, 46, 65. *See also* mothers, veneration of
Farías, Fernando, 188. *See also Ya no estoy aquí*
feeling, structures of, 11, 147, 151–57, 162–66, 169, 180, 195n10, *See also* affect; empathy; emotion; pathos, romance; sentiment
femininity, 6–7, 18–19, 48, 197n26. *See also* gender

feminism, 3, 5, 38, 108, 187, 190, 194n6
festivals, film, 7, 11, 110, 146, 150, 153, 183, 203n3, 203n7, 204n9
Fernández, Emilio, xv, xvi, 108, 191n1. *See also Las abandonadas*; *María Candelaria*; *Rio escondido*; *Víctimas del pecado*
Fernández Violante, Marcela, 196n18
Foster, David William, 204n9
Fuentes, Raúl, 151. *See also Todo el mundo tiene a alguien menos yo*

Galindo, Rubén, 201n5. *See also La banda del carro rojo*
Gamboa, Alejandro, 109. *See also El Tigre de Santa Julia*
Gamio, Manuel, 198n27
García Bernal, Gael, 37–38, 63, 188. *See also Chicuarotes*
García Canclini, Nestor, 10–11, 191n2, 205n16
Gaspar de Alba, Alicia, 194n5
Gasolina (Hernández Cordón), 149
gayness. *See* homosexuality; queerness; sexual diversity
gender: in *Batalla en cielo*, 78, 84–85, 112; and class, 2, 21, 26–30, 34; coloniality of, 31, 194n4, 194n6, 206n3; in *Heli*, 113–14, 122, 134, 138–39, 141; malformed, xvii–xviii, 2, 6–7, 16–17, 32–33, 42, 78–79, 81–82, 107, 170, 184–86, 192n6; modern/colonial system, 1–2, 6–7, 47, 193n1, 194n4, 194n6; and national cinema, xvii, 1–2, 6, 16, 21–22, 31–33, 45, 47, 81, 108, 188, 192n3, 192n6, 195n7; and nationalism, xvi, 5, 19, 21–22, 24–26, 38, 40, 42–47, 108, 112, 188, 193n4; and neoliberalism, 16, 33–34, 37, 44, 108, 155–56, 185; in

Post tenebras lux, 76, 93–97, 102; and racialization, 1–2, 6–7, 26–30, 48–49, 80–82, 175–76, 184, 188, 194n4; in *Rudo y Cursi*, 42–44, 63–71; social theories of, 22, 193n4; in *Te prometo anarquía*, 146, 148, 151, 170; in *Y tu mamá también*, 40–44, 51–62, 70–71. See also femininity; masculinity; sexuality; sexual identity
Géricault, Théodore, 90. See also *A Horse Frightened by Lightening*
globalization, 4, 33, 41, 108. See also neoliberalism
Goal! (Cannon), 199n8
Golden Age cinema: allusions to, 37, 43–44, 52–55, 59, 65–66, 70, 77, 79, 93, 186; and class difference, 29, 97; critical readings of, xvi–xvii, 25, 192n3; and machismo, xvi–xvii, 19–22, 25, 41, 44–47, 69, 79; and malformed masculinity, xvii–xviii, 28, 33, 40, 49–51, 81, 94, 96; and melodrama, xiii–xiv, 21–22, 25, 87; and mestizaje, xvii, 28, 30, 50, 112, 186; and mexicanidad, 19–22, 30, 40, 50, 186, 187, 191n2, 193n7; and nostalgia, xiv, 108; prostitution in, 87. See also national cinema
Gómez, Beto, 201n4. See also *Salvando al soldado Pérez*
González Echevarría, Roberto, 38
González Iñárritu, Alejandro, 199n7, 199n9, 200n2
González Rodríguez, Sergio, 193n3
Guadalupe, Virgin of, 47, 83, 92, 197n26
Guanajuato, 110, 112, 119, 132, 137
Guatemala, 149
Gutmann, Matthew, 22

Harvey, David, 8–9

Hasta el sol tiene manchas (Hernández Cordón), 149
Hazlo como hombre (López, N.), 185–86
Hermosillo, Jaime Humberto, 3, 203n2. See also *Matinée*
Hernández, Julián, 204n7, 206n2
Hernández Castillo, Rosalva Aída, 194n6
Hernández Cordón, Julio, 17–18, 34, 145–82, 203n4, 205n19. See also *Atrás hay relámpagos*; *Cómprame un revolver*; *Gasolina*; *Hasta el sol tiene manchas*; *Las marimbas del infierno*; *Polvo*
Hershfield, Joanne, 192n3, 194n5
heteronormativity, 2, 5, 20, 46, 55, 60, 146, 204n9
heterosexualism. See heteronormativity
Hind, Emily, 108–11, 200n1
Hollywood cinema, 11, 21, 44, 46, 111, 163, 199n9, 204n10
homoeroticism: in Golden Age cinema, 45–46, 54; and homosociality, 20; and machismo, xvi; in *Te prometo anarquía*, 150–51, 168, 182, 203n2; in *Y tu mamá también*, 38, 53–55, 58. See also homosexuality; homosociality; queerness
homophobia, xvii, 4, 19–21, 25, 32, 45, 47–48, 189; and queer studies, 204n9; rejection of, 156, 185; in *Y tu mamá también*, 55
homosexuality, 20; in Golden Age cinema, xvii, 25, 46, 79; and homosociality, 21; normalization of, 35, 152–53, 155; as otherness, 32; stereotypes of, xviii, 154–55; in *Te prometo anarquía*, 146, 149–51; in *Y tu mamá también*, 55. See also queerness; sexual diversity

homosociality, 19–22, 32, 45, 69–70, 185, 197n21; in *Batalla en el cielo*, 83; in Golden Age cinema, 21–22, 25, 45–49; and homoeroticism, 20; and homosexuality, 21; in *Rudo y Cursi*, 42, 44, 65, 69; in *Te prometo anarquía*, 147, 168; in *Y tu mamá también*, 40, 44, 51–62
Horse Frightened by Lightning, A (Gericault), 90
Huezo, Tatiana, 197n18
humanness, 6, 31, 48, 102–103, 184, 188–89, 194n4. *See also* dehumanization

Illouz, Eva, 163
IMCINE (Instituto Mexicano de Cinematografía), 183, 203n3, 206n1
imperialism. *See* colonialism
independent cinema, 11, 17, 105, 183–84, 197n18. *See also* arthouse cinema; auteurism; festivals, film
indigeneity, xvi
indigenismo, xv, xvii, 26–28, 31, 50, 108. *See also* indio
indigenous people, 1, 12, 27, 196n13
indio, xviii, 27–28, 50, 80. *See also* indigenismo; racialization
industrialization, 8, 21–22 30, 48, 112, 137
industry, film, 3, 7–9, 17, 18, 63, 105, 108, 148, 163, 184, 189, 191n2, 193n7, 194n7, 199n7, 199n9, 206n1
Infante, Pedro, xiii–xvi, 25–26, 45–46, 76–81, 94–96, 108, 185–87, 191n2, 198n2
Instituto Mexicano de Cinematografía, 183, 203n3, 206n1
Irwin, Robert McKee, 19–26

Japón (Reygadas), 77, 102–104
joto, 21, 79

Jurassic Park (Spielberg), 128

LGBTQ+. *See* homosexuality; queerness; sexual diversity
La banda del carro rojo (Galindo), 201n5
labor, xix, 4–5, 8, 11–12, 21–22, 30, 112; in *Batalla en el cielo*, 76, 79, 82, 91; and coloniality, 29–30; in *Heli*, 34, 112–14, 136–38, 143; and *Post tenebras lux*, 76, 100, 102; racialized division of, 27–30, 43; in *Rudo y Cursi*, 43
Lahr-Vivaz, Elena, 38, 40, 69, 77–79, 199n1
La jaula de oro (Quemada-Diez), 188
La ley de Herodes (Estrada), 109
La mujer del puerto (Boytler), 87
land, xix, 11, 27, 29–30, 114
Landeta, Matilde, 196n18
La otra familia (Loza), 155–56
La raza cósmica (Vasconcelos), 56
Las abandonadas (Fernández), 87
Las marimbas del infierno (Hernández Cordón), 149
La virgen de los sicarios (Schroeder), 203n2
Leon, 132
Llamas-Rodríguez, Juan, 110–11, 116–18, 201n6
Lomnitz, Claudio, 197n25
López, Ana, 78, 192n3
López, Nicolás, 185. *See also Hazlo como hombre*
López Obrador, Andrés Manuel, 9, 195n8
Los bastardos (Escalante), 202n14
Los tres García (Rodríguez), 46–47, 49, 54, 65, 69
love. *See* romance
Loza, Gustavo, 155. *See also La otra familia*

Lugones, María, 2, 31, 193n1, 194n4, 194n6, 206n3
Luna, Diego, 37–38, 63
Lund, Joshua, 27, 30, 197n25
Lund, Kátia, 111. See also *Cidade de Deus*

machismo, 18–26; in *Batalla en el cielo*, 34, 76, 111; in Golden Age cinema, xvi–xvii, 19–22, 25, 29, 45–46, 69, 79–80, 96, 191n2; in *Heli*, 138; and homoeroticism, xvi, 20, 45–46; and homophobia, 19–21, 25, 32, 45; and homosexuality, 21, 25, 46, 79; and malformed masculinity, 14, 44, 48, 69, 79, 138; and mestizaje, xvii, 26, 28, 50, 76, 108, 197n25; and mexicanidad, xix, 18–19, 96; and misogyny, 19–20, 25, 32; obsolescence of, 5, 41, 108–109, 156, 185–87; in *Rudo y Cursi*, 42, 44, 62, 65, 69–71; in *Y tu mamá también*, 38, 40, 44, 52–55, 59, 61, 68–69. See also macho
macho: in *Batalla en el cielo*, 84, 87–88; as cinema archetype, xiii–xviii, 6, 18–21, 25–26, 30, 32, 45, 47, 50, 79–80, 108, 112, 185–87; and malformed masculinity, 48, 79, 96–97; as mestizo, 26; as narco, 109; pejorative perceptions of, 61, 187; in *Rudo y Cursi*, 42, 63, 65, 67, 70; as model subject, 23–24, 32; in *Y tu mamá también*, 51, 59. See also machismo
MacLaird, Misha, 9–11
Mala Noche (Van Sant), 203n2
male bonding. See homosociality
malformation. See masculinity: malformed
Malinche, 24, 38, 47
manliness. See machismo; masculinity

Marán, Luna, 197n18
Marcos, Sylvia, 194n6
María Candelaria (Fernández), 108
Marquez, Alejandra, 197
masculinity: in *Batalla en el cielo*, 34, 75–76, 78, 82–88, 92–93, 105, 111; and capitalism, 21, 29–30, 170, 175; and class difference, 26; and coloniality, 31; crisis of, 2, 5, 42–43; defined negatively, 25; and drug violence, 16, 107–10, 196n16, 202n11; in Golden Age cinema, xv–xix, 1–4, 18–22 25, 28, 44–45, 47–51, 79–81, 96–97, 112, 192n3, 192n6, 194n7; in *Heli*, 110–11, 118, 120, 123, 130–34, 137–43; malformed, xviii–xix, 6–7, 14, 16–17, 26, 32, 44, 48, 79–81, 108, 183–84, 189, 192n6, 194n4; and modernization, 24; nationalism, 24, 96–97, 192n4; and neoliberalism, xix, 4–5, 7–8, 16–18, 33, 42–43, 82, 108, 174, 185–89, 201n2; and patriarchy, 4, 19, 32; in *Post tenebras lux*, 34, 75–76, 94, 102, 105; and power, xvi, 4–5, 7, 22, 25, 31, 33, 44, 47–48, 82, 97; and racialization, 16, 26, 28, 48–50, 81, 184; in *Rudo y Cursi*, 33, 38, 42–43, 63–71; in *Te prometo anarquía*, 34–35, 146–48, 153–54, 170–80, 205n21; and violence, 5–7, 14–16, 31, 21; in *Y tu mamá también*, 33, 37, 40–41, 52, 55–52, 69–71; See also machismo; gender
mass media: and mexicanidad, 193n7; and neoliberalism, 10–11, 13; and sexual diversity, 145, 148, 151–52, 158; theories of, 191n2; and violence, 14, 34, 110, 112–13, 118, 120–23, 127–28, 170, 173, 202n13, 205n19

Matinée (Hermosillo), 203n2
Mbembe, Achilles, 205n18
Meirelles, Fernando, 111. See also *Cidade de Deus*
melodrama: in *Batalla en el cielo*, 78; in current cinema, 155, 157, 183; in Golden Age cinema, xiii–xvi, 21, 25, 38, 78, 80–81, 87, 187; and masculinity, 21, 25; as metagenre (López, A.), 78, 199n1; prostitution in, 87, 194n5. *See also* sentiment; and specific titles
mestizaje, xvii, 1–2, 21, 26–30, 48, 50, 56, 76, 80–81, 108, 188, 194n4, 197n25. *See also* indigensimo; mestizo; racialization
mestizo, xvii–xviii, 2, 6, 23, 26–31, 48–50, 79–81, 188, 192n6, 197nn25–26; in *Batalla en el cielo*, 34, 76, 82, 92–94, 112; in *Post tenebras lux*, 94–96. *See also* mestizaje; racialization
mexicanidad, xv–xix, 18–29, 44, 47, 51, 69, 96, 105, 108, 186, 191n2; in Reygadas's work, 75, 77–78, 92, 94, 97, 111–12; in *Rudo y Cursi*, 43–44, 51, 65, 70; in *Y tu mamá también*, 38–40, 41, 51, 53. *See also* nationalism
Mexicanness. *See* mexicanidad
Mexico City, 20, 149; in *Amores Perros*, 200n2; in *Batalla en el cielo*, 82–83, 93, 112; audiences in, 108–109, 163, 200n1; as LGBTTTI-friendly, 203; in *Rudo y Cursi*, 63; spatial transformations in, 163; in *Te prometo anarquía*, 146, 157, 162, 165–66, 171, 173; in *Y tu mamá también*, 51
mise en abyme, 113, 124–25, 130, 133, 201n9

misogyny, xiv, xvii, 19–20, 25, 32, 45–48, 185, 189; and endriagos (Valencia), 174; in *Heli*, 138; in *Rudo y Cursi*, 67; in *Y tu mamá también*, 38, 41, 52, 55, 60, 65
Miss Bala (Naranjo), 201n4
modernization, xvi, xviii, 1, 6, 21–22, 24, 108; and gender system, 48, 112 and melodrama, 78; and mestizaje, 27 194n4. *See also* modernity
modernity, xvii, 2, 6, 34, 61, 76, 79, 86, 133, 193n4; and cosmopolitanism, xix; and emotional capitalism, 163; and Eurocentrism, 30; and gore capitalism (Valencia), 173, 175; and indigenismo, 50; and melodrama, 87; and mestizaje, 50, 80; and rationality, 97. *See also* modernization
Molina Enríquez, Andrés, 198n27
Monsiváis, Carlos, 191n2, 193n7, 198n2
Moraña, Mabel, 204n8
mothers, veneration of, 46–47, 49, 65–67, 69. *See also* family
My Own Private Idaho (Van Sant), 203n2

NAFTA (North American Free Trade Agreement), 7, 9, 195n8. *See also* neoliberalism
Naranjo, Gerardo, 201n4. See also *Miss Bala*
narcos, 14–16, 70, 107, 109–11, 196n16, 201n5; in *Heli*, 34, 112, 114–24, 129–32, 136; in Hernández Cordón's work, 153, 176, 203n4; Paley on, 14–16; Valencia on, 14, 176; Zavala on, 15, 113, 117–18, 201n10. *See also* criminality; drugs; violence

Narcos: Mexico, 121
national cinema: allusions to, 38, 40, 43, 54, 69, 77, 82, 87, 89, 93–94, 111–12, 198n1; current state of, 183, 206n1; expired paradigm of, 2–3, 7, 163; as ideological instrument xv–xvi, 30–31, 192n2; and masculinity, xiii–xix, 1–7, 14, 16, 19–21, 26, 28, 31–33, 37, 43, 45–50, 59, 61, 75, 78–80, 85, 93–94, 108–109, 112, 189, 192n3, 192n6, 193n4, 194n7; neoliberal reconfiguration of, xix, 3–4, 6–7, 9–11, 38–39, 68, 71, 105, 108–10, 151, 155, 162–63, 183, 189, 194n7, 199n7, 206n1; and racialization, 28, 31, 74; and rural Mexico, 108–109; women's nonacting roles in, 196n18. *See also* Golden Age cinema; industry, film; postnational cinema
national identity. *See* mexicanidad
nationalism, 1, 4–5, 18–21, 24, 28, 38, 40–44, 57–62, 69–70, 74–78, 188, 197n26. *See also* mexicanidad
Navarrete, Federico, 192n5
Necesito dinero (Zacarías), xvi
Negrete, Jorge, 79
neoliberalism: and citizenship, 10–11, 44, 133, 139, 169; cultural politics of, 3–4, 6–8, 11–14, 18, 35, 39, 43–44, 51, 60, 69, 82, 108–109, 114, 133, 139, 151, 155, 177, 181, 184–90, 195n9, 201n2; and film industry reform, 3, 9–11, 17, 194n7; and masculinity, 2, 5–7, 16–17, 33, 41, 49, 51, 59–60, 65, 69, 76, 82–83, 108, 112, 143, 146–47, 153, 174–75, 180, 184–85, 194n4; as political economy, xix, 3, 8–9, 82, 135, 148, 171–72, 195n8; and social inequity, 12, 16, 138, 145–46, 171, 174, 180, 182; and state power, xix, 6–7, 9, 13–16, 32, 82, 111, 114, 118, 122, 135–37, 181, 188, 201n10; as structure of feeling, 11, 16, 134, 155, 181–82, 195n10; and violence, xix, 6–7, 11–16, 111, 141–42, 145, 148, 153, 172, 175, 196n16. *See also* globalization; NAFTA; privatization
Netflix, 121, 185
Noble, Andrea, xvi–xvii, 192nn2–3
North American Free Trade Agreement, 7, 9, 195n8. *See also* neoliberalism
Nosotros los pobres (Rodríguez), xiii–xiv, 80–81, 92
Novaro, María, 198n3. *See also Sin dejar huella*

Oaxaca, 51, 204n13
Olaizola, Yulene, 197n18

pachuco, 23, 192n6. *See also* Paz, Octavio; Tin Tan
pacts, thematization of, 40, 44–46, 53, 55, 57, 65. *See also* contract
painting, 90–92, 200nn7–8
Paley, Dawn, 14–16, 202n12
Palma, Andrea, 87
Palou, Pedro Ángel, 24
Paranoid Park (Van Sant), 203n2
parody, 37, 42, 63, 66–67, 121, 141, 172. *See also* satire
Partido Revolucionario Institucional, 5, 11–12, 24
pathos, xiv, 21, 63, 154, 165–66, 169, 179, 181. *See also* affect, emotion, empathy
patriarchy, 2–4, 24, 32, 93–97, 138–39, 187. *See also* contract: patriarchal

Paz, Octavio, xvii–xviii, 23–24, 192n4, 197n24, 197n26
Plan B (Berger, M.), 155
pelado, xviii, 23, 192n6. See also Cantinflas; Ramos, Samuel
Pepe el Toro (Rodríguez), 187
Perezcano, Rigoberto, 152. See also Carmín tropical
Piñeyro, Marcelo, 203n2. See also Plata quemada
Plata quemada (Piñeyro), 203n2
Podalsky, Laura, 110–11, 116–18, 129, 201n6, 202n18, 204n8
Polvo (Hernández Cordón), 149
Porfiriato, 21, 27, 30. See also Díaz, Porfirio
Por la libre (de Llaca), 198n3
posthegemony, 152–53, 204n12
postnational cinema, 4, 6–7, 34, 68, 94, 97, 104–105, 148, 151, 194n7. See also national cinema; transnational cinema
Post tenebras lux (Reygadas), 33–34, 74–76, 93–105
power: and capitalism, 82, 92; coloniality of (Quijano), 29–31, 184, 198n28; and masculinity, xvi–xix, 4–5, 7, 17–19, 22, 25, 31–35, 44–48, 75–76, 82, 92, 95, 97, 102, 104–105, 135, 139–43, 174, 179; and mexicanidad, 23, 33, 51, 76, 78; neoliberal state, xix, 6–9, 13–16, 32, 82, 111, 114, 118, 122–23, 128, 132–37, 152, 181, 188–90, 201n10; and racialization, 1, 4–5, 30, 51, 112; and representation, 90–95, 102–104, 128, 189, 200n9; and violence, 116, 118, 172–75, 205n18
PRI (Partido Revolucionario Institucional), 5, 11–12, 24
privatization, 7–10, 135, 163, 171. See also neoliberalism

prostitution film, 83, 87–89, 194n5. See also specific titles

queer cinema, 151–53, 155–58, 181, 203n7, 204n9. See also homosexuality; queerness
queerness: audience interest in, 153, 157; as identity and politics, 145–46, 148, 151, 155–56, 190, 202n1; as integral to machismo, xvi; mainstreaming of, 145, 151–53; in Te prometo anarquía, 146, 150, 153. See also homoeroticism; homosexuality; queer cinema
Quemada-Diez, Diego, 188. See also La jaula de oro
¿Qué te ha dado esa mujer? (Rodríguez), 45–46, 53–54

race/racism/racial classification. See racialization
racialization, xvii–xviii, 1–2, 4, 6, 16–17, 26–32, 48–51, 78–81, 108, 112, 183–85, 188, 192n5, 194n4, 197n25; in Batalla en el cielo, 82, 84–85, 91, 94, 112; in Post tenebras lux, 34, 95; in Rudo y Cursi, 33, 42–43; in Te prometo anarquía, 170, 182; in Y tu mamá también, 33, 61–62. See also brownness; mestizaje; whiteness
Ramírez Berg, Charles, 2–3, 193n2, 195n7
Ramos, Samuel, xvii–xviii, 23–24, 26
Rancière, Jacques, 73
realism: 97, 105, 163–64, 188, 204n13; in Heli 105, 110–18, 125–28, 138–39; in Reygadas's work, 73–75, 82–87, 93, 102–105, 112; in Rudo y Cursi, 70; in Te prometo anarquía, 34, 146–49, 153, 157, 161, 167–69, 173, 182, 203n2

Retes, Gabriel, 201n3. *See also Un dulce olor a muerte*
revolution, 18–19, 30, 87, 107
Reygadas, Carlos, 17–18, 33–34, 71, 73–105, 111–12, 114–16, 150, 199n5, 200n9. *See also Batalla en el cielo*; *Japón*; *Post tenebras lux*
Rio escondido (Fernández), 108
Ripstein, Arturo, 108, 195n7. *See also El lugar sin límites*
road movie, 42, 51–52, 65, 193n3. *See also specific titles*
Rodríguez, Ismael, xiii–xv, 45. *See also A toda máquina*; *Los tres García*; *Nosotros los pobres*; *Pepe el Toro*; *¿Qué te ha dado esa mujer?*; *Tizoc*
romance, 11, 19–20, 34, 41, 65–67, 93, 119, 133–34, 145–65, 168–69, 177–78, 180–82
romantic comedy, 39, 134, 157, 162–64, 166, 169, 181, 185, 186–87, 194n7, 205n17
Rousseau, Jean Jacques, 199n6
Rubin, Gayle, 197n21
Rudo y Cursi (Cuarón, C.), 33, 37–38, 42–44, 62–71, 199n7

Salinas de Gotari, Carlos, 9
Salvando al soldado Pérez (Gómez), 201n4
Sánchez Prado, Ignacio: on affect, 204n8; on *Amores perros*, 200n2; on *Japón*, 77; on narco films, 110–11, 201nn4–5; on neoliberalism and cinema, 3–4, 9–11, 39, 69, 148, 155–56, 162, 164; on neoliberalism and literature, 195n9; on postnational filmmaking, 196n17, 194n7; on realism, 188; on romantic comedy, 39, 163–64, 169, 181, 202n16; on *Rudo y Cursi*, 43, 64, 68; on soccer films, 199n8; on *Y tu mamá también*, 38–40, 68
San Diego, 187
satire, 42–44, 62–70, 192n6. *See also parody*
Schaefer, Claudia, 42–43, 67–69
Schroeder, Barbet, 203n2. *See also La virgen de los sicarios*
Sedgwick, Eve Kosofsky, 197n21
Seidler, Victor, 97
self-reflexivity: in Escalante's cinema, 112–13, 118–20, 129–31, 133, 139, 142; in Reygadas's cinema, 34, 74–76, 84, 95, 98, 100–11; in *Te prometo anarquía*, 146, 162
sensuality, 21, 25, 73–74, 154, 158–59, 179, 205n13
sentiment: and machismo, xvi, 21–25, 47, 134; in *Te prometo anarquía*, 149, 156–58, 160–61, 164, 168, 180, 182; toward animals, 103. *See also affect; emotion; feeling, structures of; melodrama; romance*
Serrano, Antonio, 194n7. *See also Sexo, pudor y lágrimas*
Sevilla, Ninón (Emelia Pérez Castellanos), 87
sex, biological, 22
sex, depictions of, 57, 88–89, 142, 150, 159, 179
sex comedy, 195n7
Sexo, pudor y lágrimas (Serrano), 194n7
sexual diversity, 145, 148–56, 182, 204n13
sexual identity, 108, 150. *See also homosexuality; queerness; sexual diversity; sexuality*
sexuality, xvi, 5, 20–21, 26–27, 79, 151, 164. *See also homosexuality; heternormativity; sexual identity; sexual diversity*

Smith, Paul Julian, 145, 148, 150–57, 181–82, 203n7, 204n10, 204nn12–13, 205n14
spectatorship. *See* audiences
Spielberg, Steven, 128. See also *Jurassic Park*
Sin dejar huella (Novaro), 198n3
soccer, 37, 42–43, 55, 62–68, 199n8. See also *Rudo y Cursi*; sports film
Sojob, María, 197n18
Sólo con tu pareja (Cuarón, A.), 39, 41, 71
Solórzano, Fernánda, 115, 117, 127, 129, 202n14, 203n3, 203n6
Sommer, Doris, 197n20
sports film, 37, 42–43, 64–67, 199n8. See also soccer; *and specific titles*

television, xiii, xv, 11, 15, 65, 112–13, 122, 124, 131, 152, 163, 173, 202n14
Texas, 180, 182
Third Cinema, 184
Tierney, Dolores, xvi–xvii, 192nn2–3, 196n17, 199n7
Tijuana, 12, 172, 186
Tin Tan (Germán Valdés), 192n6
Tizoc (Rodríguez), xvi
Todo el mundo tiene a alguien menos yo (Fuentes), 151, 204n10
Tort, Gerardo, 198n3. See also *Viaje redondo*
Tovar Velarde, Sergio, 152. See also *Cuatro lunas*
transnational cinema, 17, 37, 46, 52, 63–64, 196n17, 203n7; audiences, 71, 77, 110–11, 205n13

Un dulce olor a muerte (Retes), 201n3
unmanliness, xvii, 6, 25. *See also* effeminacy; masculinity: malformed

urbanization, 22, 30
Urbina, Dinazar, 197n18

Valencia, Sayak, 12–14, 148, 172–80, 193n3, 196n15, 201n8, 201n11, 202n15, 205n18, 205n20
Van Sant, Gus, 203n2. See also *Elephant*; *Mala Noche*; *My Own Private Idaho*; *Paranoid Park*
Vasconcelos, José, 56, 198n27, 199n6. See also *La raza cósmica*
Venkatesh, Vinodh, 154–57, 181, 193n4
Veracruz, xv
Vermeer, Johannes, 200n8
Viaje Redondo (Tort), 198n3
Víctimas del pecado (Fernández), 87
video games, 112, 129–30, 176
violence: colonial, 31; criminal, 5, 12–16, 34, 70, 107–36, 147–49, 151–55, 162, 165, 169–70, 172–79, 182, 185, 188, 196n16, 200n2, 202nn13–14, 203n2, 203n4, 205n14; domestic, 138–40; gendered, 4, 32, 38, 61; legitimation of, xviii, xix, 5–7, 13, 47, 76, 78, 81, 95, 96, 137, 148; and masculinity, 5, 14–16, 21, 32, 38, 79, 101–102, 104–105, 141, 153, 170, 174–75, 180, 189; redemptive, 92, 141–42, 172; structural, 142, 145, 147, 164, 201n6; sexual, 24, 47; slow (Llamas-Rodríguez), 116; state, 7, 11–16, 30–31, 33, 50–51, 57, 71, 137, 148, 152, 189; toward animals, 101–103. See also criminality; power
virility, xviii, 19–25, 32, 45–47, 79, 185; in *Batalla en el cielo*, 90; in *Y tu mamá también*, 59–61. See also machismo
voice-over, 39, 56–58, 63–64, 66

westernization, 1, 6, 192n5
whiteness, 6, 28, 48, 50, 81, 192n5; of audiences, 188; in *Batalla en el cielo*, 84, 88, 91, 94; of film stars, xvii, 26, 50, 79, 87, 188; and humanness, 31, 48; in *Post tenebras lux*, 94. *See also* criollo; racialization
Williams, Raymond, 195n10
Wood, David, 42–43, 67–69

Young, Neil, 104
Ya no estoy aquí (Farías), 188–89
Y tu mamá también (Cuarón, A.), 33, 37–45, 51–63, 65–66, 68–71, 109, 185–86, 198n1, 198n3

zapatismo. *See* EZLN
Zavala, Oswaldo, 15–16, 113, 117, 188, 201n10, 202nn12–13
Zea, Leopoldo, 56